Total Discipleship

Total Discipleship

**Discipleship Training Theory
Founded upon "The Heart of a Shepherd"
that Shapes Sacred Disciplines**

John Jung-hyun Oh

Printed in the United States of America

979-8-3845-4002-1

Published by B&H Publishing Group
Brentwood, Tennessee

Dewey Decimal Classifaction: 248.4
Subject Heading: DISCIPLESHIP / DISCIPLESHIP TRAINING / CHRISTIAN LIFE

Cover design/illustration adapted from artwork by Semi Park/DMI.
Author photo taken by the author. Used by permission.

1 2 3 4 5 6 • 28 27 26 25

Contents

Part 3: Fruits of Teleios Discipleship: Practical Application of Teleios Discipleship

Prologue for the Teleios of Discipleship Training

In the first-century church, there was no separation between communal worship and the noble spiritual life of saints (Rom. 12:1–2; 1 Pet. 1:15). For them, individual maturity and corporate mission were inseparable (John 8:31–32; 20:21; Eph. 4:13, 16). As a result, they became a community that the world was not worthy of (Heb. 11:38). To the eyes of the world, the early Christians were a unique group of people possessing a special character. Their lives were attractive to people, possessing the ability to relay their faith through service and sacrifice.

If the first disciples and early communities introduced in the Bible were characterized as such, we must then ask ourselves, "Why are we not seeing the same impact or influence around us?" I believe the answer will be found in our reassessment of our efforts in discipleship. Despite hearing about many fruits resulting from generations of efforts in discipleship training, there are signs that the corners of discipleship training are gradually wearing out, showing signs of fatigue. Above all, what is more concerning is the growing voices of self-criticism within the ministry field. Somewhere along the way, discipleship training has deviated from an all-encompassing, personality-transforming discipline and become fragmented and formalized. This phenomenon has become a heavy burden on the hearts of ministers who have been long committed to discipleship training.

Why did this happen? It is because the kind of discipleship marked by a personally mature and noble lifestyle, a dynamic community, and having an alternative hope to the world—which also were the elements of the early church disciples—have become distant from us. While we taught the right doctrines, the role of the Holy Spirit was limited in the practice of the teachings. Discipleship training produced outer appearances of holiness, yet we have failed to adequately follow the heart and the mind of Jesus. Consequently, we witnessed the rise of an elite class of discipleship trainers who received training splendidly but lacked proficiency in the foundational aspects of discipleship, such as self-denial and priestly sacrifice. As a result, discipleship training became a hot potato in many churches—constantly changing out new leadership and new strategies.

However, I am not overly pessimistic; rather I am confident that we have an opportunity to reverse this trend. If the disciples of the first-century church, who had much less biblical knowledge than us, and who faced an incomparably harsh environment, could become such vibrant disciples, then we have all that we need to disciple the believers to a greater depth. We must train and raise whole and complete disciples—the Teleios disciples. I believe we can commit to such a task because "with man it is impossible, but not with God. For all things are possible with God" (Mark 10:27). How is this possible? I contend that if we can implant the "shepherd's heart," which has been largely missing in discipleship training, into the hearts of trainees, then they can strive daily toward becoming Teleios disciples, embodying the excellence of Teleios Discipleship. The shepherd's heart should become the heart of every pastor, minister, and all saints. Like the words of Charles Haddon Spurgeon, all church leaders, including pastors, carry a holy destiny that cannot rest until the lost sheep are joyfully brought home on their shoulders.[1]

Teleios Is the Heavenly Life That Only Saints Can Enjoy

The world seeks completeness in various ways. Since the fall of Adam, humanity, shattered and broken, instinctively longs for wholeness.[2] In some ways, history can be seen as a struggle for completeness. Those in power seek more power, the wealthy pursue more wealth, scholars strive for higher intellect, and artists aspire to greater talent, all in the pursuit of completeness. This relentless pursuit, despite the impossibility of achieving it, is an innate spiritual desire to return to the prefallen state of creation.[3]

However, humans cannot achieve perfect wholeness on this earth. With a sinful nature, humans inherently cannot obey God's Word 100 percent, and they do not strive for 100 percent obedience willingly either. As Augustine confessed, humans, being unable to find peace without God, pursuing wholeness apart from God is completely futile.[4] One cannot find genuine wholeness apart from God; wholeness that is unrelated to God cannot be found in the world.

The wholeness of the saints that we pursue and aim for is a journey of sanctification, relying on the "completeness of God's nature and the completeness of the gospel" in the daily progress of life in Christ. The apostle Paul expressed this in Philippians 3:12, "Not that I have already obtained this or am already perfect, but I press on to make it my own, because Christ Jesus has made me his own." Christians can attain the excellence of completeness only because of Jesus's sacrifice on the cross. The only way to achieve wholeness on this earth is through the cross, reconciling sinners with God and embracing the gospel that transforms the redeemed into God's children. For believers who regard the blood of the cross as the way of salvation and the gospel of the cross as the principle of life, "seeking wholeness every moment is both a privilege and a duty."[5]

Pursuing wholeness daily signifies living a "heavenly life" in companionship with God.[6] A minister not guiding saints on the path of completeness is neglecting their mission and duty. Disobeying the command, "Be perfect, therefore, as your heavenly Father is perfect" (Matt. 5:48 CSB), is forsaking the bestowed blessings for a believer and rejecting the command of God the Father, who earnestly desires wholeness in his people. A minister failing to teach and embody this biblical wholeness to saints, neglecting to enable them to resemble Jesus, is devoid of the shepherd's heart. The shepherd's heart of a pastor invokes ministers to commit to all they can do to bring their people to the state of completeness and wholeness that God desires—the Teleios of a believer.

The Urgency of the Shepherd's Heart in the Age of Artificial Intelligence

With the advent of services utilizing artificial intelligence, the use of AI has already become commonplace. Beyond simply searching for necessary information on the internet, we are now entering a new dimension where personalized information is provided in customized forms tailored to individual needs. While artificial intelligence currently exhibits a mechanical and rudimentary appearance, there will come a time when it approaches human likeness. Some anticipate the post-singularity era with enthusiasm; others view it with apprehension. Some even worry that if AI disguises itself as spirituality, people might perceive it as an absolute existence.

It is only through God's Word and the shepherd's heart that one can traverse the era of artificial intelligence. The Bible and the shepherd's heart not only discern false or disguised spirituality but also are the power fueled by a holy fire that melts the coldness of the world dominated by digital numbers.

We should not fear the unpredictable temptations and dominance of the age of artificial intelligence but the spiritual insensitivity that fails to recognize or even sense the "appalling and horrible thing has happened in the land," as mentioned in Jeremiah 5:30 CSB. Opening our dull hearts, unclogging our ears, and unveiling our blinded eyes (Isa. 6:10) come from the shepherd's heart, rooted in the love revealed when Jesus's heart burst on the cross. The shepherd's heart reaches out and rescues the hands of believers from the distorted sea of artificial intelligence, ensuring they do not fall into its deceptive waves. We need Teleios Discipleship in both the minister and the believers.

How This Book Is Organized

This book on Teleios Discipleship unfolds in three main parts. Part 1 delves into the shepherd's heart as the "core" and "root" of wholeness, or Teleios, discussing the mindset that pastors and believers should possess. Part 2, as the "stem" of Teleios, explores the ecclesiology and pneumatology that ministers with a shepherd's heart should grasp, along with the pastor's character on the path of Teleios Discipleship and the goals of holistic disciple training. Part 3, as the "fruit" of Teleios, practically addresses how pastors can train believers into Teleios disciples in various dimensions within the context of pastoral ministry.

In theological education, pastoral philosophy is often introduced first, followed by an explanation of pastoral work in the field. This follows the flow of Western pastoral philosophy, progressing from the head (knowledge) to the heart (emotions) and then to the hands (actions). Yet, an observation of Jesus's ministry reveals that these three aspects cannot be separated—they must coexist simultaneously. Through more than forty years of pastoral experience, I am firmly convinced that pastoral ministry that is grounded in wholeness must begin with the shepherd's heart revealed in the Bible for the church community to thrive. Without a shepherd's heart from God, even with an error-free orthodox understanding of the church, the sap of life in pastoral ministry cannot flow down to the field where the hands and feet of ministry are active.

Just as the church is the body of Christ, I aim to discuss Teleios patterning the flow of blood in a human being, starting from the heart to the head and then to the hands. The blood flowing from the passionate heart of God, who is the ultimate Shepherd, should reach the veins of the church, formulating a philosophy of pastoral ministry and ecclesiology. This philosophy, derived from the blood of the Shepherd, then translates into practical implementation across all areas of pastoral ministry upon the recognition of God's desire for Teleios in us as a foundation.

The Structure of Each Chapter

Chapter 1 of part 1 addresses the misconception surrounding the question of whether sinful humans can achieve perfect wholeness, or Teleios, through discipleship. It explores why Teleios should be the goal for believers. In chapter 2, the theological foundation of Teleios, the shepherd's heart, is examined. The chapter explores how the shepherd's heart leads believers toward the completeness found in Jesus. Chapter 3 delves into embracing Jesus Christ's wholeness as our own through a life marked by the cross and self-denial.

Moving to part 2, chapter 4 offers the framework of proper ecclesiology—the backbone of Teleios Discipleship training—from the perspectives of theological soundness, pastoral sincerity, and missional suitability. Chapter 5 emphasizes the heightened importance of the Holy Spirit in discipleship training, especially in the era of the Fourth Industrial Revolution led by artificial intelligence. It discusses the perspectives on the Holy Spirit that must be maintained from the viewpoint of Teleios in the twenty-first century. Chapter 6 explores the character of pastors ministering with a shepherd's heart for the ultimate goal of God's glory in the Teleios disciple's life journey.

In part 3, chapter 7 sheds light on how completeness in Christ within individuals unfolds across the domains of thought, emotions, will, relationships, and actions. It will treat how Teleios's spiritual formation takes place and how it is applied. Finally, chapter 8 focuses on the practical aspects of holistic discipleship training in five specified areas of worship, family, workplace, missions, and culture. Through it, Teleios Discipleship training will prove to be the avenue by which the believers can walk under Christ's kingly rule on earth.

From the new birth, we possess the sacred mission to become Teleios disciples of Jesus. We are called to live and strive daily to reflect Christ's character in every aspect of life. We are the people who live out of gratitude for Jesus's Teleios (perfect and complete) sacrifice, being committed to whatever it takes to be like, be with, and be for Jesus Christ on this earth

(1 Cor. 11:1–2; 2 Pet. 2:5). Just as Jesus's salvation is complete and perfect, our lives in discipleship must also advance toward Teleios. There is no gray zone in the life of a Teleios disciple. One must choose to live either as a Teleios disciple in all areas or not at all (Luke 18:21–22). This book presents the road map to Teleios Discipleship training. This path originates from the shepherd's heart. The journey is the self-denial that bears the cross. The fruit of Teleios Discipleship is a missional life. The goal of this discipleship is *Soli Deo Gloria*, giving glory to God alone. All these concepts are firmly rooted in the revealed Scriptures, where the heart of God as the Shepherd is fully disclosed.

Preface

"Do you love the church, the body of Christ?" This book answers the question with a pastoral awakening and a spiritual confession.

Looking back, everything has unfolded within God's providence. As the son of a pastor who planted a church in the most downtrodden neighborhood of Busan, South Korea, God engraved the love for the church on my heart even before I could comprehend what it was in my mind. Relocating to Seoul at the age of eighteen, God allowed me an encounter with the gospel and discipleship training during the most innocent time of my life. God then had a question waiting for me at a young adult's Bible study I was invited to. As a young man searching for a purpose in life, I was asked, "What do you think is the most valuable life?" The question shook my heart like a seismic event and reshaped my thoughts from the ground up. Every step thereafter became a journey led by God in search of the answer to that question.

While serving in college ministry, I pondered why the strengths of parachurch organizations outside the church were not integrated into the church and why devoted young believers were leaving the church for missions or ministry organizations rather than serving the local church. I even contemplated why I still needed to remain in the church myself.

Then I started my studies in the States, along with a college ministry in an immigrant church. I continued to ask, "Why aren't young people contemplating what a more valuable life is?" This time I was challenging about thirty college students in my ministry with that question. As we bound our hearts together, pouring out our passion in pursuit of the answer, we all opened our eyes to the heart of Jesus. This spiritual awakening became the driving force behind the growth that turned those thirty into 120 students by the time of the winter retreat, in just six months after I assumed leadership. Later, this became the original core of my pastoral ministry—the shepherd's heart.

With twelve dedicated saints, I planted SaRang Community Church in Southern California. While growing from a small to medium, medium to a large, and then a megachurch, I experienced various pastoral challenges and victories. Yet, the shepherd's heart remained the root and my archetype of ministry throughout all these pastoral journeys.

As time passed, I became the senior pastor of SaRang Church in Seoul, Korea. As the church experienced continued growth, I now reflect on the years of blessed ministries only to realize that there is a debt of love I must repay. The Korean church has experienced a truly unique blessing; I am equally a recipient of God's sovereign and abundant grace poured out to the believers in the Korean peninsula. Just under a hundred years of evangelical mission in the land, the Korean church has become the second-largest missionary-sending nation in the world. The rate of conversion and profession in the Christian faith per demographic are unprecedented in modern history. All of this fruit was made possible by the sheer grace of God and the faithfulness of the Western church. If the Korean church has been receiving for the past hundred years, I am convinced that it is now time to give back to the rest of the world, as the Korean church steps up to rekindle the fire in the Western church. The time has come to repose the question again to the evangelical world, "What are you living for? What is the most valuable life? Why are we not committed to what is more valuable?"

In any challenging environment encountered on life's journey, God lavishes his incredible grace—the "perfecting" of His children. This is the blessing I experienced firsthand, the grace I sought to impart through my ministry, and the answer to the questions I faced. Now I desire to share what is involved in God's "perfecting" grace, namely Teleios, with the co-laborers in Christ, junior pastors, and all saints who call God "Abba! Father!" (Rom. 8:15). This earnest desire led me, despite who I am, to write this book. In this sense, this book is also a sincere record of the testimony of my pastoral ministry.

Today, many foresee a dark future for the church. Skepticism of the faith has permeated not only the pulpit but also the lives of believers. For the church to rise again and witness revival, it must be fueled by the shepherd's heart of Jesus. The scarlet blood of the cross of Jesus must reflow through the veins of ministers and saints. Only then can we cut off the coldness emitted by Satan and rekindle the church, the body of the Lord, with a renewed sense of mission.

With mere "moderate efforts," we cannot break through the powerful gravity of the secular world.[1] In fact, the shepherd's heart makes it unbearable for ministers and saints to accept mediocrity. If it were not for the shepherd's heart, how could Jesus willingly bear the heavy and fearsome cross of atonement? If it were not for the shepherd's heart, how could the disciples silently walk the path of martyrdom?

I hope this book serves as a tool to implant the shepherd's heart into our hearts. The shepherd's heart will lead individuals, neighbors, and communities to the completeness (Teleios) that God desires, the ultimate destination.

I pray that each page that is imbued with the shepherd's heart becomes your pastoral insight and power, pulling ministers and workers from the first steps of faith to the strides of complete discipleship.

Many efforts went into the making of this book. There are truly numerous individuals I want to thank through this platform. I express my gratitude to the coworkers of SaRang Church who, with the shepherd's heart, labor and dedicate themselves to the heavenly family.[2] Assistance was received for gathering and organizing materials for the book. Also, I owe a great debt of love to the saints who prayed day and night for me. This book is dedicated to all members of the SaRang Church family with love.

Humbly Submitted,
October 2023
Pastoral Office of SaRang Church
"Hyegang" John Jung-hyun Oh

PART 1

The Roots of Teleios Discipleship: Biblical and Theological Origins of Teleios

"We must face the congregation with the heart of a shepherd who is in pursuit of a lost sheep. We must not rest until we find and carry the sheep home on our shoulders in joy."

Charles Haddon Spurgeon

CHAPTER 1

Why Teleios Discipleship Training?

The Path to a Discipleship-Centric Life

In the early 2010s, as the church launched its campaign for a new building project, a series of challenges began to surface. What was unearthed amid the testing time was not simply internal conflicts or external attacks. Instead, people began to doubt the fruit of SaRang's discipleship ministry. Those who spectated the difficulties of the church questioned how a church that gained recognition through intense and robust discipleship training would be susceptible to turmoil such as this. Bystanders concluded that SaRang's discipleship training was ineffective in cultivating the health of the church.

However, it is evident to me that their assessment was shortsighted. No one—especially those who talked on the sidelines—was able to see what would come out as a result. As we reflect on those times with a clearer vision, I am convinced this period granted us the opportunity to shed the layers of complacency that had accumulated over the decades. We learned to throw off the robe of "self-righteousness," including the one of my own.

The Lord saw us through. SaRang is now thriving. We have come through the tunnel, and God's faithfulness was the light. More specifically, this season of difficulty demonstrated the maturity of the members who were nurtured, raised, and commissioned as Christ's disciples through our discipleship training. Times have been difficult, but our love for the Lord and His body grew even stronger. This love led to spontaneous prayer movements, with thousands of believers participating in fasting and prayer during the building project. Amid adversity, love was even more visible as the saints came together to support the church. This could not have been possible without discipleship training, which had been undertaken by tens of thousands of people since the birth of the church.

Moreover, this period became a pivotal moment for reflecting on the essence, the foundation, and the framework of the ministry of discipleship training. During this time, we also questioned whether anything had unintentionally veered our effort for discipleship training off course, distancing it from its core. In this season, with a heart-wrenching agony that accompanied brutally honest self-examination, we inquired about the purpose of discipleship training and what the true outcome of discipleship should be.

The valuable pearl born from this painful process is Teleios Discipleship. Teleios Discipleship is discipleship imbued with the heart of Jesus, training that creates a heart-soil in a believer that is drenched with the blood of Jesus. If SaRang Church's founding pastor, Han-heum Oak's "Maniac Theory" emphasized the absolute necessity of discipleship training, Teleios Discipleship can be seen as the work that explores how discipleship should be practically carried out in the field of life. It makes the transition from the "One-Person Philosophy" to the "Whole-Person Philosophy."

While "Maniac Theory" focuses on sowing the seeds of discipleship training in a local church context, Teleios Discipleship is concerned with where and how the seeds of discipleship should be sown, so that the discipleship can achieve comprehensive transmission of the gospel that transcends social and temporal boundaries. It takes a step further from merely teaching about discipleship to the embodied practice in life, further transforming a church from a "Disciple-Making Church" to a "Disciple-Making Mission Church."[1]

A minister should pursue discipleship training that goes beyond human conventions or methodology, seeking the complete discipleship formation that is immersed in the blood of Jesus.[2] As general orders for soldiers' attention with a thunderous shout, we must aim to call all believers to an attentive posture before the Lord, immediately standing up straight, sharply fixing our eyes on the blood-drenched cross of Jesus Christ. This is the discipleship training a minister must strive for. Striving for Teleios Discipleship overcomes the traps of imbalanced, bureaucratized, and institutionalized forms of discipleship, melting away all that is peripheral in the blood of Jesus. In short, it is the work of transforming the inner fabric of a believer to become the one who trembles—anytime, anywhere—just at the thought of the blood of Jesus shed for them, carried out by the minister's shepherd's heart.

Teleios Discipleship Is Training That Believes in the Holy Potentiality Contained in the Seed of Life

There are times when discipleship training loses its balance and deviates from its course. This happens when we either perceive discipleship as a form of self-help or fail to recognize the hidden potential for growth in discipleship training. Jesus's call to go and make disciples already affirms the possibility of kingdom expansion. Discipleship training is a means to actualize such potentiality through missional living.

The Bible clearly shows how life has the natural potential for expansion, and it contributes to the advancement of God's kingdom. Jesus elected the twelve disciples, but the discipleship soon expanded to seventy evangelists. The seventy evangelists expanded to 120 in Mark's upper room. The 120 did not remain in that number because five hundred witnessed the resurrection of Jesus. And in the book of Acts, three thousand people were saved in one day. In the Old Testament, there were three hundred warriors under Gideon, and there were seven thousand who did not bow to Baal. These numbers are eventually followed by the "multitude" in Revelation 19. Why did the Bible record these numbers in such detail? It is because the holy expansion of the kingdom of God is not an abstract concept; these numbers show that God's work is real. The small become a thousand, and the weak become a mighty nation (Isa. 60:22).

Teleios Discipleship goes beyond just talking about possibilities. God, through His written Word, demonstrates and confirms the expansion of the gospel witness and the fruit of life rising like a fire. Believing in the holy expansion of the kingdom of God, furthermore teaching it, witnessing it, experiencing its fruition in real life, and committing one's life to see it spread, is what Teleios Discipleship is all about.

To Actualize the Expansion, Like-Minded Coworkers Are Essential

While some factors make ministry successful, the support and encouragement from co-laborers in Christ are a nonnegotiable absolute necessity in discipleship training ministry. Today's discipleship training ministry urgently requires deep spiritual camaraderie that carries each other as in a three-legged race. True partners in ministry, those who can genuinely spur one another on until the end, are sometimes forged in the face of death.

Pastor Han-heum Oak has been my mentor in ministry since the late 1970s when he first visited Naesoodong Church's college ministry as a guest speaker. He graciously took me in since that time. He and I began to share both questions and convictions we have developed in disciple-making ministries over the years. Yet, our relationship entered another level of depth through an event that occurred in 2001. This transformed our ordinary mentor-mentee relationship into a lifelong ministry partnership. It took place when Pastor Oak and I traveled to Oregon in the United States for two weeks. During our time there, we shared daily devotions through our meditations on 1 Thessalonians, visited different places, and engaged in enriching conversations. Then one day, Pastor Oak and I went down below the cliffs on the beach in Oregon to take pictures of the waves. In a quick instance, we were almost swept away by the sea, as we ventured too close on the slippery ocean rocks. I still have a photo from that day we nearly lost our lives. After that close call, we forged a new bond. We became vulnerable with each other, sharing stories we had never revealed to anyone. Together, we poured out our experiences and our faith to each other. After tasting a moment of death together, our sense of camaraderie became stronger than ever before. Our pastoral relationship had escalated to a partnership in ministry, into a new level of spiritual solidarity.

Pastoral life requires becoming a true shepherd, which also requires the sacrifice of life. The journey of pastoral ministry is often so challenging that we can feel like giving up. In such times, true ministry partners are necessary for the pastoral task at hand. Disciple-making ministers hence should ask themselves, "Do I have a true ministry partner who can truly resonate with my heart?" before asking, "Do I have what it takes to minister well?" One must then resolve to be that friend, partner, and comrade for someone else as well. When that happens, a minister will be able to expand the kingdom of God even in the harshest soil.[3]

What Are We Pursuing Through Discipleship Training?

The purpose of discipleship is to become like Jesus, and the starting point of that training is the heart of God, who is the Shepherd. Discipleship training begins with God's heart, whose desire is for no one to perish but for everyone to come to repentance and faith. Our Shepherd God desires those who are in Christ to continue growing to the likeness of His Son through the power of the Holy Spirit. Since we have already received the grace of the "spring of water welling up to eternal life" (John 4:14) that enables continued growth, growth through obedience should likewise continue in us.[4] A disciple who understands the heart of the Shepherd God seeks wholeness as taught in the Lord's Prayer—a full stature embedded in God's name, God's kingdom, and God's will (Matt. 6:9–10).

Discipleship training has been defined in different ways depending on the era, culture, environment, and situation. However, over the past forty years in ministry, there is one definition of discipleship training that has not changed and cannot be compromised. Discipleship training is training that places believers in the "mainstream of grace." The term "mainstream of grace" refers to a place, an environment, and spaces where spiritual blessings flow in abundance. However, this blessing must be firmly grounded in orthodox faith, based on the Word of God. It must be experienced by blessings found in the reformed doctrines of Martin Luther and John Calvin, the faith of martyrs like Pastors Joo Gi-cheol and Kil Sun-ju, and the lordship of Christ that proclaims Jesus as the Lord of life.

Though many show up at a church gathering, not everyone stands in the mainstream of grace. The incident in Numbers 16 demonstrates this phenomenon. Korah, who rebelled against Moses's leadership, perished with his followers (Num. 16:33). When one person, like Korah, moves out of grace, the entire group falls into the path of destruction. Satan has three ways of making saints stand outside the mainstream of grace. First, he blinds the saints spiritually, causing them to be shortsighted about the kingdom. Second, he stirs up worldly pride, leading the saints to fall from a peak of arrogance. Third, he makes them spiritually insensitive, rendering them powerless and inactive.

However, Jesus placed those who were in the blind spots of grace back into the mainstream of grace. A prime example is Mary Magdalene, who had seven demons and led a miserable life to the extent that she could not even carry out a normal daily life. However, after being invited to live in the mainstream of grace, she became the one who cared for those who met Jesus. This is a vivid picture of what the goal of Teleios Discipleship must be.

The Primacy of Life of Discipleship, Not a Formality of Discipleship Training

Even when the term *discipleship training* was not commonly used in the Korean church, there were devout women who knelt on the cold wooden floor of the sanctuary every early morning to pray, who faithfully kept the Lord's Day holy, who gave to church out of their meager provisions with grains of rice. These ladies of faith frugally managed their living expenses to contribute to the church and bore abundant fruits of evangelism through their lives and character. They matured in the process of becoming more like Jesus through the Word, the sacraments, and a life of prayer—all this without formally structured discipleship training. Their lives stand as living testimonies of the importance of a discipled life conceived by the local church. It was the local church that matured these spiritual mothers.

If the context is removed from discipleship training, that training is reduced to individualistic education. This is why the concepts of the church and ecclesiology must be urgently reestablished. Phrases like, "The church is one. The church is holy. The church is universal. The church is apostolic," are beautiful and profound confessions of faith. However, without adding new spirit, discoveries, and movements to these statements, they will merely be words and will not fully function as a true description of a vibrant active church.

While studying in the United States, I led the college ministry at a church where Rev. Kim Dong-myung was serving as the senior pastor. As the new pastor, I engaged in discipling the students from 8:00 a.m. to 1:00 p.m. every Saturday. The training was intense, but as intense as the training was, the result of the training became visible through a rapidly growing number. Spiritual reproduction was taking off like wildfire. Then one day, Pastor Kim Dong-myung announced that he was leaving for South America for mission work. While preparing to leave, Pastor Kim was exposed to the power of a discipleship training program. After returning, he approached me, along with the college group leaders, to undergo another set of discipleship training under him. I was quite baffled. I could not understand why he wanted to put me in a discipleship training group when I was leading one. Neither could I understand why he would put me in a group with the students I had trained through my version of discipleship training. Nevertheless, I decided to go through the training under Pastor Kim, along with my students; and this lasted for almost seven to eight months.

Contrary to my preconceived skepticism, this season of discipleship training offered a major awakening in me. Through this experience, I ultimately realized that if the goal of discipleship is to become like Jesus Christ and undergo a transformation in one's character and personality, this goal will not be attained merely by getting the trainees to submit to a set of disciplines or subscribe to certain principles. I was convinced that principles or disciplines alone cannot change people. During the discipleship training with Pastor Kim, I was sweetly broken, just like the college students I had been leading. If I had not gone through this set of discipleship training periods myself, I would not have understood what it means to be broken before the Lord or experienced what true discipleship training should involve. This experience had a significant impact on my approach to discipleship training. I learned to distinguish between a life of discipleship and formalized discipleship training. This experience schooled me to see that the key to genuine disciple-making was to invite the people to the life of discipleship, not a formality of training.

The Argument for Teleios Perfection

For over a decade, I have been giving the lecture titled "Teleios Discipleship" during the Discipleship Training Leader's Seminar, referred to as the CAL Seminar (Called to Awaken the Laity Seminar). In this first session of the week, people often ask, "Why did you have to use the word *perfection* (Teleios) to describe discipleship, among the many other adjectives?" Many seminar attendees found the term burdensome. Others ask whether there is such a thing as "imperfect" discipleship, and if so, what that would look like. No matter how one answers those questions, perfection, or Teleios, is often considered to be a term that does not fit well with discipleship, especially since it involves people who are still struggling with the weakness of the flesh in this world, whether a disciple-maker or a disciple in training.

However, Teleios goes hand in hand with discipleship. Strictly speaking, the term *Teleios* is an exclusively suitable word to describe the outcome of discipleship training. One cannot truly address discipleship training apart from discussing wholeness or perfection—Teleios. This is because the goal of discipleship (becoming like Jesus), the process (maturity through inner transformation), and the fruit (bearing the fruit of righteousness in all aspects of life) are all related to our wholeness or perfection. In the following, I present a case for Teleios as the goal for discipleship from four perspectives: theological landscape, ministry context, social culture, and pastoral ministry. These discussions will greatly aid the understanding of the new theory of discipleship training, the theory of Teleios Discipleship.

Theological Argument for Teleios Discipleship

In disciple training, Teleios, or "perfected wholeness," is a theologically significant concept for five key reasons. First, to understand the original language of the New Testament concerning Christ's disciples, one must explore the concept of Teleios. In the Gospels and the book of Acts, the word *disciple* is mentioned 263 times. However, interestingly, the term *disciple* is not mentioned in the epistles of the apostles; instead, terms like *believers*, *brothers and sisters*, *saints*, *followers*, and *Christians* are used.

The absence of the word *disciple* does not mean discipleship or discipleship training has disappeared. Instead, what we see is the term *Teleios one* replacing the term *disciple*. In other words, in place of the term *disciples*, the one who "follows," but more significantly, the one who is "Teleios" appears in replacement. The reason for this change is easier to understand when one considers the cultural context. The term *disciple* would have had more resonance with those of Jewish background. Yet, the term *Teleios one*, in contrast, would have had a better resonance with those in the Greco-Roman cultural context, as the apostles emphasized the idea of following Jesus in their epistles.[5] If this is the term the Bible uses more frequently in discussions of discipleship, it certainly warrants a deeper exploration. Likewise, we must not be hesitant to refer to disciples as the Teleios ones. Have we not heard it said that the language is the home of existence? When our language changes, the eyes through which it portrays reality also change.

Second, if one desires to achieve spiritual maturity, one must establish the theological concept of Teleios under the lens of biblical theology. For those who live under the cultural influence of Confucianism, the understanding of Teleios automatically gets associated with personal and moral perfection. For those under the influence of Western education, the word may denote an abstract ideal. However, the Teleios mentioned in the context of Teleios Discipleship training does not refer to such abstract concepts. Teleios Discipleship training is a practical process of sanctification, where saints are raised as "perfect ones" in Christ Jesus (Col. 1:28–29 KJV, NKJV, ASB, NLT). This journey of sanctification differs significantly from the self-realization often promoted in the world. Contrary to secular works of self-help, it is rooted in the grace of Jesus Christ who bore the cross to make the saints perfect. It is starkly different since its goal, motivation, and means are all found in Jesus alone.

When the goal of discipleship training becomes the elevation of the individual to a noble and virtuous believer, the results are discord, conflicts, and division rather than the transformation of individual saints and the subsequent cultivation of a healthy community. Even just to remove the subtle residues of Confucian influence that have subtly infiltrated our understanding of discipleship training—or any other cultural influence, for that matter, we must reimagine the concept of discipleship as Jesus envisioned it. He envisions Teleios in us.

Third, after serving more than eighty CAL seminars, several aspects of discipleship training surfaced as urgent needs to improve upon the first-generation discipleship training program. To attain holistic discipleship training, we needed to delve into the inner being of a person—especially reflecting on the transformation of the five components of character: mind, heart, will, relationships, and actions. Additionally, we needed to illuminate what authentic discipleship looks like in worship, family, work, mission fields, and various sectors of culture. If the first-generation discipleship training primarily focused on planting one's life on sound doctrine, we now need to thoroughly revisit and explore how they are standing and walking the discipled life under the banner of discipleship training.

Fourth, we must emphasize Teleios in discipleship because wholeness is necessary to supplement the element of experience in spiritual formation. When one observes the way Jesus Himself nurtured His disciples, we can find that it essentially was a field education—taking them to preach the gospel of the kingdom, touring different cities and villages with Him, and providing experiential learning. The disciples learned from Jesus during those journeys. Little by little, the disciples sometimes grasped the teaching, at times rejoiced in it, and other times were perplexed by it. Similarly, Teleios Discipleship training goes beyond the delivery of information. Instead, the training modules for discipleship must expand into all aspects of life, bridging personal life into a spiritual ecosystem. The horizon of our followership must be stretched beyond a compartmentalized part of a believer's life. This is not to dismiss a need for systematic learning of biblical knowledge that takes place in a traditional classroom or throughout an academic calendar. It is to progress beyond classroom-based pedagogy into experiential formation in discipleship training.

Last, incorporating Teleios in discipleship is crucial because of the need to reconstruct ecclesiology from the perspective of wholeness. Traditional ecclesiology has often emphasized that people should "come" to the church, hear the Word, "repent," and be "trained" to become disciples. However, the "come-and-see model" is encountering significant barriers in modern society. People simply do not find reasons to "come and see" at a church. It is now essential to consider an ecclesiology that is shaped by the notions of "going" together or "being with" others. Just as God the Father sent His Son to become Immanuel in the world, the church needs to relearn that its mission is to "be with" people who are groaning in meaninglessness, weariness, pain, and death. The church must become a sending center that both stands as a witness to the gospel and a companion to the lost. Teleios in discipleship emphasizes the missional calling embedded in a disciple's identity.

Teleios, hence, is an indispensable factor in reshaping ecclesiology that is true to the metanarrative of God's salvation. It leads to the reestablishment of the dynamic view of the church that continues to put together mosaic pieces of transformation stories of God's work in the world.

The Pursuit of Teleios in Discipleship Is to Look Beyond the Abstract Attribute of God

God's love demonstrated through the cross is perfect; it is a perfect love. Similarly, the sacrifice that Jesus offered on the cross is perfect as well. The salvation offered through the cross is also perfect. The purpose of Teleios in discipleship training is to manifest God's perfect nature to the church, the saints, and the world. Without comprehending God's perfect wholeness, how will we wholly address the question of life, including pain and suffering? The world asks, "If God is good, why does evil exist? If God is love, why is there so much suffering and pain?" Just as the Pharisees and scribes tested Jesus with questions over two thousand years ago, the world is challenging the church and believers today with questions that are not easily resolved by human reason, intelligence, or sentimentality.

Jesus countered those who tested Him with responses that transcended worldly wisdom and understanding. Teleios Discipleship seeks to answer the challenges of the world similarly. How is this possible? By more deeply, vividly, and supernaturally pursuing God's perfect way of saving the world. Clinging to His Word for us to "be perfect, as your heavenly Father is perfect" (Matt. 5:48), Teleios in discipleship training aims to cultivate disciples who will overcome the challenges of the world with divine means, just as Jesus surpassed worldly expectations.

To be obedient to the command "Be perfect," we must understand what God's perfection entails. What is at stake is not perfection in and of itself. Instead, when we come to comprehend God's perfect nature, this understanding enables us to see the purpose of God when he says, "Be perfect." Alister McGrath once compared discovering God to finding a pair of glasses that helps us see the world more clearly.[6] Discovering God is not the end goal. The greater goal is found in using those glasses to see the endless wonders of God with reverence and fascination and sharing it with the rest of the world. Teleios Discipleship operates similarly. Its goal is to enable believers to apprehend the meaning and significance of God's perfection in all that He is and all that He does.

Argument from Ministry Context

I have offered theological backing for the reason the term *Teleios* is an apt descriptor for discipleship training. Yet, several additional questions must be addressed to further substantiate the incorporation of the term in discipleship. One of those questions is to assess whether such pursuit of Teleios in discipleship training is suitable for ministry. For Teleios Discipleship to be practical and not merely theoretical, it must be able to present a convincing answer to the following question.

I have heard ministers say, "The zeal of Christians has been diminishing over time, and the church is experiencing a sharp decline in membership. Despite incorporating many programs that have been considered effective for church growth, it is not stopping the steady decline of church attendance and involvement. Furthermore, many churches are experiencing a sharp decline in the number of students in the children and youth ministries. The decline of the church is not a baseless anxiety but an objective fact, as shown by statistics."[7] This may hold some truth. Yet it does not offer any reason why one must look for other ways or reasons to discount Teleios Discipleship training. On the contrary, this assessment is precisely why wholeness (Teleios) should be integrated into discipleship training, offering a fresh approach to making disciples. We must remember that the circumstances should not drive the mission; rather, the mission should guide us in navigating through the circumstances. Why is this so? Nothing changes the mission we have to make disciples. Critics of discipleship training often claim that discipleship training makes no real difference in the real lives of believers. Why do these types of criticism surface? Or better yet, why do believers seem to lack the ability to have a beautiful impact on society beyond the boundaries of the church? Is there a fundamental issue with the calling to discipleship to begin with, or is it because discipleship training simply is an outdated form of nurturing Christ's followers today?

No, the reason for the lack of genuine change in a believer even after discipleship training is that it remains superficial. Such training never penetrates the heart and character of the believer. We must reexamine to see whether we have labeled mundanely repeated religious routines as "training." The programmatic and nominal approach to discipleship training requires a thoughtful reevaluation. When discipleship training is misused as a volunteer management strategy rather than a catalyst for personal transformation, it can inadvertently produce self-centered and spiritually close-minded individuals. Even if the discipleship curriculum includes teachings on self-denial and living a cruciform life, we must critically examine whether it indeed yields the fruit of self-denial in practical life, particularly in how disciples relate to one another within the church and how they treat fellow believers.

Moreover, we must revisit the essence, motivation, and methods of discipleship training. Rather than trying to fit discipleship training into the cultural and church context, we should thoroughly examine what discipleship training looked like in the New Testament, sharpening our strategy to take the next step forward by looking back. We must reflect on how to adapt biblical discipleship training aptly to our ministry context. Discipleship training should ultimately move toward meeting a global standard—a horizon of ministry that surpasses regional boundaries—in raising biblically holistic disciples.[8] Discipleship and the proclamation of the kingdom of God were not two separate agendas for Jesus. He continually taught and examined His disciples to ensure that the kingdom's reign and power would overtake their character, virtue, and daily living. We must do the same. For our disciple-making efforts to be pleasing to the Lord, they must completely resemble the training approach that Jesus modeled as our standard, regardless of circumstances, situations, or context. We care not what numerical success we may see. We leave the results to the Lord and sow the seed today, though sometimes we will do so with weeping (1 Cor. 3:6; Ps. 126:5–6). Even when all seem pessimistic about the future of the church and when all signs point to the further decline of Christianity, what we must see instead is an excellent opportunity to reexamine the foundations of discipleship training. This offers us a unique chance to realign the purpose and the process of discipleship and disciple-making ministries.

What Happens When Ministers Pursue Teleios in their Ministry Context?

J. I. Packer writes, "Wholeness in worship means that every worshiper participates without exception and adopts the most open posture towards God. Wholeness in ministry means not only performing spiritual gifts but also discerning and utilizing all capacities available for service. Wholeness in fellowship, shared among believers, means generously giving oneself and one's possessions to help others, to an extent that might seem extravagant."[9] In this sense, Teleios goes beyond quietly seeking faith on a personal level; it is a passionately communal pursuit. When Teleios is passionately pursued, the temperament of the church will undergo a fervent transformation. Pursuing Teleios fervently will shatter the frozen voice of the "frozen people of God," breaking the ice of frozen voices in praise, the cold formalism, hardened hearts, and the absence of loving service toward one another.[10]

We must earnestly pursue Teleios because it is the essence of faith. When we strive to recenter what is essential, all that is peripheral to ministry smolders as the church is invigorated with renewed fire. Putting out the peripherals in ministry produces the transformation of the local body. Many people may come in and out of the church, but the church does not experience vitality and become cold because congregants stand next to a "fire that is not the fire of the Holy Spirit, warming themselves on the strength of their own."[11] Churches today are unable to experience real fire while standing next to fake ones.

Teleios is the fire from the furnace that embraces the pursuit to find answers to the essential questions that ask what the church is, what ministry is, what worship is, and what mission it possesses. Teleios is the engine of pastoral ministry that allows one to align with fidelity to the essence and grants flexibility in nonessential matters. It is a powerful magnifying glass that allows ministers to focus the energy of ministry on the essence.

Argument from Sociocultural Considerations

Teleios must additionally answer whether it possesses sociocultural applicability. One may be convinced that Teleios was the training methods and goal Jesus used to train His disciples, but it is another matter to be convinced that such vision is suitable in the sociocultural surroundings that the church in the twenty-first century finds herself in. The twenty-first century is characterized by unprecedented changes in speed, direction, and relationships compared to previous eras. The pace at which information is generated today is incomparable in terms of quality and quantity to what was happening just a generation or a century ago.[12] What makes all these changes worse is that human reason cannot predict the direction of the future.[13] Moreover, society is more hyper-connected through social media than ever before.[14] Yet at the same time, this connection spawned more isolated relationships than ever before.[15] Hence, discipleship for the twenty-first century must be tailored to be effective in the rapidly evolving landscape. "God does not change, but human culture inevitably does. There is no guarantee that what resonated with Billy Graham in the 20th century will necessarily resonate with us in the 21st century."[16] "Our goal is not to reproduce the 1st-century church in the 21st century but to embody the present reality of Jesus and biblical values today, moving toward a 21st-century church that embraces the future as a divine gift."[17]

We face two main challenges in the modern world. The first is the deconstruction of the transcendent and metaphysical concept of existence, which traditionally served as the basis for every moral, ethical, philosophical, and legal framework. In my younger days, people believed in a higher power of some kind. Just a generation ago, it was not difficult to find people looking up to the sky in an indirect hope for help in times of need. No longer do people of the present generation look to that sky. The existence of a sacred order such as a higher being, conscience, or virtues seems absent in the minds of average people.

The second challenge is the "modern self" that has emerged in the place of the sacred order.[18] The sacred order upheld by this modern self is moral and cultural relativism. This modern self would worship overt individualism at every moment. In the absence of an absolute sovereign, a new sovereign has taken its place—the individual. Now, there is nothing sacred that can touch the rights, potential, and inviolability of the individual. Not even religion has the authority over this individual. To claim, "As long as I maintain a personal relationship with God on my terms, nothing else matters," is a subtle propaganda of overt individualism infiltrating the church. Furthermore, this modern self-unleashed a powerful force known as the sexual revolution. Fueled by the sociocultural atmosphere that denies absolute truth and embraces only relativistic truth-claims, the sexual revolution ruthlessly deconstructed the traditional view of sex, bringing about support for homosexuality. Individuality of faith has poisoned the essential understanding of discipleship.

In abandoning the sacred order, modern individuals have not gained freedom but reaped greater confusion, a loss of purpose, and a crisis of meaninglessness. Despite advancements in technology and knowledge, there has been a significant regression, confusion, and loss when it comes to discerning what constitutes a good life and what life to pursue. Seen from a Christian perspective, the outcome of these changes is spiritual illiteracy. The loss of clarity and discernment is so severe that hesitation and confused contemplation are commonplace. Moral absolutes have been dethroned, yet people cannot shake off the feeling of being always scrutinized.

I am confident discipleship that strives for Teleios wholeness can serve as an antidote to contemporary confusion and unrest. Teleios Discipleship is a guiding principle of discipleship and a philosophy of ministry that offers the timely hope found in Esther 4:14: "And who knows whether you have not come to the kingdom for such a time as this?" Above all, it is a foundational principle that every believer should pursue throughout their lives. The Teleios we aim to attain through discipleship is the integrated formation of Christlike character in a believer. Teleios is not a new obligation we need to supplement or develop. We must reawaken the believer to cherish, nurture, and progress in this Teleios, calling them toward a life of continuous obedience, taking up their cross.

Furthermore, Teleios Discipleship introduces a holistic self that can replace the modern self. The Teleios self is the self that overcomes the delusion of cultural relativism. It is the identity that abhors blatant individualism in Jesus Christ through the recognition of a new birth and subsequent connection to the community of faith. It is also a "holy self" that does not let "sexual immorality and all impurity or covetousness . . . even be named" among them (Eph. 5:3). This self, born from the Spirit of Jesus Christ, remains humble and empty, directing its will not toward the self-given meaning of life but toward God's will. The Teleios disciple is the one who gazes at the cross as the centerline on the highway of life, putting to death the old self that only sought to cave into sinful desires.

Will Teleios Discipleship Still Be Viable in the Age of Artificial Intelligence?

In a time when everything is changing rapidly and artificial intelligence and virtual reality are becoming common, can discipleship training continue to minister effectively? *Singularity* is the term that refers to the point at which humans may no longer be able to control artificial intelligence, and some have suggested that it will arrive by the year 2045.[19] At such a time, it will be the beginning of an era that brings unprecedented changes to human civilization through the self-dictated evolution artificial intelligence generates on its own, often described as the "intelligence explosion." Can Teleios Discipleship have practical significance in such a period? What similarities or differences in challenges the church faces in the age of artificial intelligence have from historical ones such as early Christian Gnosticism, the Enlightenment of the eighteenth century, twentieth-century communism, or postmodernism since the 1960s?

While all of these major threats share commonality as an attempt to dismantle the foundational meaning of the cross and resurrection, the context of the current challenges is unique. The era of artificial intelligence is characterized by an unprecedented global flow, free from the constraints of space and time. Therefore, Christianity can face an identity crisis and a crisis of faith in an instant, all the while failing to detect these undermining effects under our radar. We do not readily recognize that the convenience, innovation, and omnipotence inherent in artificial intelligence serve to substantiate a secular narrative that humans have progressed beyond a need for a God. How can we ensure that discipleship remains steadfast amid the enormous upheaval of the modern world? How can the church safeguard the fundamental aim and heart of Christian ministry as the staff of Moses and the sling stones of David once delivered God's people from such gigantic perils?

To address this, those in ministry must have a dual perspective, looking both in and outside the church. Focusing solely on the church's internal issues leads to neglecting the imminent danger from the deluge of the secular world. This is why the true heart of the minister is so important. When a minister's heart aches for the lost as he searches for it all night and day long and pulsates with a sense of mission toward that one soul, the church will blossom internally and overcome the world externally. No matter how the turbulent storms of the secular world rage, the church's future will be determined not by any of the externals but by how many genuine agents of the divine calling—those who consider the mission given by Jesus Christ more precious than their own lives—exist within us. We hear this heartbeat best expressed in this confession; it is of the apostle Paul when he says, "I do not account my life of any value nor as precious to myself, if only I may finish my course and the ministry that I received from the Lord Jesus, to testify to the gospel of the grace of God" (Acts 20:24).

Argument from Pastoral Theology

Even after hearing the argument for Teleios Discipleship from theological, pastoral, and sociocultural perspectives, one significant question remains. It is the question that arises from the sense of doubt. If we are not capable of attaining the full stature of Teleios ourselves, how can one compel others to pursue it? While it is true that no minister will ever be perfect in this life, it cannot mean we simply give up this pursuit altogether. So, how can imperfect and unqualified humans like us pursue Teleios?

Augustine found the answer in God's nature that delights in lavishing his grace: "Grant what you command, and command what you will."[20] When God commands us to "be" or "do," it will surely come to pass because he places the means to obey the command in our hands. Moreover, what God commands us is also what he desires. In this light, if it is the Lord who calls us to "follow [Him]," we can also be certain that he will be the one to supply us with the desire, strength, wisdom, and agility to follow Him (Mark 1:17–18).

God delights in lavishing His grace (2 Cor. 9:8). He invites us to walk with Him, even before we fully understand what it is like to completely commit ourselves to discipleship. Discipleship is an experience of the presence of the God "who daily bears us up" (Ps. 68:19). Discipleship is arduous but beautiful. The process brings about changes in character and life, though they are accompanied by cost. But the journey of conforming back to the life He desires and lavishes is worth the payment and is full of hope and expectations. The cost involved in this change can never outweigh the glorious gift of the transformation.

Discipleship is solemn and beautiful. If you were to listen to Beethoven's symphony and take a music theory exam, it might feel quite overwhelming. However, consider the experience of enjoying a performance of Beethoven's work by a famous orchestra with someone you love.

You might immerse yourself in the beauty of the performance. It will be enchanting. The growth in discipleship works the same way. The Lord does not twist our arms to force a life of new moral codes and obligations for the sake of the law, but leads us on a path of change befitting his children. As we walk in steps befitting our status, the beauty and glory of God's perfection will evoke a sense of awe and reverence in us. We will come to marvel at His gift of perfection taking root in us.

Discipleship brings about specific changes in life, but it is not an endless program of behavioral change. Discipleship training must not operate this way. Instead, we are inviting the believers to "participate in the process of change, not as a redemptive program but a personalized redemption journey by a redeemer himself."[21] Therefore, discipleship training is not just a curriculum but a personal encounter and fellowship with the living Lord that transforms us. The path of faith is solemn but eternally joyful.[22] Therefore, discipleship training is a path one can walk with the joy found in following the Lord's footsteps.

Pastoral Ministry with a Sincere Heart for People and a Whole Heart for God

I have always prayed, "God, grant me a ministry that can only be explained by Your power." Churches everywhere have faced numerous challenges in recent years, especially with the pandemic. The call to return believers to in-person worship evoked a sensation akin to the discomfort experienced when using a muscle that had long been inactive. This circumstance placed considerable strain on local churches and prompted inquiries into the sustainability of conventional forms of ministry.

In the 1970s and 1980s, the Korean church rallied around the slogan "Plant Christ in the hearts of every Korean people and make this land a field of abundant spiritual harvest." However, the early 2000s marked a visible decline in the zeal for evangelism and revival. In light of these challenges, Korean churches began to contemplate how to navigate an increasingly hostile environment and how to fulfill their mission in the era of the Fourth Industrial Revolution. They focused on how to pass on the faith to the next generation, given the influences of secularization and religious pluralism.

The National Pastors Conference at SaRang Church began as a response to these pastoral concerns. We initiated midweek daily prayer meetings to prepare for this time. Some were skeptical about the prospect of having more than five thousand ministers attend during these challenging times. As we started the prayer meetings, however, we noticed that various problems seemed to vanish, like melting snow, and that the obstacles began appearing as stepping stones.

Why did this happen? People had various interpretations, but for me, one conviction emerged as clear as daylight: "We sought the Lord with undivided hearts!" This awakening and revelation felt as if my body had been struck by lightning. From that moment, the slogan for the National Pastors Conference, "Sincere Heart for People and the Whole Heart for God," burst forth, gaining national attention beyond the walls of my church. This slogan resonated not only in the churches but also in society at large. "Sincere Heart for People and the Whole Heart for God" was a divine blessing that came because of responding to God with undivided hearts and sincere faith. It unlocked a new chapter in the ministry. Teleios became the source of enthusiasm and dynamism in our pastoral efforts, opening new horizons of ministry. Teleios enables a ministry that possesses a "Sincere Heart for People and the Whole Heart for God."

The Human Nature Drawn to Teleios

The Origin of the Heart's Desire for Wholeness

Humans are well aware of their own imperfections. What is astonishing is that though humans are fully aware of their imperfections, they are driven desperately to pursue wholeness. They relentlessly seek Teleios, even though, if they understood their imperfections, they would stop dreaming of perfection.

The Bible reveals the origin of the human nature that seeks Teleios. We begin to find clues as we reflect on the image of God. What does it mean to be made in the image of God? In Genesis 5:3, Adam has a son, Seth. Seth was like his father Adam—"his own likeness, after his image." The name "Seth" means "resemblance" or "likeness." The son, Seth, is like the father, Adam. When we consider the relationship between Adam and Seth, it becomes clear that when we say humans are made in God's image, it means that humans are created to resemble God in a special sense. John Calvin, for this reason, said, "Man is like God, in whose image he was made. Within man, the glory of God is manifested as though in a mirror."[23]

In what ways does mankind resemble God? We can list a few aspects. First, unlike other creatures, humans possess reason, spirituality, and the ability to know and worship God. Furthermore, the fact that humans were created as male and female means that when men and women unite as couples in love, they reflect the image of God (Gen. 1:27; 5:1–2). God has given humans the authority to rule over creation in His place, and their dominion over creation is another reflection of God's image (Gen. 1:28). Moreover, the New Testament emphasizes that humans can have covenantal communion with God in righteousness and holiness (1 Cor. 1:9).

However, the image of God within humans has been significantly marred (Rom. 3:23). By rebelling against God, the righteousness and holiness that were originally in them were shattered, and the image of God within them was also seriously damaged. Without Christ, humans would never have become new creations who are "after the likeness of God in true righteousness and holiness" (Eph. 4:24). In Jesus Christ, as the second Adam, humans have been recreated in the image of God (2 Cor. 5:17). This renewed image holds the ultimate goal of growing to the "measure of the stature of the fullness of Christ" (Eph. 4:13). Our yearning for wholeness stems from this nature. Even though this nature makes us aware of our imperfections, we cannot help but desire wholeness. Thus, wholeness is both an ideal and a holy burden for creatures.

A Proper Understanding of Teleios Wholeness

We often approach the term Teleios with reservation because we often understand it in secular terms rather than from a biblical perspective. In Hebrews, the Greek adjective 'τέλειος' (teleios) meaning "complete" or "perfect," along with its noun form, 'τελειότης' (teleiotēs), and the verb 'τελειόω' (teleioo) altogether appear a remarkable twelve times. Despite the seemingly straightforward nature of these words, their usage proves unexpectedly intricate, making their interpretation not easily discernible. The word *complete*, contrary to our common understanding, was employed with diverse meanings in the first-century Mediterranean context, encompassing Jewish society and various aspects of daily life along the Mediterranean shores.[24]

Let us explore some common usages. First, in some Hellenistic Jewish literature, *Teleios* referred to the physical and emotional maturity that could only be achieved later in life. This sense of wholeness is closely related to the notions of maturity and wisdom attained with age. To translate in modern terms, "seasoned, experienced" would be the best equivalent. Second, it also referred to a moral or ethical superiority that resulted from rigorous training. In other words, the term was also associated with the idea of moral perfection. Achieving such a state necessitated strict personal discipline. Rigorous self-cultivation was the only way to reach moral superiority. Third, in the context of Greco-Roman religious cultures, the term *Teleios* was used to describe becoming a full member of some mystery cults or religious groups, suggesting initiation into hidden knowledge.

The fourth category requires further treatment. Though *Teleios* was used in the Septuagint to denote moral excellence (Gen. 6:9; 1 Kings 15:3) and unblemished sacrifice (Exod. 12:5), there was one additional and unique use. The term *Teleios* was used also to express the concept of "ordination" concerning priestly duties.[25] Korean translations of the Bible translate *Teleios* as "entrusted to the priest." But when translated directly, it means that the "hands of the priests are made whole." It conveys the idea that the priests' hands are being made "whole" by becoming authorized and qualified for the priestly service. The context allows us to understand that the term was used not merely to describe moral quality but befitting or being qualified to the position.

The Path to Holiness for the Saints

When we understand *Teleios* not as moral perfection but as "prepared for the duty to be delegated, fitting for the performance of the duty," one can interpret difficult passages like Hebrews 2:10, "For it was fitting that he, for whom and by whom all things exist, in bringing many sons to glory, should make the founder of their salvation perfect through suffering." Here, God brings about the salvation of God's children. In doing so, Jesus becomes "perfect through suffering." However, the idea that Jesus becomes perfect through suffering is not easily comprehensible. Does this mean that Jesus was not perfect before enduring the cross? If perfection implies moral excellence, does it suggest that Jesus, the source of all goodness and righteousness, endured the disgraceful cross only to achieve moral excellence? Trying to understand *Teleios* in the usual sense, it becomes challenging to accurately grasp the meaning of this verse. However, interpreting it as Jesus, in the role of the spiritual high priest, fulfilling the duty of salvation "most aptly" and being delegated as our eternal high priest, aligns with the context and naturally unfolds the intended meaning.[26]

The idea that Jesus became perfect does not mean "Jesus became morally perfect," but rather "He perfectly fulfilled the duty of the high priest who brings us salvation, with no need for further adjustment or refinement." Considering the perfection of saints should be done in relation to Jesus's perfect work. Simply put, the perfection of saints does not mean that they are "morally perfect" all the time or that they must be "without blemish" in the futuristic sense. Instead, it is more appropriate to view the perfection of saints as an ongoing state of anticipation of the perfection already granted as a status as well as nearing closer and closer to glorification. Teleios of a believer is the journey to eschatological perfection. Teleios denotes the fittingness of the saints as it correlates to their identity and status in Christ.

Then, what does it exactly mean to be fitting as a saint? "If God aims for our transformation, then faith and repentance become the way of life that we receive through His calling."[27] The image of a saint's fittingness is found in the one who steadily walks the path of repentance and faith, who, throughout their life, continuously follows the Lord through repentance and faith. It is becoming like Simon of Cyrene, who initially carried the cross for Jesus without knowing what it entailed, but ultimately owning the cross on his own as a follower (Mark 15:21; Luke 23:26; Rom. 16:13).

True Transformation: The Identity of Those Who Are on the Path to Teleios

There is a reason saints continually walk the path of repentance and faith, even though they have already received great salvation through the cross. Although we have been saved from God's wrath and judgment, the redemptive power has not yet fully been actualized. While our status has changed from being slaves of Satan to being the people and children of God (already), the full restoration of our inner selves has not yet occurred (not yet). What is required of disciples living in the space and time between "already" and "not yet" is daily progress toward the embodiment of perfection in their present circumstances.

We are the recipients of the light, a new creation (2 Cor. 4:6; 5:17). However, becoming a new creation and living as one are entirely different issues. Nowhere in the Bible does it promise that we will automatically live as new creations simply by remaining still. Because we have entered the new dimension (the kingdom of God) by receiving the light, deliberate and comprehensive efforts toward transformation are necessary. Discipleship is about wholeheartedly pursuing, choosing, and acting.[28]

We must remember what Teleios Discipleship seeks is not mere appearances of holy but an outworking of holiness. This is a reflection of some aspects of today's churches and believers. The appearance of obedience was present both in Cain, who killed his brother, and in King Ahab, one of the evilest kings in the history of Northern Israel; yet, they both missed genuine obedience. Similarly, from a Korean perspective, the Confucian culture's emphasis on maintaining face has contributed to the separation of church and life, making it difficult for individuals to integrate their behavior in public and private. There is no need for internal blaming for Koreans; rather, they must realize that the Teleios Discipleship is the source code that casts out Cain and Ahab within ourselves. The same source code cures this Cain and King Ahab imposter syndrome that Christians in the world face.

Some people fall into a deeper pit of despair while trying to change. This is because they attempt to change through their own strength. Self-transformation is as impossible as self-salvation. Even if we have a renewed status and position, it remains impossible. The Bible does not say that our change depends on our abilities (Jer. 4:6). Our transformation is planned, accomplished, and applied by God alone.

For those who were destined to perish and die within the first Adam, God, who is rich in mercy, restores us to the astonishing reality of being "the image of the heavenly one" (1 Cor. 15:49 NABRE). The new person we are to put on is already present within us (Eph. 4:24). If God demonstrated power, beauty, and faithfulness in the first creation, the second creation (redemption in Christ) is an awe-inducing work that involves being renewed even "in knowledge" (Col. 3:10). This is the goal and content that we should believe in and anticipate through discipleship. The transformation, possibilities, content, and goals of our change through discipleship are missions worth pursuing and cherishing eternally. Even unbelievers can change a few habits and adopt a few rules for a better life, but we have the guarantee that God's zealous commitment will see us through.

We are sinners who can pursue change with wrong motives. This is entirely possible still as Christians. There may be hidden desires to prove

I am a good person to God, to others, and even to myself. However, there is nothing that angers Jesus more than doing the right thing with wrong motives.[29] If I were to become the judge examining the degree of my transformation and scoring it, it would truly be a paradox. Pursuing change for the sake of earning approval before God and others and any attempts to change for the sake of self-satisfaction are both pursuits driven by wrong motives, and they can never be successful.

True transformation arises from our being and our identity. Transformation that is aligned with the biblical definitions of our identity—"children of God" (Gal. 3:26 KJV; Rom. 8:14 NABRE), "the bride of the Son, Jesus" (Rev. 19:7–8), "the temple where the Holy Spirit dwells" (1 Cor. 3:16, author paraphrased)—is the only endeavor for change that aligns with our identity. When we do so, transformation does not become a burdensome and daunting task but a delightful duty of the saints with the promise of life (Mark 8:34–37). The primary agent with the greatest desire to transform us is God (Ezek. 36:25–27). God sees our transformation into the likeness of His Son as the crucial task of His redemptive work. Knowing that God comes near to us for this purpose is both a comfort and a strength even in the dark valleys of death, a source that frees us from all of life's burdens.

The Biblical Truth About Teleios

Diagnosis of the Goal of Teleios as the Imitation of Christ

In Ephesians 4:13 and 15, Paul twice emphasizes the right standard for reaching Teleios. The first is, "Until we all attain to the unity of the faith and of the knowledge of the Son of God, to mature manhood, to the measure of the stature of the fullness of Christ," and the second is, "Rather, speaking the truth in love, we are to grow up in every way into him who is the head, into Christ." Hence, maturity is at the core of a Teleios Discipleship. The

Teleios we pursue is the growth that reaches Christ, and it is maturity that imitates Jesus while doing what is true in everything.

If becoming like Jesus is the goal of Teleios, and the process of becoming like Jesus is the journey, how does one achieve such goals? The answer lies in Jesus. The Bible records several instances of people coming into contact with Jesus. When Jesus touched a leper, the wholeness of Jesus flowed, and the leper became clean. When a woman with an issue of blood touched the edge of Jesus's garment. Even though touching an unclean woman made a man unclean, the opposite took place. The power that made the woman whole flowed, and she was instantly healed. Similarly, this is how we attain Teleios. The wholeness of a believer can only come through contact with Christ. Therefore, Teleios Discipleship is about creating points of contact with Jesus and incorporating those touchpoints into the way of life.

True Teleios wholeness is achieved when one wholeheartedly obeys Christ's words in areas they had not engaged in discipleship. In Matthew 19:16 and following, a rich young man comes to Jesus and asks, "What good thing must I do to get eternal life?" (v. 16 MSG). Jesus tells him to keep the commandments. The rich young man says he has kept them all but still asks what he lacks. At this point, Jesus says, "If you would be perfect, go, sell what you possess and give to the poor, and you will have treasure in heaven; and come, follow me" (Matt. 19:21). The key phrase in this passage is "If you want to be perfect." If you desire to be whole, it means obeying Jesus's words and following Him.

The rich young man would probably have been challenged to consider what true obedience involved for the first time in his life. Jesus is now asking the rich young man to obey in an area he may not have thought about before. Obedience is the hammer that breaks the pull of the fleshly desires dragging us toward the world. Teleios is given when obstacles to obedience are overcome. In this sense, true discipleship trains believers to overcome the hurdles of unfamiliarity in unreserved, unrestricted obedience. God's work is often accomplished not by the multitude who know obedience in their minds but by individuals who, no matter what the cost, learn to soar over the high wall that obstructed obedience.

Wholeness of Saints Versus Wholeness of the World

The wholeness of saints is not optional but essential. It is God's will that must be fulfilled (Matt. 5:48). The Teleios that God demands for us is different from the wholeness pursued by the world. First, the subject of wholeness is different. The world pursues wholeness with oneself as the subject. However, biblical wholeness has God as its subject, not self (Ezek. 27:4; 1 Pet. 5:10; James 2:5). Second, the method of achieving wholeness is different. The world operates under the notion that as long as the deficient parts are filled, the issue is resolved. However, the Teleios of a Christian involves acknowledging one's absolute inadequacy and ignorance, denying oneself, obeying the Word, and becoming more like Jesus. This is how one attains true wholeness in Christ. Third, the purpose of the pursuit is different. The world seeks wholeness to stand out, but the Bible emphasizes pursuing Teleios to fulfill God's will. For this reason, God desires to "equip you with everything good that you may do his will, working in us that which is pleasing in his sight, through Jesus Christ" (Heb. 13:21). Becoming whole is not to boast in oneself but to be better equipped to fulfill God's will.

The Worldly Tolerance Falls Short of Attaining the Teleios of Saints

The world seeks wholeness through tolerance and inclusivity. It believes that by filling a blank canvas with every color of the world, one can achieve wholeness. The worldly pursuit of wholeness believes that by embracing all differences without discrimination and consolidating all distinctives on one big empty canvas, humanity will reach wholeness. The world teaches that such undertaking is noble and the key to creating a harmonious society.

However, underneath this teaching lies an implicit presupposition that Christianity should be rejected. The idea of love is proliferating in the world today, yet it is devoid of God. Much in the same way, the concept of tolerance in the world is merely a term that has already eradicated God out of all its conversations. The new tolerance is based on the idea that "all truths are created by humans, and all truths created by humans are equal, and each belief is equal."[30] The world believes that by filling shelves with human-made truths, someday humanity will reach wholeness. However, without God who is the origin of truth and perfection (John 15:5), no one can reach or attain true Teleios.

The Invitation to Wholeness, Your RSVP[31]

The invitation to "attain to Teleios" should bring joy and gladness to the saints. "Speaking the truth in love, we are to grow up in every way into him who is the head, into Christ, from whom the whole body, joined and held together by every joint with which it is equipped, when each part is working properly, makes the body grow so that it builds itself up in love" (Eph. 4:15–16). From this passage, we can understand that the "whole person" we seek to become is growing into the likeness of Jesus Christ.

This message provides great comfort regarding Teleios in two aspects. First, Teleios grows progressively. One does not become whole overnight. It takes time. Past habits may still linger, and previous attitudes can continue to influence our lives. Even despair may set in as we continue to battle the lingering effects of sin. There may come a time when we question, "Am I a true follower of Christ?" We may be discouraged or disappointed by lack of instantaneous growth out of our immaturity. Yet, we must understand that our immaturity is not meant to be resolved quickly, and the journey to maturity takes a lifetime.[32]

Second, Teleios occurs in stages. No one starts walking right after birth. Spiritual growth works the same way. John speaks of stages for believers, referring to them as "little children," "young men," and "fathers" (1 John 2:12–17). Through training, believers progress through the stages of Teleios, discovering their spiritual immaturity. Further being exposed to the hidden roots of sin, Teleios believers eventually resolve rebellious habits against God. Even now, the Lord invites all believers to Teleios. He does not expect us to turn into angels overnight. Our only task is to respond with an RSVP, indicating our attendance by saying "Yes!" and adding our name to the invitation.

The Process of Teleios Taking Root

Spiritually immature individuals are "tossed to and fro by the waves and carried about by every wind of doctrine, by human cunning, by craftiness in deceitful schemes" (Eph. 4:14). An immature Christian is constantly swept away by the waves of the latest spiritual hype. They lack discernment and may not realize dangers promptly. Believers who are still spiritual infants may insist, out of their pride, that they would never be prone to stumbling even as they age. Peter, for example, made such claims (Mark 14:29–30), but in reality, he was quite immature. In short, Teleios had not yet taken root in him.

What then does Teleios rooted in a believer look like? Ephesians 4:15 mentions how we are to "speak the truth in love" (NLT). These two ideas, "speaking" and "in love" in Greek are one word, which can also be translated as "living in truth with love." In this phrase, two aspects are observed in a person attaining Teleios. Passively speaking, it involves moving beyond the level of a child and progressing toward maturity. It entails living out the truth in love. By embodying such a lifestyle, one distances oneself from pride, becomes sweetly broken, and discovers oneself anew. The person who pursues wholeness focuses less on the opinions of others, grows steadily more mature, and lives actively within the context of love and truth. As a result, arrogance diminishes, and self-awareness as self-denial increases. The person who continues to take root in Teleios adopts a new way of life, one that is radically distinct and often shockingly contrary to the culture. For instance, they pray for those who persecute them (Matt. 5:44), while the world advocates an eye for an eye and competition for self-fulfillment (Matt. 5:38). The Teleios believer unveils their true self before the Lord, acknowledging that this moment of disclosure is the most hopeful time in their life because the Lord accepts them as they are.

The journey to Teleios for a believer is vastly different from the path the people of the world are on. The journey Christians take toward Teleios holds immeasurable value. While the world's path often results in disappointment as one approaches the destination, the Christian journey becomes increasingly filled with hope as it nears the ultimate destiny. This is because the Christian's life unfolds in astonishing delights, reaching greater heights of holy contentment. Through this process, the life of a believer becomes whole.

Teleios Ultimately Leads to a Missional Life

The Bible reveals that thinking and knowing are not as crucial as acting in faith (2 Cor. 5:7). However, even acting in faith is considered secondary when compared to the transformation that occurs when becoming like Jesus. The invitation to the Teleios transformation includes goals for personal maturity (Eph. 4:13), establishing community (Eph. 4:16), and engaging in ministry through service (Eph. 4:12).

Jesus calls us to a righteousness, a broader love, a deeper devotion, and a purpose that is higher than any worldly calling. To pursue such wholeness, unity with other believers is essential. We are designed to be connected and united, caring for one another (Eph. 4:16). In Christ, we become interdependent, realizing that our existence is incomplete without one another. When we love one another in this connected way, the world recognizes us as disciples (John 13:34–35). This is the essence of the Christian mission.

The reason Teleios leads to a missional life is that a whole gospel inevitably leads to a holistic mission. John Stott describes it as "the Whole Church taking the Whole Gospel to the Whole World."[33] When one person goes through the process of Teleios, dozens or hundreds can find life because of that one person. Observing those who have undergone discipleship training and now serving as the discipled disciple-maker, it is evident that wholeness reaps a profound impact. The pursuit of wholeness by believers is not merely for the sake of individual maturity and noble faith; instead, it is for the cultivation of missional life. This is the reason the church, ministers, and believers must wholeheartedly engage in the pursuit of Teleios through Teleios-driven discipleship training at all costs.

The Horizon of Salvation for Teleios in a Believer

Path to Teleios Beyond the Forgiveness of Sin and Imputed Righteousness

In the 1980s and 1990s, slogans such as "The Gospel Stained with Blood" and "Unaltered Gospel" became popular in the South Korean church. Following such phrases, commonly heard statements included, "Jesus did not hesitate to be crucified for us. The blood shed on the cross covers our sins and resolves them eternally. Only by believing and receiving Jesus, who shed His blood for us on the cross, can we obtain eternal salvation!"

Such a statement is completely error-free. In the 1970s, I traversed numerous university campuses, proclaiming the gospel as articulated above, witnessing with my own eyes the countless souls coming forward to receive Jesus Christ for salvation. However, while forgiveness and redemption are crucial aspects, if we consider only these components and treat them as the entirety of the gospel, our focus will be on a passive defense—solely avoiding sin. If we limit the gospel to mere topics of personal forgiveness and righteousness, it will look no different than a child who contentedly plays in the dirt in a narrow alleyway, oblivious to the magnificent golden sandy beaches and the enchanting seas glaring with silver-colored lights that await just a few more blocks away.[34]

To Walk the Journey of Teleios, One Must Unfold the Full Panorama of the Gospel

Salvation is the missional outcome of the gospel. To fully realize the salvation of Jesus in our lives, we must grasp the entire picture of the gospel. The reason we assess our position from this vantage point is that relying solely on a fragmented understanding of the gospel prevents us from walking the journey of Teleios. This signifies that with a faith that confuses a few glimpses of grace as the entirety, we cannot ascend to the summit of Teleios as God desires it. We fall into a deformed and imbalanced faith that is isolated. We do not experience the joy of the feast and banquet found in the gospel, missing out on the celebration it brings.

To walk the journey of Teleios, we must unfold the entire panorama of the gospel. Paul did not present the complete picture of the gospel to his audience all at once in one sitting. He presented the gospel truths in various orders, argued upon different premises, and applied them in diverse ways.[35] The believers in the early church enjoyed limited access to the other parts of the Scripture before the final canonization of the Bible.

Hence, having access to the complete gospel message and the entire canon is a privilege for contemporary Christians. It is then the crucial responsibility of pastors to unveil the comprehensive picture of the gospel to believers. This enables us to grasp the mystery of providence interwoven in the journey of a believer's life and to advance in faith. This panoramic view of the gospel manifested in every facet of life will activate believers to walk toward the destination of Teleios in this journey of faith no matter where it takes them.

CHAPTER 2

The Fountain of Teleios: The Heart of a Shepherd

After graduating from Talbot Theological Seminary, I was asked to deliver a chapel message a few years later. In the audience were renowned professors. I felt an immense burden, wondering, *How can I preach before these distinguished individuals, and in English, no less?*

However, one mentor-like professor leaned over to me and said, "John, feeling burdened? Do not try to impress anyone. Just share your convictions and what you firmly believe. That is all that matters." Regardless of whether the sermon was good or bad, if I could not be convinced of what I was delivering, how could the recipients be sure? If I could not believe it with my life on the line, how could the congregation respond in faith? From that day on, I focused on delivering the one idea I would commit the entirety of my pastoral ministry, the concept I would hold onto even unto death—the shepherd of God.

The shepherd's heart is the source of my pastoral ministry. With the realization that this heart is at the core of what ministers do, I experienced sufficient grace in difficult times, experienced the explosive growth of my ministry, and overcame seemingly impossible obstacles. When facing the challenges of pastoral work, even in the darkness of the precipice of heaven's path, I was able to rise again to the calling, all because I did not miss the compassionate heart of God the Father who deeply cares for me.

The Shepherd's Heart of the Triune God

Genesis of Teleios: The Shepherd's Heart of God the Father

God the Father is a true Shepherd. It is commonly conceived that Jesus is the great Shepherd (Heb. 13:20), and we rarely associate God the Father, being the Creator, as having a connection with shepherding. However, that is not the case. The shepherd's heart has emanated from God the Father since the time of creation.

This is evident in various Old Testament passages. For instance, David portrayed God as a Good Shepherd in Psalm 23. The depiction of God as a Shepherd in Psalm 23 is connected to God's true shepherd-hood mentioned in Ezekiel 34:11 and following. God's role as a Shepherd is revealed in various places in the Old Testament as being a protector and guide for the marginalized, the poor, and the oppressed. The expression in Job 5:15, "But he saves the needy from the sword of their mouth and from the hand of the mighty," is similar to David's expression in 1 Samuel 17:37, "The LORD who delivered me from the paw of the lion and from the paw of the bear." The biblical understanding of God's shepherding act to protect the weak is consistent. This highlights that the understanding of God's role as a Shepherd is a transcendent inspiration that was intuitively and organically revealed to the biblical authors, all the while originating from the Father's heart.

God is a rescuing Shepherd. The Hebrew word *natzal* (נצָלַ), used in the verse "delivered me from the paw of the lion and from the paw of the bear" (1 Sam. 17:37), carries the meaning of rescuing from the jaws of fierce and wicked beasts, including instances such as Jacob's rescue in Genesis 32:11 and the Israelites being rescued from Egypt in Exodus 3:8. This term is used more than two hundred times in the Old Testament, consistently revealing God's shepherd heart throughout the entire Old Testament.

How does this shepherd heart of God lead His children to Teleios? The final paragraph of Leviticus 27 provides a crucial clue about the perfection of the believers. Leviticus concludes with the commandment, "A tithe of everything . . . belongs to the LORD" (v. 30 NIV). However, the manner of the tithe is unique: "Every tithe of herds and flocks, every tenth animal of all that pass under the herdsman's staff, shall be holy to the Lord" (v. 32). In the Old Testament, the tithe symbolizes wholeness without blemish. The tenth animal passing under the shepherd's rod appears unchanged from before it passed. However, the moment it passes under the shepherd's rod, it becomes the Lord's possession.

In this way, God is a gracious Shepherd. Our becoming Teleios is like the tenth animal passing under the shepherd's rod. It is not anything we earn or achieve on our own. Simply being under the shepherd's rod of God, we are graciously given the status of being whole—Teleios. This is the shepherd's heart of God. He desires that all pass under the shepherd's rod and that they all, like the tenth sheep, be sanctified and made whole.

The Path to Teleios Begins: The Shepherd's Heart of the Son, Jesus

The shepherd's heart of Jesus flows from the blood that is shed on the cross. "The cross is an event where the heart of love is poured out. It is the place where Jesus, crying out to God, all the while embracing all our sins, died as he connected our hands in his one hand and God's hand with the other. The cross is where the heart of love bursts opened for all."[1]

The cross of Jesus lays down the entirety of His being to save sinners (Eph. 5:2). His life-giving starts from the shepherd's heart. This establishes the foundation understanding that to serve in Christian ministry is to replicate that heart. Ministering with the shepherd's heart rooted in the cross means sacrificing oneself for the saints, offering one's life as a fragrant aroma to God, just as Jesus has done for us.

What is crucial for a genuine walk in Christian life is coming to full grips with the heart of God who did not spare His own Son for us, hence giving everything (Rom. 8:32). God's heart is the shepherd's heart (Pss. 23; 80:1), and the shepherd's heart is the heart of Jesus flowing as blood on the cross. This heart cannot be awakened through emotional awareness or intellectual understanding but by innovating the paradigm of pastoral care.

Luther further articulated this idea. "The essence of the theology of the cross lies not in understanding but in perception. For this reason, the theology of the cross prioritizes experience over mere thoughts or theories."[2] The shepherd's heart is not understood but perceived with the heart and experienced in life; otherwise, it cannot be truly known. The theology of the cross resists all attempts to understand theology through intellectual reasoning and considers all concepts as vain attempts. Luther presents a vision of Christians' presence in the dark wilderness of a fallen world, as well as how to respond to a deep anxiety about existential and metaphysical uncertainty as those who have embraced the heart of God.[3]

The shepherd's heart, grounded in the cross, is not just an emotional expression but a spiritual vision and source that enables believers to live as faithful individuals in the uncertain and anxious realities of this world. The cross is the source that enables the understanding of the love of Christ. It further discloses the love's breadth, length, height, and depth (Eph. 3:18–19). Knowing the shepherd's heart allows one to experience the blessings of understanding these dimensions in Christ's love. This spiritual awakening also influences human perception. Therefore, those who understand the shepherd's heart can see the world with open eyes and have a broader and deeper perspective on people, times, and civilizations, as informed by the Scriptures. In this way, the shepherd's heart, originating from the eternal heart of Jesus, becomes an inexhaustible source of depth in ministry.

The Power that Enables Teleios: The Shepherd's Heart of the Holy Spirit

Just as the Father and the Son are shepherds, the Holy Spirit is also a shepherd at heart. After Jesus ascended, the Holy Spirit came to fulfill the role of guiding disciples as the Shepherd, as Jesus had foretold (John 14:26; 16:13). The events recorded in the book of Acts vividly portray the Holy Spirit's role as a Shepherd. In the Old Testament, The Holy Spirit ministered with the heart of a shepherd (Gen. 1:2; Isa. 44:3; Job 33:4). In the New Testament, the Holy Spirit, who imparts pastoral gifts to the church's shepherds (Eph. 4:11), continues to bestow the shepherd's heart abundantly. Furthermore, the Holy Spirit provides the church with the fruit of the Spirit (Gal. 5:22–23), the truth of the Spirit (John 15:26; 16:13), and the freedom of the Spirit (2 Cor. 3:17).

The shepherd's heart of the Holy Spirit is expressed well in Romans 8:26: "Likewise the Spirit helps us in our weakness. . . . The Spirit himself intercedes for us with groanings too deep for words." Human frailty, inherent in the fallen nature, is an inescapable characteristic we have. This vulnerability originates from the state described by the words of Solomon, "The hearts of the children of man are full of evil, and madness is in their hearts while they live" (Eccles. 9:3). Left unchecked, it tends to accelerate toward a state where individuals grow "worse than" the worse (Jer. 16:12). Redirecting the humanity entangled in sin from sure judgment is impossible through human efforts alone.

At the core of the Spirit's groaning over human frailty is the shepherd's heart. A. W. Tozer described it as "the cry of a mother in labor about to give birth to a child."[4] Humans lack any ability to turn themselves back and are destined to die if left as they are. The Spirit, aware of the wretched fate of humanity enslaved by sin (Rom. 7:14), seeks to liberate us from the "law of sin and death" (Rom. 8:2), which is driven by the shepherd's heart. The Spirit's groaning beyond words originates from the shepherd's heart that lays down his life to seek the lost. Echoing this boiling groaning of the Spirit within the hearts of believers should be the earnest desire of every faithful Christian minister.

If the Spirit did not groan over our weakness and intercede "for the saints according to the will of God" (Rom. 8:27), we, as Christians, would be unable to pursue the embodiment of perfection that God desires. There are two aspects of perfection demanded from Christians: one is the "perfection through justification" achieved in the person of Jesus, and the other is the "perfection through sanctification" realized within the believer's heart through the Holy Spirit.[5] Without the Teleios in view, many are quick to fall into the current of the world and drift away from the path to God's plan for perfection. This aligns with the stern warning from the apostle Paul, "Are you so foolish? Having begun by the Spirit, are you now being perfected by the flesh?" (Gal. 3:3). The fact that there is no more wretched person than a Christian who has deviated from the path toward perfection vividly demonstrates why the Spirit helps in our weakness with the fervent shepherd's heart. The Holy Spirit's shepherd's heart is for saints to receive the perfection of sanctification.

Connecting Pastoral Insight with the Shepherd's Heart

The shepherd's heart results in pastoral insight. Reflecting on the prodigal son's story from a legalistic perspective, one sees the son's punishment as a deserved consequence. But when viewed through the father's heart, the discipline becomes a means of purification for future restoration. The shepherd's heart offers insights for pastors on whether to engage in a ministry focused on the past or one that illuminates the future.

The general impression of the phrase "shepherd's heart" is positive and warm, evoking empathy from people due to the emotional and pastoral associations of the words. However, to truly understand the shepherd's heart, one must enter the heart of the Israelite shepherds of that time. To possess the genuine heart of a shepherd, one had to taste and swallow the bitter experiences of being a shepherd in that context. Resonating with such a cold reality of the shepherd's life is the only path to understanding the true calling of pastoral ministry. In ancient Israel, shepherds were not esteemed. Being a shepherd was considered a lowly occupation, barely above that of a humble servant and even lower than a slave.[6]

The news of Jesus's birth first being conveyed to shepherds dwelling in the fields of Bethlehem carries profound significance and reveals the depth of God's heart since it signified that God came first to the lowest of society.

Just as the news of Jesus's birth did not bring joy to every shepherd in Israel, the shepherd's heart of God does not bring joy to pastors or believers who do not share the heart of the cross. While phrases like "disciple training should be done with the shepherd's heart" may be appropriate expressions, they can become a burden rather than a joy for those who do not embrace the true heart of the cross.

The shepherd's heart can never be a claimed right or privilege. To grasp the shepherd's heart, one must open their eyes to the fervent heart of the Father who allowed His Son to be wounded (Isa. 53:10).[7] The shepherd's heart is the heart of God who delighted in wounding His Son to give everything for His flock. For this reason, congregations pastored by ministers who hold such a heart at the core of their ministry are blessed. Contrarily, the absence of such a shepherd's heart in a minister brings pain and sorrow to the Lord's church.

The Shepherd's Heart of God Flowing Through the Old and New Testaments

The shepherd's heart of God clearly flows through Genesis to Revelation. In Genesis 48:15, Jacob confesses, "God . . . has been my shepherd all my life long to this day." Jacob makes this confession at the end of his life while blessing his son Joseph and his grandsons Ephraim and Manasseh. At the scene of the blessing, Jacob recognizes God as his compassionate shepherd and utters a profound meditation on the essence of faith, inviting us to appreciate the depth of faith.

The shepherd's heart permeates the life of Jesus. God, the King of kings, incarnated as Jesus on this earth, bore the sins of the world on the cross, even though He was without sin. Jesus, who intercedes for us even now in His prayer (Heb. 7:25), exhibits the overflowing shepherd's heart in all His ministries. Jesus became the "Shepherd of Israel" (Matt. 2:6). For thirty-three years, He served as the Good Shepherd, ultimately "[laying] down his life for the sheep" (John 10:11). The Bible records that when

Jesus returns, He will be the Shepherd for the saints, "[wiping] away every tear" (Rev. 7:17).

Jesus referred to Himself as the "good shepherd" (John 10:11), and Peter, His disciple, called Jesus the "chief Shepherd" (1 Pet. 5:4). Peter witnessed the miraculous catch of fish, experienced the risen Lord preparing breakfast, and, most notably, denied Jesus but later experienced restoration. Now, what we must note is that all these events occurred around the Sea of Galilee. Despite this cultural background, Peter never called Jesus the "great fisherman" but rather the "chief Shepherd," and this should hold significant meaning.

Confessing God as a Shepherd has been a central theme in the faith tradition of Israel. The reason to pay attention to the portrayal of God as a Shepherd throughout the entire Bible is that it contains the profound intentions of the Godhead and shows the fervent desire toward us. One powerful expression of the shepherd's sentiment is found in Matthew 9:36. Jesus, seeing the crowds, "had compassion for them." The Greek word used for "had compassion" is "σπλαγχνίζομαι" (*splanchnizomai*), which is having a heart of deep compassion, literally describing tearing apart of intestine in the gut. This word is used twelve times in the New Testament—five times in Matthew, four times in Mark, and three times in Luke.[8] This is the word used to describe Jesus's feelings when He saw the people of Israel wandering like sheep without a shepherd. If the disciples are called to imitate Jesus, then placing such sentiment and emotional commitment at the core must be the goal.

Now, let us journey through the entire Bible, exploring the flowing stream of God's heart, entering the heart of God who reveals Himself as a compassionate Shepherd seeking to return the fallen humanity from the misery of sin and death.

The Shepherd's Heart of God Encountered in the Pentateuch

The Heart of God that Comes to Adam (Gen. 3). From the beginning of human history, the heart of God as a Shepherd is evident. God personally prepared the best dwelling place, the garden of Eden, for the sheep. He called humanity co-laborers in His ministry, assigning them the shepherd's mission to cultivate and keep the land (Gen. 2:8, 15).

In Genesis 3, humanity is found in sin, and God seeks out Adam. This is done not by natural phenomena like earthquake or thunder, but God first seeks Adam with his personal voice, asking, "Where are you?" (Gen. 3:9). Within God's question lies the incarnational heart of the shepherd God, desiring to restore and dwell together again with His people (John 1:14). The essence of the shepherd's heart is found in the act of seeking. It is God who first looks for Adam first as a shepherd. "A shepherd should not harbor a hope that a lost sheep will find its way back or will be calling out for their shepherd on their own. To find the sheep, one must go to where the sheep are lost. This is the shepherd's duty. If God wants to find us, he must first come to us himself."[9]

Just as the shepherd God comes to his sheep, just as the pastor goes to the people, the pastoral incarnation is the key that opens the door of the heart of a shepherd. God seeks Adam first. God entered the space marred by sin to find Adam who was already in the realm of sin. In this movement of God, we find the heart of mission, the essence of the gospel.

In my early years, when I read the question, "[Adam,] where are you?" my heart sank. The question made me afraid of God. However, as I studied theology and delved deeper into the Bible, I came to realize that at the heart of this question was the heart that did not intend to shame, condemn, or punish Adam. If discipline were the purpose, there would be no need to ask. Why did God ask where Adam was? It is not because God did not know where Adam was. God knew. Instead, this question is a poignant inquiry from God's heart expressing His deep sorrow, all the while revealing His desire to restore Adam to his rightful place despite his fallen state. This heart, dwelling in the King of the entire universe, is the starting point of redemption. Only when we begin to grasp this heart of God, we can truly engage in proper discipleship.

From encountering Jacob as a shepherd in Genesis (Gen. 48:15) to becoming the sole shepherd of the Israelite nation from the exodus onward, God guided their steps every day with a compassionate fatherly heart. Even during their forty years in the wilderness, God ensured that they were not abandoned or forsaken as orphans (Pss. 77:20; 78:52–54).

The Shepherd's Heart Revealed in Moses' Prayer (Num. 11:12). Luke describes Moses's life in three distinct periods: forty years of upbringing and education in Egypt, forty years of solitude and growth in the wilderness, and another forty years leading God's people in the wilderness (Acts 7). In Genesis, God had already revealed to Abraham that his descendants would be enslaved in a foreign land for four hundred years (Gen. 15:13–14). Through Moses, God orchestrated the liberation of the Israelites from Egypt and guided them through forty years of wilderness living.

The Israelites needed a shepherd to guide them on the right path. The fact that the Israelites had been shaped by the life of slavery implies a complete addiction to worldly customs. Mentally and physically entrenched in the secular system, they were described as "stiff-necked people" (Exod. 32:9) who had to traverse "through the great and terrifying wilderness, with its fiery serpents and scorpions and thirsty ground where there was no water" (Deut. 8:15). How did God prepare Moses so that he would lead the Israelites to stay on God's path and not deviate during this perilous journey?

God prepared Moses by appointing him as a shepherd in the wilderness for forty years. Moses, despite being the son of a princess and educated in all the wisdom of Egypt, did not rely on his worldly knowledge and powerful leadership to guide the Israelites. The most crucial qualification needed to care for the oppressed slaves was a shepherd's heart.[10]

The shepherd's heart enables one to fight against the wild beasts in the wilderness to protect the sheep (1 Sam. 17:34–35). It is the heart that allows one to spare no effort, even risking one's life for the sheep (John 10:15). God made Moses live a shepherd's life, risking his life to protect and guide his flock. God transformed Moses from someone who relied solely on his own strength (Exod. 2:12) into a person who truly loves the nation and embodies the shepherd's heart.

So, what is the shepherd's heart that God caused to flow through Moses's veins? Numbers 11:12 vividly and passionately illustrates this: "Did I conceive all this people? Did I give them birth, that you should say to me, 'Carry them in your bosom, as a nurse carries a nursing child,' to the land that you swore to give their fathers?"

The shepherd's heart reflects the pain of a mother giving birth and the toil of a father caring for his children. However, this shepherd's heart is not an inherent characteristic of Moses; it was poured into him by God for the sake of Israel's exodus and wilderness journey. Moses's shepherd's heart is evident in his desperate intercessory prayer, where he pleads for forgiveness for the fatal sins committed by the Israelites, even offering to have his name blotted out from God's book if forgiveness is not granted (Exod. 32:32).

The Shepherd Heart of God Encountered Through Historical Books

The Heart of God Revealed Through the Judgment on Achan. One of the shocking scenes during Joshua's conquest of Canaan involves the crime of Achan, who violated God's command due to greed. When teachers instruct children in Sunday school, they would hope to avoid discussing the scene where Achan is stoned to death for stealing a cloak, silver, and gold from Jericho. However, even this passage reveals the shepherd's heart of God. Instead of immediately punishing Achan with a sharp instrument, God provided him with several opportunities for repentance and confession of sin.

In Joshua 7:16–18 (NASB), the concept of bringing someone "near," and that person being "taken" is repeated four times. The Bible emphasizes the process of Achan being chosen from the tribe of Judah, the family of Zerah, the household of Zabdi, until Achan was finally singled out. Through this repetitive process of "coming near" and being "chosen," God's desire for repentance is clearly expressed (2 Pet. 3:9). Casting lots was not a means of punishment but a reflection of God's heart, waiting for Achan to repent.

The repetition of the selection process reveals God's desire for repentance, emphasizing that the casting of lots was not a punitive procedure but an expression of God's heart waiting for Achan to turn back. The story is written to expose the broken heart of the Father who desires to see the Israelites rise again to continue their priestly mission through repentance. If pastors teach the shepherd's heart of God in this passage, starting from an early age, it can shape individuals into lifelong believers who would deeply understand the compassionate heart of the Father God. Through this, the foundation of faith for children can be elevated, and it can serve as a sacred stimulus for disciples, awakening them to see the shepherd's heart of God afresh.

The Shepherd's Heart Revealed in the Israelites' Spiritual Amnesia

After completing forty years of wilderness life, the Israelites entered the Promised Land of Canaan. The lives of the Israelites began to deteriorate significantly during the period of the Judges following the era of Joshua. They became even more corrupted, forgetting the Lord, and falling victim to spiritual amnesia (Judg. 2:10). Disobedience led to suffering, followed by a cry to God, receiving salvation from God, and peace returning to the Israelite nation. However, as the era of the Judges prolonged, Israel's spiritual state did not recover but deteriorated further, ultimately leading to destruction (Judg. 17:6; 21:25).

Nevertheless, God, as the Shepherd of Israel, did not abandon His sheep under any circumstances. "As a result of disobedience, Israel struggled in poverty for centuries. Yet, God chose a young shepherd named David as their leader."[11] God, having learned the shepherd's heart from tending sheep since childhood, established David as the king of the Israelite nation (1 Chron. 11:2; Ps. 78:70–72). David served as a king resembling a shepherd throughout his life. Regardless of the era in Israel's history, a true leader needed to possess the shepherd's heart in alignment with God's heart (Acts 13:22), for the scattered Israelites were like sheep without a shepherd (1 Kings 22:17; 2 Chron. 18:16).

The reason God repeatedly saved Israel from their sins was not because of their good deeds or repentance. Rather, it was due to God's absolute shepherd's heart and compassionate mercy toward them (Neh. 9:16–17; 1 Sam. 12:22). God did not break His covenant with Abraham and continued to embrace them. Through the book of Judges, we can witness God's passionate heart for Israel, hoping for their repentance.

The Shepherd's Heart That Redeems Sinful Deeds (1 Kings 21:8–28). The shepherd's heart of God does not merely mean showing mercy and reaching out to the fallen humanity. When David's kingdom prospered, Satan provoked the latent pride in his heart. In response, David, wanting to assess the strength of the army he ruled, conducted a census. The census revealed a massive army with 1.1 million men capable of bearing arms, including 470,000 men from the tribe of Judah, totaling 1.57 million soldiers. Why was the census problematic? David believed that salvation depended not on human strength but on God's hand (1 Sam. 17:47). However, his mistake was relying on his military might and seeking personal glory rather than trusting God. The census was an outward expression of the inner motivation and source of true reliance. As a result, 70,000 Israelites died from a plague. David, realizing his sin, fervently prayed to God, acknowledging his wrongdoing. He pleaded for mercy for himself, his family, and his people. In response, God instructed David to build an altar on the threshing floor of Araunah where he answered with fire on the altar of burnt offering. God had opened the door to salvation.

The threshing floor of Araunah, where David built the altar, later became the site where Solomon built the temple in Jerusalem (2 Sam. 24:20–25; 1 Chron. 21:20–22:1; 2 Chron. 3:1). The repentant offering made by David became the foundation for the temple in Jerusalem. Furthermore, Jesus carried the cross of redemption on Mount Calvary, near the temple in Jerusalem.

What was once a scene of heinous sin became the very place of God's redemption. God's shepherd's heart does not leave human frailty as it is; instead, this heart desires to transform wounds and despair into healing and hope, turning the threshing floor of Araunah into a temple where all nations pray and a place of the cross for the salvation of the world. This reflects the shepherd's heart of God, converting the sinful into redemption.

The Shepherd's Heart in Psalms

The Pinnacle of the Shepherd's Heart, a Song of Jesus (Ps. 23).[12] Psalm 23 is a messianic psalm. It goes beyond simply singing about the relationship between the shepherd God and David, who is a shepherd himself. Rather, it is David's poetic and prophetic expression of the love he had for God the Father, a heart the Christian sees echoed in Jesus. We explore how Teleios appears in this text as follows.

- Complete Satisfaction of the Soul: "The LORD is my shepherd; I shall not want" (v. 1). This confession brings to mind the time when Jesus was ministered to by angels sent by the heavenly Father, ensuring that even in the wilderness, there was no lack (Mark 1:13). Jesus found true satisfaction in His soul due to God's caring love.
- Perfect Guidance of the Soul: "He makes me lie down in green pastures. He leads me beside still waters" (v. 2). Though Jesus had nowhere to lay His head, when He went to a quiet place to pray early in the morning (Mark 1:35), He experienced the grace of God the Father, who prepared green pastures and peaceful waters.
- Complete Restoration of the Soul: "He restores my soul. He leads me in paths of righteousness for his name's sake" (v. 3). When Jesus was distressed in the garden of Gethsemane (Matt. 26:38–39), his soul was restored, enabling him to walk steadfastly

on the "paths of righteousness" (Matt. 3:15) prepared by the Father for His name's sake.

- Complete Protection of the Soul: "Even though I walk through the valley of the shadow of death, I will fear no evil, for you are with me; your rod and your staff, they comfort me" (v. 4). Although Jesus was led to the valley of the agonizing Golgotha, the Father protected Him amid numerous sufferings, raising him from the dead (Acts 3:15).
- Abundant Supply for the Soul: "You prepare a table before me in the presence of my enemies; you anoint my head with oil; my cup overflows" (v. 5). As the Son of God, Jesus was full of the richness and abundance of the Father, receiving an anointing from above (Acts 13:33; Ps. 2:2–9). Jesus, as the Messiah, ascended to heaven, partaking in the feast prepared by the Father (Rev. 19:9). Just as Jesus stated on earth, "Man shall not live by bread alone, but by every word that comes from the mouth of God" (Matt. 4:4), He, as the Shepherd, received infinite supply from God instead of earthly sustenance.
- Perfect Dwelling Place for the Soul: "Surely goodness and mercy shall follow me all the days of my life, and I shall dwell in the house of the LORD forever" (v. 6). Finally, Jesus obtained an eternal dwelling place for His soul. He ascended to heaven to dwell forever in the house of God (Mark 16:19; Col. 3:1). Jesus revealed Himself as the Shepherd of God throughout eternity. Despite facing severe trials in the wilderness, including the darkness of Gethsemane and the agony of the cross, Jesus

> willingly endured and overcame it all because he understood the shepherd's heart of God was with Him (John 10:15).

Shepherd's Heart That Rescues and Preserves, Even if Covered in Blood (Ezek. 16:6). After becoming the senior pastor of SaRang Church, I met various challenges. One came as the church began to undergo a new building project, which was an unprecedented undertaking in Korean church history. It involved an enormous amount of finance, human resources, and difficult decisions. We had simply outgrown our previous site. After consulting with the late pastor Oak, our founding pastor, we embarked on a journey to relocate.

When we announced our decision, more than thirty thousand members of SaRang Church contributed to purchasing the current site of land in Seocho-dong, a neighborhood in Seoul. Yet, during this process, the church experienced division. I was torn as well. At that time, many people believed the deep wounds I received were irreparable. In the middle of unspeakable attacks, a word saved me and kept me alive. "I said to you in your blood, 'Live!' I said to you in your blood, 'Live!" (Ezek. 16:6). In these words, the heart of God as a shepherd was flowing like a hot stream of blood running down from the cross.

"Live, even though you are covered in blood" is a thunderous word from God. Israel, though was trampled by the armies of the world and miserably abandoned, was never forgotten in God's heart. His words ring, roaring over the heavens and the earth, resounding everywhere to sound His vehement desire that Israel will live again. Desperately wanting to see such helpless Israel, who without constant care would surely be doomed for bloodied death, God echoes these words because of the shepherd's heart for her.

As they reflect on the shepherd's heart of God, those who understand the attacks and challenges pastors or leaders face in various seasons of pastoral ministry will come to understand that they are not forgotten either. The shepherd's heart convinces us that even if we may be in a state "covered in blood," we are safe in the arms of God. Our worth is not determined by people but by the words that are uttered when we are in the Father's embrace.

Shepherd's Heart, Where Righteousness Is Swallowed by God's Loving Mercy (Hosea 11:8–9). In pastoral ministry, there are moments of despair. In Hosea 11:8–9, the shepherd's heart of God overflows like a downpour. "How can I give you up, O Ephraim? How can I hand you over, O Israel? How can I make you like Admah? How can I treat you like Zeboiim? My heart recoils within me; my compassion grows warm and tender. . . . For I am God and not a man, the Holy One in your midst, and I will not come in wrath." This passage can be considered God's desperate plea toward northern Israel that has forsaken Him. Due to rampant wickedness that surely deserved destruction as they continued to reject God's law, Israel deserved to be left to its own devices, facing a path of destruction like an unruly son who rebels against his parents (Deut. 21:18–21). At that time, Israel persistently turned its back on God (Hosea 11:7).

We can see a fierce collision between God's righteousness and God's loving mercy. The burning love of God swallows up and consumes even the rebellious acts that should logically and rightfully be unforgivable. This is the shepherd's heart—His burning love engulfs and melts away even the darkest wickedness that deserves death. This is expressed symbolically as "bowels are troubled" in Jeremiah 31:20 (KJV), portraying the aching heart of the Shepherd. In particular, the statement "I am . . . the Holy One in your midst" (Hosea 11:9) reveals the spine of the shepherd's heart. This statement brings to mind the destruction of Sodom and Gomorrah, where not even ten righteous people could be found. We are no better than Sodom and Gomorrah. However, the reason we can survive without perishing as sinful beings is that, amid those deserving death, God personally stood as the "Holy One."

Even though we are rebellious children who persistently turn away from God, the shepherd's heart is the burning love of God that embraces us. Despite the perilous sin we accrue, it is God who personally stands among us as the Holy One, preventing our destruction. To see how God's love swallows up his righteousness, one must see the enduring wounds in God's heart—a wound inflicted by His own children, a wound sustained because of His relentless love. This wound is the starting point of the shepherd's heart.

The Shepherd's Heart in the Gospels

The Father's Heart Waiting for the Prodigal Son (Luke 15). The parable of the prodigal son encompasses the framework of creation, fall, and redemption. Understanding this allows us to discern the pastoral nature of God's heart toward humanity. The Father seeks and waits for lost souls missionally. In short, this parable bundles together theological, pastoral, and missional insights.

When Jesus looks out to the crowd with compassion in Matthew 9:36, we see the Father's heart we find in Luke 15 as the father looks out to the horizon to wait for the prodigal son. The father, seeing his son from afar, "ran and embraced him and kissed him" (Luke 15:20). Before the son could request to be a hired servant, the father commanded his servants to clothe him in the best robe, put a ring on his hand, and sandals on his feet. The father restored the son from prodigal to heir. In this sense, the main character of this parable is not the returned prodigal son but the prodigal father. Despite the deep wounds in His heart caused by His rebellious children, God the Father sustained unjust treatment. Father God, who waits with compassion, is merciful and always resides in his mercy.

Along with this idea, we must exercise our spiritual imagination to further explore the father's heart in God's heart. Upon witnessing the extravagant feast, the returning son might have thought, *Why did I not understand my father's heart? I thought being under my father meant losing my freedom, and I tried to escape, but I was mistaken. My father waited for me with love. Now that I know, I should live not for myself but for my father's joy. How can I bring joy to my father's heart? How can I love my father more?* It is at this moment that the prodigal son would have experienced a transformative turning point in his life. This emotional turning, or repentance, is crucial; without it, we are still prodigals even if we never leave home.

The essence of all ministries is not about what we can accomplish. It is about asking ourselves, “Why did I not understand the heart of God the Father? How can I please the Lord out of gratitude?” These are the convictions appropriate for a disciple who understands the heart of the shepherd.

The Shepherd’s Heart Unveiled at the Miracle of the Five Loaves and Two Fish (John 6). Jesus feeding the multitude with five loaves of bread and two fish is found in all four Gospels (Matt. 14:13–21; Mark 6:32–44; Luke 9:10–17; John 6:1–13). After hearing Jesus’s teachings, the day had now passed, and the people were hungry. The disciples tried to send away the crowd that was there. However, for Jesus, this was both an opportune moment and a divine place. This event was not only a place of heavenly manna and provision but also a moment when God’s people experienced His power. Through this event, the disciples experienced a revolutionary shift in their values. “It was a moment of moving from death to life, from fear to love.”[13]

Jesus told the disciples, “You give them something to eat” (Matt. 14:16). In John 6, Philip, lacking the shepherd’s heart, complained that even two hundred denarii would not be enough. However, Andrew still obeyed Jesus’s words, searched for something to eat, and found a boy with five barley loaves and two fish. Witnessing this scene, other disciples might have silently mocked, thinking, *What can we possibly do with such a meager thing?*

Yet, having the shepherd’s heart, Jesus did not ignore or dismiss the small offering. Instead, Jesus instructed the disciples to distribute them. Andrew might not have fully grasped Jesus’s heart. However, witnessing the Lord bless and break the small barley loaves must have left a lifelong impression of awe. Seeing Jesus, with compassion, feeding the hungry crowd and caring for the lost sheep, Andrew must have understood the shepherd’s heart. The shepherd’s heart became the source that empowered Andrew to minister effectively in any situation. Through this episode, the shepherd's heart culminates with spiritual compassion for those who had bread on earth but missed out on the bread of eternal life.

If we fail to cultivate this posture, we may end up spiritually damaging or discouraging those entrusted to us for discipleship. Who are we to serve these souls? What qualification do we have to motivate others to walk as disciples of Jesus? It is only when we carry the earnest desire and poignant heart that lifts a desperate cry, "What shall I do to feed the souls I serve? What loaves of bread and fish do I have to offer?" can we become shepherds caring for souls for the sake of the great Shepherd, Jesus. In those moments, we become the small shepherds, sharing in His shepherd's heart.

The Heart of Jesus in Forgiving the Adulterous Woman (John 8). A woman caught in adultery was brought to Jesus and thrust before Him, creating a moment of the most contrasting personalities in human history: "A woman and a man, a sinner and the sinless Son of God, an adulterous woman and the holy God!"[14] Pharisees questioned Jesus, saying, "Now in the Law, Moses commanded us to stone such women. So what do you say?" (John 8:5). This incident might have been one of the events that greatly unsettled the crowds following Jesus at that time. If Jesus commanded to stone her, it would cast doubt on His teaching of love. If He let her go, the One who came to fulfill the law would seemingly contradict it—a truly perplexing question of profound dilemma.

Yet, Jesus began writing on the ground with His finger. Looking up, He said, "Let him who is without sin among you be the first to throw a stone at her" (John 8:7b). Then, He stooped down again and continued writing. Observing that only the woman remained, He said, "Neither do I condemn you; go, and from now on sin no more" (John 8:11b).

Commentators have pondered this event all the while missing the true focus by frequently debating what Jesus wrote rather than why Jesus did what He did.[15] After writing, Jesus looked at the woman. She was alone and cowering in fear, on the brink of being stoned to death. This was truly a scene overflowing with the loving heart of Jesus like a waterfall, the heart that is saturated with compassion for sinners, and the heart that desires to make the darkest sins as white as snow. The words of Jesus became an inspiration for His portrait: lifting a fallen woman in the brutality of life; a mural image left in the catacombs of Rome depicts the Good Shepherd carrying a frightened lamb through a perilous world.[16]

The Pharisees sought to use this woman to prove their righteousness, but the heart of the Lord was different. Jesus declared that whoever was without sin could cast the first stone. Furthermore, He touched the wounded heart of the woman, freeing her from a lifetime of shame and guilt. His words that announced His forgiveness and recommissioned her back into righteousness embody the shepherd's heart: "I also forgive you; now forgive yourself and sin no more." In the tragic scene where stoning was imminent under the law, God turned it around to showcase a scene where His profound grace covered the profound shame of sin.

The woman's shame became a metaphor for human dignity tarnished by sin, and Jesus' forgiveness became an analogy for his liberation of humans enslaved by sin. "Even in our moments of shame and disgrace, Jesus redeems us from self-condemnation, offering freedom from it all."[17] R. A. Torrey insightfully expressed, "Christ hanging on the cross delivers us from guilt. Christ sitting on the throne delivers us from the power of sin. The second coming of Christ delivers us from the presence of sin."[18] Through the shepherd's heart of Jesus, the woman's body has become a sanctuary where God Himself dwells.

The Shepherd's Heart Calling Simon of Cyrene (Matt. 27:32). "His name [is] . . . Wonderful Counselor." This is the title the prophet Isaiah used to refer to Jesus (Isa. 9:6). God's marvelous nature is a reality, and this is vividly revealed in the shepherd's heart. Simon, from Cyrene, came to Jerusalem for the significant Jewish festival of Passover. Many Jews living far away dreamed of one thing throughout their lives: observing a festival in Jerusalem. Simon of Cyrene was one of them.

Something, however, happened to Simon that both bewildered and infuriated him. He was surrounded by a tumultuous atmosphere. He witnessed a prisoner, lashed with a whip, covered in blood, struggling to carry a heavy cross, repeatedly falling. He saw a prisoner condemned to the Roman crucifixion, barely able to bear the weight of the gruesome cross. Observing this pitiful scene, a thought might have crossed Simon's mind, *What grave sin has this unfortunate prisoner committed to endure the dreadful punishment of the cross?* As he shivered at the gruesome spectacle, a Roman soldier called him with a cold voice, seized him, and forced him to carry the blood-stained cross of Jesus (Matt. 27:32). Simon's face must have contorted significantly due to the disgrace suddenly thrust upon him. The world either mocked or turned away from the misfortune that befell him. Yet, it was precisely at that moment that the overflowing time of God's shepherd heart toward Simon of Cyrene began.

At the time when the disciples who had been with Jesus for three years fled and the seventy disciples whom Jesus had appointed deserted Him, God's heart was already directed toward Simon of Cyrene. Through Simon a grand ministry was planned and foreseen. It is God reaching out His hand to grasp us in the moments when the world turns away and even when our loved ones forsake us. Such a shepherd's heart of God is beyond comprehension by worldly wisdom or reason. Later, the apostle Paul would refer to Simon's wife as his own mother, indicating that Simon's household in Cyrene became a pillar in the Roman church (Rom. 16:13).

It may seem that Simon was unexpectedly forced to carry the cross. But in reality, it was the fervent love of Jesus that was leading Simon to the gate of salvation. Through the calling of Simon of Cyrene, the shepherd's heart reveals that his heart is not monochromatic but full of colors, not one-dimensional but multidimensional. On life's journey, sometimes God grabs hold of our lives and makes us carry the cross. But this is when the burning heart of God, the complete shepherd's heart that loves us, reaches us boundlessly. Some may regard Simon of Cyrene as someone who had a unique experience in a specific situation, seemingly unrelated to our present selves. However, every Christian today is Simon of Cyrene.[19] Therefore, the passionate shepherd's heart of God expressed to Simon of Cyrene still flows for each one of us in this very moment.

Shepherd's Heart Revealed in the Epistles

God's Heart That Preserves Us from Destruction. The shepherd's heart is missional. If there is a verse that summarizes the shepherd's heart, it has to be 2 Peter 3:9: "The Lord is not slow to fulfill his promise as some count slowness, but is patient toward you, not wishing that any should perish, but that all should reach repentance." God is not someone who warns sinners once or twice before unleashing punishment. He patiently waits, aiming to persuade and convince us (Exod. 34:6). God's patience stems from His love for sinners, and that is the shepherd's heart.

Knowing the shepherd's heart of the Father, Jesus also bore the shepherd's heart by taking up the redeeming cross for sinners as the Good Shepherd (1 Pet. 2:24). The ministry of the cross was a voluntary choice with a willing heart. This simply shows what kind of heart a pastoral minister must possess. A true shepherd's heart will willingly choose even the agonizing ministry like the cross.

The story of Jonah's dispute over the withered plant in Jonah 4 illustrates a practical example of the shepherd's heart. When Jonah complains of the heat because of worm-eaten plants, God rebukes Jonah, comparing the plant to the Ninevites. God did this because He wanted Jonah to know God's burning compassion for sinners (Jonah 4:5–11).

When speaking of the shepherd's heart of God that longs for sinners to repent, this heart illuminates a new light regarding the concept of penal substitution. As a Presbyterian, I believe the cross Jesus bore was a result of penal substitution. The doctrines we believe in should be centered on the gospel that brings life, not legalistic regulations (2 Cor. 3:6). This doctrine should be infused with the shepherd's heart of God and the atoning blood of Jesus on the cross.

When we engage in a fresh reading of this doctrine with the heart of God, we have fresh insight into the burning heart of God for sinners. We must now read the text with the underlying understanding of God's heart that wishes "that all should reach repentance" (2 Pet. 3:9). If we can penetrate the doctrine of penal substitution with the shepherd's heart, the pastoral ministry will rise to an unparalleled level of capacity.

The Shepherd's Heart Found in Paul's "Debtor" Identity. "I am under obligation both to Greeks and to barbarians, both to the wise and to the foolish" (Rom. 1:14). This verse provided me with insights that expanded my pastoral paradigm. Paul proclaimed the gospel to Greeks and barbarians, and they heard his message and believed in Jesus. So, who is the obligated debtor here? It would be those who heard the gospel. However, Paul, who ministered with the heart of a shepherd, thinks entirely differently. He reflects, "They are the reason for my identity as the herald of the gospel of Jesus Christ. I am who I am because there are those who need to hear this news. I consider my life of no worth; I simply am grateful to be able to run this race. Therefore, I am the debtor, indebted to them."[20]

A minister with the heart of a shepherd will never dominate over the flock but rather serve with humility, finding value and meaning in their pastoral role through the very people they serve. By nurturing disciples with the debtor's heart, as Paul did, the church becomes more equipped and humble. It prevents pastoral ministers from falling into the trap of self-righteousness and condemning fellow believers, a pitfall occasionally observed after going through seasons of discipleship training (Rom. 12:16). Hence, discipleship training can be seen as a thorough process of imparting the shepherd's heart to trainees. Without a debtor's heart, discipleship training will risk descending into the production of legalistic criticism or becoming an idealistic critic, losing the essence of true discipleship.

Shepherd's Heart Evident in Priestly Responsibility, Not Prophetic Criticism

Having examined the shepherd's heart flowing throughout the entire Bible, we have observed its vital importance biblically and pastorally. If the shepherd's heart is as crucial as this, how can a minister assess whether they possess the shepherd's heart or not? What pastoral qualities should be present in one's life to minister with a shepherd's heart? The true heart of a minister will be assessed where the plumb line of the heart lies between prophetic criticism and priestly responsibility.

A healthy sense of critical assessment is helpful for all. However, a prophetic criticism that is solely interested in judging others without a clear purpose can lead to cold cynicism. In this state, everything around them—including fellow believers, fellow members of the church, and fellow leaders—becomes an object of disdain. There are times when criticism becomes helpful in discerning what is good, but criticism alone will not produce good and abundant fruit. Ministry driven by a sharply critical judgment of others might capture popular attention initially, but over time, it often evolves into a fruitless endeavor. Over time, ministries driven by such interest simply fizz out. Hence, believers entrenched in prophetic pessimism or criticism must balance it with a sense of priestly responsibility.

How can one shift from prophetic criticism to a priestly sense of responsibility? This involves assessing whether the solution to the current problem is theologically sound, genuine in the pastoral context, and appropriate for missions. The pastoral solution to these questions is the shepherd's heart. I have witnessed in numerous ministry contexts that neglecting the heart of God permeates the entire Bible and in shepherd Jesus, turning discipleship training into a formidable weapon asserting superiority.

If we fail to understand God's heart is to bring sinners out of darkness, our ministry will turn into self-destructive harm no matter how sound the doctrine or how impressive the testimony is. Ministry should begin with a heart full of desperation, desiring to draw even one more soul out of darkness. Neglecting this heart in discipleship training leads to mechanical behavior correction, doctrinal legalism, and distortion into self-affirmation and self-promotion instead of self-denial. True discipleship training originates from God's heart. It involves calling sinners, granting them a new spirit and qualification, allowing them to live in obedience to the Son, and fulfilling "all that I have commanded" (Matt. 28:20). All this begins with the identification of one's heart with God's earnest longing found in His heart.

The Heart of a Shepherd from the Perspective of the Christian Faith

The Heart of a Shepherd Hidden Behind the Wrath of God

Why is it important to emphasize God being a shepherd? It is because of the common error people make in perceiving God. Many Christians view God the Father as holy and majestic yet, at the same time stern, punitive and wrathful. In my childhood, I was tremendously fearful and intimidated when thinking about God. If someone had taught me about the shepherd's heart of our Father God earlier, I would have spent my adolescent years with less burden of fear and instead learning to enjoy God more. It was only later in life, as I learned how to meditate on the Bible and delved deeper into theological truth, that the fear disappeared. What set me free was understanding the heart of our shepherd God.

If one does not understand God's wrath correctly, one cannot understand God's love either. There is no inconsistency between God's love and wrath. Martin Luther contended that gaining a true understanding of God's love necessitates undergoing a profound sense of despair, acknowledging one's deserving standing as a recipient of God's wrath.[21] This conveys the idea that even within God's righteous wrath lies the shepherd's heart.

There is insight that corrects our misunderstanding of God as a fearsome figure of wrath and Jesus as the true appeaser of such a God. It is found in the "remarkable paradox beyond our comprehension that the cross is the outpouring of God's wrath and simultaneously the outpouring of God's love. Because of His love for us, God, in Christ, absorbed His wrath against sin."[22] One truly understands the shepherd's heart when one understands that God's profound love has swallowed up His wrath. Those who comprehend this can approach God with holy fear and joyful delight even in acknowledgement of his righteous wrath. If Adam had understood the grace of the shepherd's heart, realizing that God's love swallows God's wrath, he would never have fled from God.

The Shepherd's Heart Hidden in God's Jealousy

When the Bible mentions that God hated Esau, we must be able to see the shepherd's heart of God as well. We read this verse as an expression of God's shepherd's heart, eagerly awaiting Esau's return to the point of jealously hating him. Understanding God's shepherd's heart equates to apprehending His jealousy for us.

It might be challenging to comprehend why God would be jealous of His creation. God pays attention even to the smallest idols we easily justify. God was jealous even of the small snacks carved out to imitate the goddess that symbolized the queen of heaven at that time. How can we fully come to terms with the fact that even these small idol-looking snacks caused God's jealousy and wounded His heart (Jer. 7:17–18; 44:19)?

Why is God jealous? It is because of our relationship with Him. God opposes anything that hinders our relationship with Him. The crucial point is that God's jealousy aims to protect us, and this is what sets His jealousy apart from the worldly sentiment. "God's jealousy is like a safety device that prevents us from missing out on the best in life and harming ourselves."[23] Remarkably, God's jealousy is connected to the concept of covenant. "Take care, lest you forget the covenant of the Lord your God, which he made with you, and make a carved image, the form of anything that the Lord your God has forbidden you" (Deut. 4:23). "For the Lord your God is a consuming fire, a jealous God" (Deut. 4:24). God does not want to share His love with anything in the world.

The Desperation of a Poor Mother with Many Children

If we were to find the shepherd's heart in the sentiment of Koreans, we might find it in the heartfelt desperation of a poor mother who has many children. A mother would not sit idly. She would do whatever it took, even cutting her hair or begging with no regard for dignity, if she could just feed her children.

As children of God, we do not fully understand the heart of God. Parents have the heart to willingly sacrifice their lives and love their children to the end. However, the heart of our Father God cannot be compared to the intentions of mere human parents. Isaiah 49:15 says, "Can a woman forget her nursing child, that she should have no compassion on the son of her womb? Even these may forget, yet I will not forget you."

Discipleship training is not just about creating ten thousand teachers but about creating spiritual fathers with the heart of a shepherd. This kind of heart is evident even in the letter the apostle Paul wrote to the Corinthian church. In 1 Corinthians 4:15, he says, "For though you have countless guides in Christ, you do not have many fathers. For I became your father in Christ Jesus through the gospel." Discipleship training is all about instilling in disciples the profound fatherly and motherly love, the love deeply rooted in the heart of God, even before laying the foundation for discipleship with biblical knowledge.

The Urgent Heart of a Shepherd That Transforms Mundane Ministries into Extraordinary Ministry

During challenging economic times in Korean modern history, there were individuals in the Jagalchi Fish Market in Busan who worked and raised families in the most difficult circumstances. Immediately after surviving the Korean War, they carried mackerels on their heads, traversing alleyways and shouting, "Mackerels for sale!" They were trying to reestablish life upon ruins. These were the kinds of people marked by adverse challenges and economic hardships. Their immediate difficulties included the inability to send their children to college. However, among those who sold mackerels, working those low-paying meager jobs, many mothers managed to send their children to prestigious colleges and raised them to be socially successful individuals. Despite challenging circumstances, these mothers desperately desired to put a stop to the economic hardships in their time, vowing not to pass on poverty to the next generation. Instead, they sent their children to college so they could open new doors for their family lineage, wanting to chart a better future for the next generations.[24] When we think about these hardworking moms, we can sense the deep urgency and desperation of moms who are resolute to give their children the best of opportunities, passionately desiring to grab them out of destitute life. These moms could not stop working; they were tirelessly seeking the welfare of their kids.

Does this kind of urgency and desperation exist among pastors today? Is there a sense of urgency that if they let go, if they stop ministering, the congregation will succumb to the devil's prey? In a war, a commander will not keep his people alive if he fails. In today's spiritual warfare, many pastors are surrendering their necks to the devil. The reason for this danger is a lack of urgency. The devil prowls like a hungry lion seeking prey.

In this sense, Martyn Lloyd-Jones asserted that not recognizing how desperate our spiritual condition is constitutes the most glaring sin of our generation.[25] The heart of a shepherd is one of desperate determination, like the shepherd who diligently searches for the lost sheep until it is found (Luke 15:4). Sheep, by nature, are unable to save themselves. If shepherds do not find them now, they are destined to perish. "A person who does not feel the burden for the souls of the lost cannot truly pray desperately. What we must never lose sight of is precisely this sense of urgency."[26]

Discipleship Training with the Spirit of Martyrdom and the Shepherd's Heart

Not everyone who claims to be a Christian is necessarily a Christian. One becomes a Christian by wholeheartedly believing in the Bible as God's Word. But does one become a genuine Christian simply by believing in the Bible? One must go a step further. A true Christian is someone who harbors in their heart the heart of God revealed in the Scriptures.

The Pharisees knew and kept the law better than anyone, yet they received severe rebukes from Jesus because they lacked the heart of God. They lacked the shepherd's heart. What did Jesus consider most crucial when training His disciples? This is the fundamental question. Asking what Jesus would consider to be most crucial is the key that should always be kept in the forefront and contemplated when facing difficulties in discipling others. Even when discipleship training does not seem to be effective or when reevaluating the direction of discipleship training, one must use this fundamental question to reset the course.

The supreme command and commission given by Jesus to His disciples presuppose laying down one's own life (Matt. 16:24–25; Mark 8:34–35; Luke 9:23–24; John 12:24–25). Jesus first showed them this pattern of laying down His life through the death on the cross. Without the shepherd's heart, the essence of fulfilling the Great Commission is impossible. The only reason for Teleios Discipleship training is to become like Jesus. This involves willingly standing in the place of death, choosing the path of martyrdom. No one can avoid a crisis of faith; and when it happens, all masks will be stripped away. We train disciples so that in moments of crisis, their training will lead them to choose the martyrdom faith. We train disciples so that their resolute choice will arise as an instinctive response from a transformed nature—holy, innate, and renewed instinct so deeply cultivated in them that it does not require second thoughts. A Teleios disciple whose heart inhabits the heart of a shepherd ultimately strives for martyr-like faith.

The world abhors the saying, "There is no salvation outside the church," and the unbelievers have ridiculed and caricatured the church and believers with all sorts of clever words. The warning contained in 2 Peter 3:3—that such scoffers will come in the last days to mock the church and believers—speaks to us like a sharp-edged sword that seems to cut across our reality today.

CHAPTER 3

The Path to Teleios: The Cross and Self-Denial

Whether one has recently converted or is a seasoned pastor with years in discipleship training, what should be the motivation, method, and goal of discipleship training for a follower of Christ? What spiritual principles and basic driving force should captivate and sustain a disciple without stagnation? It is the life of carrying the cross, denying oneself, and following the Lord (Luke 9:23). The essence of a Teleios disciple lies in self-denial that takes up one's cross. There is no genuine discipleship without the cross of self-denial as the ultimate means and goal. Self-denial is a spiritual warfare occurring within oneself, and taking up the cross is its outward expression of such warfare.

As seen in Galatians 2:20, self-denial and a life that takes up the cross are inseparable. "I have been crucified with Christ" is synonymous with "I live by faith in the Son of God." In short, it can read, "I live by self-denial." Rather than pointing to two separate realities, they mutually reinforce each other like the two sides of a coin. We must stand before the cross continually because the cross reveals our marrow. The cross recreates our sinful heart into the likeness of the Lord's heart. "The view of the cross, reinforced by Word and communion, constantly renews the Christ-like mind created within us by the power of the Holy Spirit."[1]

Jesus's cross is the key that opens the path to Teleios for grave sinners like us. "At the cross, Jesus became the most wicked and abhorrent sin for us, taking on all our sins."[2] John Calvin expressed this in *The Institutes of the Christian Religion*, "If we truly participate in His death, our old selves will be crucified with His death, and the sinful nature within us will die, so that our corrupt original nature will no longer regain vitality."[3] All of this thunderously echoes that no one can tread the path of Teleios without the cross. Chapter 3 is a confession that emerged after I experienced the dire tunnel of self-death and encountered the profound mystery of the cross.

In the Veins of the Shepherd's Heart Flows the Blood of the Cross

The cross is the source from which the shepherd's heart, the origin of Teleios, springs forth. Understanding the shepherd's heart in its true essence is not easy for modern people including the believers, as their thoughts and mindset are often entrenched in secular philosophies or principles of life. Such a mindset is not fully susceptible to embracing the shepherd's heart, which operates based on the principles of grace.

There is a common danger one must not overlook. It is the danger of stopping at the abstract understanding of the shepherd's heart merely as something contained in the vessel of God's love. Alternatively, one might approach the shepherd's heart as a means for healthier ministry within a specific area of pastoral care, simply viewing it as a useful tool for a vigorous ministry. However, both perceptions would be a misunderstanding and misapplication of the shepherd's heart. Just as the "theology of the cross gives birth to a practical theology shaped after Christ's life and death, which outlines the life that compels the concrete love for neighbors rather than abstract doctrines about God," the shepherd's heart is an applied principle of shepherding that guides the saints to live as Christ would on earth.[4]

Different people have different appreciation for what the cross of Christ has accomplished. This is because the breadth and depth of the cross are so vast that it does not flatten out as a matter of data or facts. The same applies to the way we train disciples. Disciple-makers' apprehension and appreciation of the cross are directly proportional to their grasp of the shepherd's heart, which is the backbone of Teleios disciple training; hence the significance of the cross simply cannot be overstated as it relates to raising Teleios disciples.

The Cross as the Centerline of Teleios

People seek an unchanging standard for life, much like the North Star. In the mid-1990s, I traveled to Stellenbosch Theological Seminary, which is located thirteen hundred kilometers south of Cape Town. Driving alone on a deserted road in the early dawn, I suddenly found myself unable to discern whether I was going in the right direction or driving in reverse. I had driven on the right side all my life, so I could never get used to driving in a country where the steering wheel was on the right. At that moment, the thought crossed my mind, "The centerline is always next to the steering wheel; that's all you have to remember to stay on the right track." And sure enough, it kept me on the journey. If the centerline is not adjacent to the driver's seat, it means you are driving in reverse.

The Cross Is the Centerline of a Life Leading to Teleios

The key for Christians not to live life in reverse is to make the cross the centerline of life. Placing the cross at the centerline of life in any situation allows one to stay on the track of faith without deviating. Two individuals illustrate this truth: Peter and Judas. If one does not have any prior knowledge of who these figures are, the sin Peter committed does not look any more grievous than the one Judas committed. Whether it is someone who denied and cursed Jesus or someone who betrayed Jesus for thirty pieces of silver, the difference is not substantial. Both Peter and Judas suffered from their mistakes, and both regretted their actions. Ironically, Peter, who was one of Jesus's disciples, denying Jesus three times could be considered an even greater scandal that greatly unsettled the disciples at the time than Judas.

However, Peter prostrated himself before the cross, while Judas fled from the cross. Peter eventually received the keys to the kingdom of heaven, and Judas heard the verdict that it would have been better that he had never been born. Peter finished his race; Judas finished his own life. What changed their life paths was an awakening to the cross. Placing the cross at the centerline of life means confessing and practicing love for Jesus in any situation. The dialogue between the resurrected Jesus and Peter in John 21, revolving around the love of Jesus and the cross, was perhaps the most significant conversation in human history. That conversation molded Peter's soul, paving the way for someone who denied Jesus to walk as a Teleios disciple.

After encountering Jesus on the road to Damascus, the apostle Paul centered his life around the cross. In 1 Corinthians 2:2, he boldly declares, "For I decided to know nothing among you except Jesus Christ and him crucified." For Paul, Jesus Christ is primarily the one crucified on the cross. He found the power and wisdom of God in the cross, which was considered foolish by the Jews and a stumbling block to the Greeks (1 Cor. 1:23). The Christianity Paul introduces centers around the cross, forming a relationship with the triune God. The cross serves as the archetype of Christian spirituality, the standard of faith (Gal. 2:20), and it is the absolute reference point and the core of faith (Phil. 3:10). The journey to the Teleios of saints begins with, penetrates through, and culminates with the cross. Without the cross, there can be no discipleship. Without discipleship there is no Teleios.

The cross as the central line remains immovable. Yet, many believers are shifting the cross according to their preferences, altering standards for faith, ministry, and life. This is not placing the cross at the center; rather, it is an endeavor that emerges when the church is contaminated by relativism. The prevalence of relativism in Christian practice and the interpretation of Scripture within the church is not always apparent. It seems to concern minor differences in punctuation or accents. However, the consequences in life are profound, akin to the world's downfall caused by the first sin.

Believing in the grace of forgiveness through the cross but lingering in sin might seem absurd, but it was a grave issue in the early Christian community. This is the misuse of the cross that Paul warns (Rom. 5:21–6:2).

Do not find it strange to say that the cross is taken hostage. It is already happening. Compromising the Word to justify one's thoughts instead of aligning one's thoughts with the Word is becoming commonplace. Os Guinness refers to this as the act of "holding truth hostage," or aligning truth with one's desires.[5] Making the cross the center of life means aligning our desires with the cross, not adjusting the cross to our desires.

How can desires be aligned with the cross? Is there any other way other than, as Jesus said about washing our feet daily? For those seeking to align desires with the truth, confession is the key avenue to center one's life back on the cross: Confession serves as a crucial practice, providing a middle track that allows us to realign with truth whenever needed.[6] In sum, confession makes the cross the centerline again, and selectively choosing words to suit our desires, compartmentalizing life in a way that skewing the cross with our desires is the act of taking the cross hostage.[7]

Teleios That Treads the Execution Field of the Cross

The apostle Paul did not discourse high-flying theology or ethics in his letters. Instead, he wrote letters to shape or correct the behavior of newly believing individuals. Having believed in Jesus Christ, he now instructs them to live in a certain way or correct their shameful and fruitless actions in other ways. No matter what aim, Paul consistently presents an absolute standard—the cross. He asserts that the process of conformity and adjustment of all values, thoughts, attitudes, and behaviors toward the cross is the journey of faith. This journey unfolds through faith, hope, and love. The reason a life of conformity to the cross makes us whole is that the blood of the cross leads us to "true heart and full assurance of faith" (Heb. 10:19–22 ESV, KJV, NRSV, ASV).

On the other hand, Satan, knowing that the cross makes the saints' lives whole, does everything in his power to make them turn away from the cross. For example, the enemy is interested in getting people disinterested in the preaching of the cross. "The cross has always offended people, and the people of the 1st century did not like the cross. Preaching about Christ's cross always led to persecution."[8] Justin Martyr, a martyr who wrote in the second century, records that preaching about Christ crucified resulted in the displeasure of Alexandria and intellectual citizens as they considered it a "crazy act."[9] Yet, the core of the apostles' preaching was the cross. Paul essentially declared that "the crucifixion of Christ on the cross is the center and essence of his preaching."[10]

Although the cross has always been offensive, it is crucial for the maturity and holiness of believers. It can be expressed as "mature holiness."[11] The reason the cross leads us to mature holiness is that Jesus, the author of salvation, was made "perfect through suffering" (Heb. 2:10) and "learned obedience through what he suffered" to be "made perfect" (Heb. 5:8–9). The perfection of Jesus means the fulfillment of His duties as the High Priest who will save us, not just an achievement of some moral perfection.

Connection Between the Cross and Internal Transformation

Is the fact that the cross transforms our inner selves an abstract assumption or a genuine reality? There is a text in the Bible that might cause readers tension as they engage with its content. In Mark 10:35–45, the sons of Zebedee, namely James and John, requested Jesus, saying, "Grant us to sit, one at your right hand and one at your left, in your glory." This was a serious matter to the extent that it would have angered the rest of the twelve disciples. It is undoubtedly a scene where the immaturity of their inner selves is revealed in an instant.

How did Jesus look upon their immaturity and heal it? One must take note of the fact that the discourse on the cross appears before and after this incident. More particularly, one must detect what intent is present in placing this episode sandwiched between the discussion of the cross.

Before experiencing the inner transformation through the death of Jesus on the cross, the disciples "spoke different languages, manifested different spirits, and expressed different ambitions."[12] This remains true today. With more than forty years of pastoral experience, there is something that still arouses my curiosity. Why is there so much disagreement among the people of God, despite claiming to believe in Jesus, actively participating in worship, having a deep spiritual experience, and even being leaders in the church with significant theological fame? Could it be because they have not truly experienced the cross, instead remaining in their different languages, different spirits, and different ambitions?

Few individuals have confessed the cross-enabled inner transformation as profoundly as the apostle Paul. Before encountering the cross, he trusted in his lineage, knowledge, and position of honor. However, after experiencing the cross, he considered all these things as "loss" (Phil. 3:5–7). Experiencing the cross means the outer walls of the soul shatter, and the inner self undergoes a complete transformation. It is the creation of an entirely new creation. Believing in Jesus and becoming a new creation is not just an epic, distant narrative but a tangible reality.

Paul not only witnessed the third heaven (2 Cor. 12:2), but his experience of the heavenly power was so intense that handkerchiefs touched by him could heal the sick and drive out demons (Acts 19:12); he still boasted only in the cross (Gal. 6:14). Why? Because the cross was the source and origin of everything he had gained, the very cause of his transformation into "Paul."[13] The fractures and discord in the church today, both among ministers and individual believers, can be attributed to this reason.

Teleios Discipleship training aims to train individuals to boast only in the cross instead no matter what situation. To achieve that, one must experience the cross and live beneath its shadows. What happens when you truly live beneath the cross? You experience God's power when you are weak (2 Cor. 12:9). You experience God's deliverance within the suffering. You realize that facing persecution or shame for the sake of faith is not shameful. You experience hope, looking beyond death with anticipation of life after death.

Living a life centered around the cross is adorned with repentance and faith. Disciples not only deeply contemplate Christ's grace but also earnestly examine their sins. If sin was not serious, God would not have taken such radical measures to send His Son for us (Rom. 8:32). As we deeply reflect on our sins, we long for the grace revealed through the cross (Rom. 7:24–25). This leads to profound repentance. Repentance with a contrite heart is a fruit that is produced through ongoing reliance on Christ's work on the cross for us.

Continuous transformation in life occurs when the idols deeply rooted in our hearts are exposed and destroyed. It happens when we cast out the idols and rely solely on Christ. The only possibility of transformation for believers lies in carrying the cross and following Christ. We must shatter down our idols (repentance) and delight in the work of Christ done for us.[14] The life bearing the cross and the inner transformation of character are inseparable results of faith and repentance. The primary place where transformation through the cross occurs is within the human heart. Therefore, transformation in these areas signifies our becoming biblically Teleios.

In my experience, the advice from those who have gone through the cross and the counsel of those who guard their own honor were different. When I had to face deep pits of agony in ministry, the advice from those who have undergone the cross of their own, experiencing their feelings of death, was invaluable. They live with unwavering confidence that, just as the cross leads to glory, excruciating suffering is the entrance to the new Jerusalem. Just as Good Friday gives way to Easter, the hardships, pains, and contradictions in the lives of believers will inevitably be resolved and transformed. They live with this vision in their perspective and a firm conviction that the day is coming.[15] These are cross-centered disciples who stand on an unwavering foundation.

Teleios Through the Cross Alone

What is the basis for the maturity of a believer to Teleios through the cross? The cross is the only means that fully satisfies the unapproachable holiness of God and God's profound love, while simultaneously resolving humanity's inevitable sin and restoring the irreparably damaged personal image of God. The complete sacrifice of the cross made it possible for the complete restoration of humanity.

To ensure our complete restoration through the cross, Jesus, at Golgotha, received three cups.[16] The first cup was received when Jesus arrived at Golgotha (Matt. 27:33–34). It was the cup of mercy, containing sour wine to alleviate suffering, which Jesus refused. The second cup was the cup of compassion, as a soldier moistened a sponge with sour wine on a reed and put it to Jesus's lips when he cried out that he was thirsty (John 19:28–29). The third cup was the cup of sin that Jesus drank in its entirety (Matt. 26:39). Erwin W. Lutzer writes about the third cup, "Jesus wanted to drink this cup without spilling a drop, and He wanted to drink it fully and in one gulp. This cup was the cup of sin that the Lord emptied entirely for you and me."[17]

Thus, Teleios achieved through the cross is given by Jesus's complete sacrifice. Through His offering, He has made His children complete forever (Heb. 10:14). The Teleios achieved only through the cross of Jesus is perfect and cannot be added to or subtracted from. As recipients of the complete redemption accomplished by Jesus through His perfect sacrifice on the cross, we have the responsibility to walk the path of sanctification, the path of the cross, so diligently "lest the cross of Christ be emptied of its power" (1 Cor. 1:17).

Martin Luther, who realized the truth that the cross makes the life of saints whole, said, "The cross alone is our theology" (*crux sola est nostra theologia*).[18] Denying oneself, carrying one's cross, and following Jesus—these three are the core of our faith. The cross is the only hope that humans living in misery and despair due to sin can look to, the ultimate standard of faith that the church and saints should ultimately pursue. Without the cross, there is no Teleios. The cross is Teleios itself.

The Path to Completeness: Passing Through the Gallows of the Cross

Carrying the cross in the arena of life carries a much deeper meaning. The spectacle of crucifixion was a common sight in Roman colonies. A convict sentenced to crucifixion had a task to bear. The prisoner had to carry the cross on their back to the place of execution. Keeping this historical fact in mind, the commonly used expressions like "carry your cross" or "I will carry the cross" nowadays have lost their original meaning for those expressions intended to communicate, "I will carry the cross to the place where I will be executed and die."[19] This is because, as Dietrich Bonhoeffer expressed it, "If you bear your cross on your shoulder and follow Christ, there is only one place we are headed, bidding us to come to die."[20] The cross undeniably leads us to the path of Teleios, but one must first pass through the execution field full of gallows of the cross to get there.

"But though we had already suffered and been shamefully treated at Philippi" (1 Thess. 2:2a), Paul faced disgrace for driving a spirit out of a slave girl, thus ruining her owners' income (Acts 16). If he had not chosen the path of the cross following the Lord, he would not have faced such trials. Paul says, "For the sake of Christ, then, I am content with weaknesses, insults, hardships, persecutions, and calamities" (2 Cor. 12:10). Paul handed down to Timothy, a faithful disciple, the purpose of enduring hardships in 2 Timothy 3:12 by saying, "Indeed, all who desire to live a godly life in Christ Jesus will be persecuted." Whether a new believer or one baptized, if you have pledged to participate in the Teleios of Jesus by following Him, you must pass through the place of disgrace, the execution field where the cross stands, to attain that wholeness.

Teleios Through the Death of the Cross

No one in the Christian faith denies the absolute importance of the cross or the power and vitality of the cross in Christianity. Why then is it challenging for the church or believers to readily confess that they are living by the power of the cross?

Even among ministers, there are cases where people consider the cross merely as a concept, a theological artifact, or a cultural symbol. They fail to recognize life, the experiential reality of the cross. "To understand the life-giving power of the cross is like confessing it in our lives, like flesh and bone clinging to our bodies."[21] Teleios Discipleship involves training that goes beyond the conceptual understanding of the cross. It is a process by which one embraces and confesses the power of the cross and lets it operate in them as their bones and flesh. The goal of discipleship training is to activate the confession of saints as to what the cross means in their lives as well as how this meaning of the cross would impact their lives and the surroundings. If such confessional training that produces the cross-shaped life is realized, it could potentially address many challenges arising from faulty discipleship training methodologies in the church.

The Teleios offered by the cross becomes more concrete when one understands the paradoxical nature of faith. When the scribes and Pharisees sought a sign, Jesus replied, "An evil and adulterous generation seeks for a sign, but no sign will be given to it except the sign of Jonah" (Matt. 16:4). The reason He said this was to indicate the cross that they would soon have to bear. Jonah spent three days and nights inside the belly of a fish, and his destiny changed. Death turned into life. True discipleship is all about living as the one, like Jonah, passing through the belly of the fish, experiencing the power that turns death to life, then rather than living as a fugitive, instead now living each day as the one who has been commissioned with a calling. This is the portrait of the Teleios Discipleship, a discipleship produced through the training that gets them fixed on the view of the cross.

Teleios Discipleship Training and Death

For a Christian, the pinnacle of Teleios on this earth is death.[22] This statement not only implies that, while the world sees death as the end of life, believers view it as the beginning of eternal life. Of course, for a Christian, death is shedding of the tent of the flesh and entering the kingdom of glory, awakening in the eternal morning.

However, if death is only seen in this light, one might leave behind the current life, merely waiting for death, dwelling solely in the dimension of yearning. However, this is not the fullness of life that regards death as the climax of existence. The Teleios sought by believers involves living the present life to the fullest while looking toward eternity. The Teleios of a Christian is the fruit bestowed upon those who understand and practice that life on this earth continues in heaven.

A person who loved God while on earth will continue to love Him in heaven after death. Someone who found joy in beholding Jesus on this earth will find joy in heaven through Jesus after death. People who love and practice truth and goodness on this earth will dwell in a city of pure gold, in the center of the city where only holy and perfected persons can enter.[23]

To understand the fact that death brings Teleios for Christians, it is essential to examine the Teleios achieved by Jesus through His death. Jesus accomplished a threefold ministry through His death: "He perfected himself, perfected his nature and character; and he perfected our redemption. Through his perfected wholeness, he drew us to his perfected wholeness."[24] The understanding that Jesus's death led the saints to Teleios becomes a holy impetus, shifting our perspective on death from fear to anticipation.

The apostle Paul achieved the most balanced view on life and death. He expresses that departing from this world would be good for him, but living on this earth is also for the benefit of others (Phil. 1:23–24). To summarize the life of a Teleios disciple in one word, it is an investment in eternity. Discipleship is for this purpose. Living in the present while keeping our gaze constantly toward eternity allows us to walk in the orbit of a Teleios life. We search for a good life, but if our search is only on the present life, we may find ourselves diverted off course when we look back on our lives.

The shepherd's heart desires that his sheep live to the fullest on this earth and yearn for spiritual success in the eternal world. To welcome death, one must invest and practice life for eternity on earth. So, what is eternal? God is eternal (Heb. 1:12), the Word is eternal (1 Pet. 1:25), and the one who does the will of God will be eternal (1 John 2:17). To live to the fullest on earth means to remember these three eternal entities. Teleios Discipleship is the work that inscribes this pursuit of eternity in the present reality of a believer.

Training like Artificial Flowers, Training like Real Flowers

Discipleship can be compared to either artificial flowers or real flowers. This difference seems to continue to influence the disciple's lifetime even after a period of formal training. How is discipleship like artificial flowers? Once the attractive appearance is peeled back, it wriggles with the spirit of competition, self-righteousness, and condemnation. It lacks the force that brings life to others. Biblically speaking, discipleship like artificial flowers is like choosing a "tree of the knowledge of good and evil" (Gen. 2:9). On the other hand, discipleship, like real flowers, is full of vitality. It is training that saves and uplifts others, bringing happiness. It possesses fragrance, growth, and, most importantly, abundant fruits. In short, it can be described as discipleship that chooses the "tree of life" (Gen 2:9; Rev. 2:7).

No one would want to avoid discipleship that saves people, full of vitality, to choose discipleship filled with competition, condemnation, and self-righteousness. However, like the Adam and Eve of the garden of Eden, the reality is that discipleship training like artificial flowers is not uncommon. This is because sometimes artificial flowers seem more genuine and beautiful than real flowers, and fakes disguise themselves to appear more real.

Depending on the touch of the disciple-maker's hand, the tender shoot of the disciple may grow twisted into discipleship like artificial flowers, capable of critical spirit and harshness, or it may grow into discipleship like real and live flowers, embodying holiness and vitality as sacred instincts. Therefore, the disciple-maker must always keep in mind God's lament, "When I looked for it to yield grapes, why did it yield wild grapes?" (Isa. 5:4), so that their effort to raise disciples will not end up being like artificial flowers. The essence of discipleship like live flowers lies in self-death. There is a saying, "A flower is a flower because it dies."[25] One cannot think that a real flower will stay beautiful forever. Sacrifice and service are essential for self-death; otherwise, it is not discipleship like real flowers.

Self-Denial and Self-Righteousness

A fatal ailment that manifests in the inability to crucify oneself is self-righteousness. Self-righteousness, much like cancer, is a lurking presence that turns disciple training into idle inaction. In the minds of those captivated by self-righteousness, there is a misconception that completing the training process earns them a certification of qualification for Christian living. This misunderstanding has emerged as the discipleship training models from parachurch ministry organizations have been integrated into the church. As these models of disciple-making entered the church, they brought forth good fruits but also unforeseen problems, and one of them was the poison called self-righteousness. Even those well-versed in the Bible tend to exhibit this tendency after completing discipleship training. This is evident in the case of Saul, who, having a thorough background in Jewish tradition and religious training, displayed such traits (Phil. 3:4–6). True discipleship training begins after completing the curriculum of the training process while self-righteousness emerges when one diverts from genuine discipleship training that is rooted in "growing in the Lord."

Critical Ailment Undermining the Life of Discipleship

The fruits of discipleship training are so abundant that they cannot all be listed. Discipleship training involves becoming a body resembling Jesus Christ, commissions people to live a missional life, and opens the way for others to become servants of God. Discipleship training is like sowing seeds in the field of our hearts, resulting in a tree where birds nest, fruits that nourish the souls of others, and the solid timber for the temple of the Lord.

However, there is a disease that can afflict such a flourishing tree. Growing a good tree takes decades if not centuries. However, once afflicted by certain diseases, a tree can succumb within months or years, unable to endure. In the case of discipleship training, a disease that can rot a well-trained and nurtured tree in a short time is none other than self-righteousness. When a tree is infected and decaying, anyone can recognize that it has succumbed to a fatal disease. In contrast, when it comes to self-righteousness in discipleship, even if others notice, the individual affected is often unaware. Paradoxically, while causing harm to others, those individuals may believe they are healthier than ever.

Self-righteousness undermines the church. "Even those who believe in orthodox doctrine like Calvin did or acknowledge the total depravity of humans like the true Baptists can still fall into arrogance and self-righteousness. If you were to ask a Pharisee, 'Is everyone a sinner?' they would respond, 'Of course, except for us.'"[26] This is a characteristic of those captured by self-righteousness—they see everyone else as sinners but themselves.

Characteristics of Self-Righteousness

A person trapped in self-righteousness is thoroughly disinterested in the lives of others. Their concern may revolve around doctrines or religious ideologies established within their own framework, much like the Pharisees. In Luke 14, contrasting figures appear—one side featuring law teachers and

Pharisees, and the other, a man with dropsy. Jesus asked them whether it was lawful to heal on the Sabbath. The Pharisees were knowledgeable in quoting Scripture. The Scripture they quoted was all correct. Surely, they were neither adherents of false religions nor fanatics. They believed in orthodox religion and taught people as they sat in the place of Moses. However, their problem was being ensnared by self-righteousness. Here, we must face a crucial question: "Can a person who believes in orthodox religion, holds sound doctrines, remains loyal to their denomination, and is faithful to the church of their ancestors become blind, stubborn, and wicked?"[27]

Individuals dressed in the attire of self-righteousness might paradoxically be deeply committed to their religious beliefs. They know the Bible and understand doctrine, but their decisive issue is the fact that they are disinterested in true life.

If there is an example in the Bible that vividly illustrates the characteristics of self-righteousness, it is the first son in Jesus's parable of the prodigal son. Earlier, we discussed the characteristics of self-righteousness, emphasizing their lack of interest in the life that Jesus gives. When the father threw a grand feast for the prodigal son who had returned, the first son could not comprehend it. All he could see was that his father's undivided attention was now focused on the returning son. He felt angry about the perceived injustice of his father's attention being directed toward the wayward brother. He affirmed his self-righteousness as he compared his moral excellence to his brother's waywardness.[28] The first son was entrenched in merit consciousness, blinded to the grace consciousness given through his father's love.

Self-righteousness is persistent. Those dominated by a strong ego are ignorant of God's grace (Rom. 10:13). When one grasps the profound mystery of the cross, merit consciousness and self-righteousness naturally fade away. The path for the church to recover the gospel and fulfill its mission may lie in shedding merit consciousness and self-righteousness. This recovery of vitality will take place as one dons grace consciousness and is clothed with the righteousness of God.

True disciple training is about putting on the righteousness of God, not the righteousness of self. Self-love, self-confidence, self-righteousness, self-indulgence, self-absorption, self-pity, self-sympathy, and self-fulfillment are not the characteristics of a person becoming like Jesus. Among these, self-righteousness is the greatest hindrance to God's grace. This is because one cannot cleanse oneself in the fountain of grace. Self-righteousness is like the enemy who sows weeds among the wheat while people are spiritually asleep (Matt. 13:25).

In the New Testament, Paul points out to the Galatians how they worshipped God zealously but lived a life full of self-righteousness, and how that led to manifestation of jealousy and strife within the church. Self-righteousness is the exhibition and natural outcome of the fallen human nature. How does self-righteousness appear in a believer's life? Generally, it stems from a sense of merit but can manifest in entirely different ways. In other words, "Resolving sin in one's own way is also a form of self-righteousness."[29]

Antidote to Self-Righteousness

Self-righteousness poses a significant obstacle to entering into God's mainstream of grace. Self-righteousness suffocates the soul because, "within the framework of a self-righteous person, there is no room for the sinner's Savior."[30] The desire to gain attention to oneself is the inherent nature of sin embedded in us since Adam's transgression, making any human effort to thwart that as merely a futile endeavor. The desire to prove oneself through pride is a sweet temptation that enslaves us. The only way to resolve this is through grace. As stated in Romans 6:14, the sense of pride disappears when we experience the liberating grace.

How can one navigate the journey of becoming a Teleios disciple without falling into the trap of self-righteousness? Charles Spurgeon asserted that the hammer of the first and greatest commandment, "love for God" spoken by Jesus (Matt. 22:38), can shatter self-righteousness into pieces.[31] Since self-righteousness is probably as fatal a sin as any, it carries a deadly poison within itself. Self-righteousness is a lethal poison that kills believers, and the only antidote to this poison is found in loving God and cherishing the soul.

Detoxifying from self-righteousness involves developing an interest in loving others and gaining life. Self-righteousness is the harm and aftermath of misguided discipleship training. Therefore, Teleios Discipleship training must guard against sprouting self-righteousness from the beginning. The smashing of self-righteousness with the hammer called Jesus's great and first commandment is the essence of Teleios Discipleship training.

Self-Denial That Leads to Teleios

If the cross is the only path to Teleios, then self-denial is the unique way to bear the cross. The Bible clearly states that anyone who desires to follow Jesus as a disciple must deny themselves to walk the path of the cross (Matt. 16:24). Self-denial is the cornerstone of the life of a Teleios disciple. In today's context, all the fractures resulting from misguided discipleship training, particularly the most malignant presence—self-righteousness—emanate entirely from the absence of self-denial. Jesus became the very example of self-denial because no one can walk the path of the cross without self-denial. How did Jesus deny himself? Jesus is eternally equal with God and one with Him (John 10:30). But Jesus Himself laid aside His status (Phil. 2:6). Jesus willingly obeyed the Father who desired His Son to bear the cross. Jesus denied Himself to give Himself to us. That logic applies in the same way to those who follow Jesus.[32]

While self-denial is a gateway to the path of a complete disciple, it is necessary to emphasize that self-denial itself is not the goal. Self-denial is required to follow Christ and bear the cross. Self-denial is sometimes perceived as more of a Stoic practice.[33]

Discipleship Is Not About Self-Realization

Transforming our bodies into spiritual temples by controlling our corrupted human nature is a daunting task, requiring an absolute ingredient called time. Discipleship training is about subjecting the body of sin to the fire of the Word, sculpting it, refining it, and molding it into a redeemed being resembling Jesus. Would Jesus, who rules over all creation, spend three years in close association with sinful disciples if not to transform their nature?

Teleios Discipleship training seeks to engrave the holy nature in the lives of believers. While it is impossible to change overnight, it is possible to incorporate daily elements of holiness rooted in the attributes of God. The goal of investing time to dissolve and purge the essence of sin through the Word is self-denial. It is crucial to reflect on whether discipleship training within the church today is being used as a tool for self-realization rather than self-denial. If there are fractures within a disciple-training church, one must assess whether the strife is rooted in the venting of desires for self-realization. If that is the case, discipleship training is only being used as a façade, offering opportunities for self-fulfillment.

In this regard, when judgments and criticisms surface within the church, it is crucial to examine whether it is the fruit of self-denial or an explosion of self-realization. Despite Jesus opening the door limitlessly to brotherly love, we must revisit the strict warning against standing in judgment of brothers (Matt. 7:1). The Bible portrays self-realization as the beginning of corruption. In Genesis, the reason Adam and Eve succumbed to the temptation of Satan was because he whispered the idea of self-realization. Adam and Eve's attempt at self-realization led to the downfall and destruction of humanity.

Those involved in discipleship training must remember that discipleship is a spiritual refining process that transforms individuals into a firm disposition of self-denial. In any case, disciple-makers should be vigilant to ensure that trainees do not fall into the path of self-realization. Discipleship trainers should constantly remind themselves that the path they are on is the path of self-denial, and they should regularly and constantly assess whether they are unintentionally veering off toward the path of self-realization.

The Uncharted Path of Discipleship: Self-Denial

"And calling the crowd to him with his disciples, he said to them, 'If anyone would come after me, let him deny himself and take up his cross and follow me'" (Mark 8:34). Jesus spoke these words to "the crowd" and "his disciples." He addressed everyone listening to Him, not singling out specific individuals. Hence, this statement applies universally to everyone present before Jesus. The requirement for becoming a disciple starts with self-denial. The path of self-denial is not one of comfort, higher status, or easy walking.[34] Asking the modern people who are accustomed to protecting and showcasing their status to deny themselves to follow Jesus is a radical and staggering summons.[35]

Commonly, self-denial is thought of as self-contempt, self-negation, or ignoring and abstaining from one's uniqueness. But in the original language, self-denial means "to sever the connection between oneself and a particular object or interest." From this perspective, self-denial is a firm and resolute decision to say no to the profound idolatry of self-centeredness.[36] The term *denial* in *self*-denial is used in the same Greek context where Peter denied Jesus three times, stating, "I do not know Jesus." Peter's denial meant, "I have no connection with Jesus."[37]

Mark 8:34 may sound like an extraordinary and irrational statement beyond the scope of common sense and experience. Even for those who claim to be Christians while desiring to maintain a moderate and nominal Christian life, this verse poses a challenging dilemma. Following Jesus is not about adopting a moderately gentle and culturally neutral position. Christian discipleship is radical and unconventional. It involves a transition from death to life, darkness to light, Satan's dominion to God's kingdom, and a complete surrender of self to God. This radical nature stems from a discipleship that transcends worldly norms and principles, overthrowing them with its radical fervor.

Self-Denial and Selfhood

The command to deny oneself refers to denying one's selfhood. However, interpreting this solely as understanding the self as inherently evil would be a mistake. John Stott aptly argues, "The self is neither entirely good nor entirely evil, and it does not have to be entirely good or entirely denied."[38] The self is a complex reality mixed with good and evil, glory and shame.[39] It is an existence that, at times, bears the image of God and, at other times, pledges allegiance to the devil.

Therefore, we must approach the concept of selfhood with delicacy and caution. The self that we must crucify on the cross is the self that resists the Lord, ensnared by the gravity of sin. Even after the fall of Adam, human selfhood still consists of both an image of God and an irreversibly damaged self because of corruption. "The self that we must deny and surrender on the cross is the fallen self, the self that is entangled in sin."[40] Once we accept Jesus as our Savior, a profound transformation occurs in our selfhood. While the prefaith self was a "created and fallen self," the post-faith self is a "created, fallen, and redeemed self." We do not have to nail the redeemed self to the cross. The redeemed self is the restored image of God, recreated and renewed by the redemption of Jesus (2 Cor. 5:17). The fallen self cannot worship God or give glory to Him, but the redeemed self can worship God and offer Him glory. Biblical self-denial means denying the fallen self, not denying the redeemed self. Due to the lack of clarity between these two, many church-goers are experiencing confusion. Without this understanding of selfhood, how can one confess to being a "sinner worse than a worm" and, at the same time, readily declare themselves a "prince in the heavenly throne"?

If we interpret selfhood only literally, we risk giving birth to a deformed self, known as the "religious self." This is as dangerous as viewing selfhood only as evil. The religious self-ignores the spirit of the words found in the Bible by legalistically regarding the worth of the written text. This self remains captive to self-righteousness. Outwardly, it may seem to follow the Scriptures, but in reality, it is a person who has never denied oneself to take up the cross and follow Christ.[41] "When we stand before the cross, we see both our worth and worthlessness simultaneously. This is because we realize the love of the One who died for us and the great sin that led Him to death."[42] The reason we need to understand selfhood in both aspects is to ensure a proper understanding that leads saints to have a correct identity and walk the path of Teleios Discipleship.

Self-Denial and the Priorities of Life

In Luke 9 and the following, three groups of people express their desire to become disciples of Jesus. Jesus, in response, delivers what may seem like stern words. The first person declares, "I will follow you wherever you go" (v. 57). Instead of a warm affirmation, Jesus says, "Foxes have holes, and birds of the air have nests, but the Son of Man has nowhere to lay his head" (v. 58). The second person states, "Let me first go and bury my father" (v. 59). Surprisingly, Jesus responds, "Leave the dead to bury their own dead. But as for you, go and proclaim the kingdom of God" (v. 60). The third person wants to say farewell to his family before following Jesus. However, Jesus asserts, "No one who puts his hand to the plow and looks back is fit for the kingdom of God" (v. 62).

Jesus offers because the path to being a Teleios disciple may not lead to a safe and comfortable life. It is a path of living counterculturally challenging even commonly accepted lifestyles and cultural norms. It is not about being "nice." Instead, it requires sacrificing one's life for the Lord and the gospel—a path of "martyrdom."[43] Jesus, from the beginning, lays out the exact challenges that those desiring to follow Him must face.

The words of the Lord given to the three individuals who expressed their desire to follow Him can be summarized as explaining that the path of discipleship is dangerous, radical, and requires a readiness for martyrdom. These ideas are explicitly restated as declarations in Luke 14:26 and 33. "Anyone who comes to me but refuses to let go of father, mother, spouse, children, brothers, sisters—yes, even one's own self!—can't be my disciple" (Luke 14:26 MSG). "So then, you cannot be my disciple unless you give away everything you own" (Luke 14:33 CEV).

These verses should not be interpreted literally, as it would conflict with Jesus's command to "love your enemies." Jesus does not give conflicting commands. So, what do these words mean? These words emphasize the priority of love for the Lord—establishing the priority of love. If the priority of love is not correctly set, meaning if the love for the Lord is not the source from which all other legitimate loves flow, one cannot love oneself or others correctly. Placing the love for the Lord as the highest priority sets the correct order for the ranking of love for everything else.

Teleios Discipleship training is the process of consistently readjusting the priorities of life. The importance of priorities lies not only in their being the best strategy for a successful life but in revealing where a person's true interests lie. Encouraging trainees or believers to continually adjust their priorities is crucial so that in decisive moments, at the crossroads of life, genuine interests and true love should be reserved for Jesus alone. If one claims that reading books is the favorite activity but chooses to play games at a crucial moment, reading is merely an occasional hobby. The same can happen in spiritual life. One may claim to love spiritual life, but if one consistently chooses worldly pursuits in decisive moments, it shows that spiritual priorities are merely noble preferences.[44] True self-denial involves an immediate and wholehearted process of kneeling. Therefore, without immediate and wholehearted obedience, self-denial cannot be proven to be genuine.[45]

Self-Denial and Isolation from Relationships

Denying oneself is the act of surrendering the right to be one's own master, trusting and relying on the Lord as the ultimate decision-maker in life. This is the essence of self-denial for Christians, representing a radical form of isolation from relationships.

There is no word in the Bible that more accurately expresses the idea behind the relinquishing of relationships as precisely as the term *waste* (Phil. 3:8). Paul does not consider things that were somewhat pleasant to him in the past, things he considered preferences, or things that were neither good nor bad as waste. Instead, he regards as waste those things that were "beneficial" to him. The word *benefit* used here, "kerdos" (κερδος), is the same word used by Paul in Philippians 1:21 when he says, "For to me to live is Christ, and to die is gain." Therefore, the benefit Paul considers as waste is truly something desirable, akin to what we might call a valuable item in contemporary language. To isolate oneself from worldly things to have a better relationship with Jesus involves considering my former interests in the world as waste, regarding them as filth that brings shame.

The reason for taking such radical measures to live as a true disciple is to counteract the accelerating gravity of sin. Sin, if left unchecked, grows to the point where it becomes uncontrollable. "Good and evil increase exponentially. That is why the small decisions of today are infinitely important. . . . Today's seemingly trivial desires open the door to the devil, providing him with a fortress or a bridge, and eventually, one ends up under attack from the enemy through that road."[46] Isolation from relationships in self-denial means breaking the relentless cycle of sin.

While the theoretical meaning of self-denial is clear, it is challenging to live that out practically. Therefore, the first experience of self-denial is crucial. Once a disciple gains the experience of cutting off the corrupted self, a new horizon for the spiritual life opens up. Discipleship can be seen as a process of training that allows one to enjoy spiritual freedom in daily life by accumulating these experiences of self-denial. Why do we get hurt, resent others, and close the door of our hearts? It is because there is something we are unwilling to let go of in the space between being who I am and the Lord's ultimate decision-making authority. However, at this moment, the person who realizes the cross and denies oneself finally offers the ultimate decision-making authority to the Lord. This is the heavenly wisdom acquired in Teleios Discipleship training. When you surrender the ultimate decision-making authority to the Lord, you begin to gain the freedom to maintain an appropriate distance from people and events. It may seem like I make all the decisions for my life, but in the end, you come to realize that I cannot exercise the ultimate decision-making authority if I am a disciple. Imagine being on an operating table. The surgery is for you, but the consent form is signed by the guardian. Just as you are not able to sign your own death certificate just before imminent death, the final authority of my life is in His hands.

Self-Denial and the Glory of God

The Lord does not command us to deny ourselves and entrust the ultimate decision-making authority to Him because He somehow plans to dominate us. Through self-denial, we receive the qualification to stand before God as righteous—this not through self-realization. Yet, many believers regard Jesus as a third party, considering themselves as the ultimate decision-makers. They act independently from the Lord, pouring significant attention onto themselves. Constantly, phrases like "I decide, I determine, I command" flow effortlessly from the insignificant mouths of human beings. A. W. Tozer aptly expressed the image of believers who exercise self-decision-making authority without realizing that they have no right to do so. He writes, "They prostrate themselves before Him all the while still striving to conceal and unwilling to let go of the crown they have put on their heads."[47]

This is essentially reversing the course of life. Surrendering oneself before God while holding onto the crown on one's head is not an act of handing over authority. I frequently reflect on the lyrics of a praise song that speaks of complete and utter surrender of all that I love, all that I adored, and all that I claimed as my own. Only when a disciple makes these lyrics a confession of their lives can they continue the path to Teleios.

Without the training to eliminate sin, discipleship training can end in dismal failure. Instead, it may produce individuals adept at using discipleship training as a guise for manipulation and inflicting wounds. In true discipleship, we can no longer lead a double life, a spiritual life not distinct from the worldly life. We must choose to live as Teleios disciples in every aspect of life. In short, "No one can remain neutral before the cross."[48] We must distinguish between religious life and biblical life. Religious life is for those who straddle the fence, but Christianity is for those who are fully committed to God's truth.[49] Teleios Discipleship cannot be attained through a religious life compromised with the world.

When You Fear Self-Denial

The term *self-denial* can instinctively evoke a callous attitude or a defensive reaction. This may be because self-denial is perceived as giving up worldly pleasures and achieving them through austere self-restraint. Therefore, when some hear the term *self-denial*, they react with anxiety, much like the rich young man in Matthew 19:22 who showed a "sorrowful" response. Is self-denial truly a somber message?

Some may pose the question: "How is it possible to accept self-denial while acknowledging it as the source of joy and as the driving force in one's faith life?" Jonathan Edwards argued in response to such a question that not only is self-denial not contradictory to seeking joy but is practically a way to pull out the roots of sorrow. "Self-denial may seem grievous to believers. . . . Nevertheless, anyone who has experienced self-denial can testify that there is no greater joy and delight than the life lived in self-denial. Self-denial removes the roots and origins of sorrow. Self-denial is like surgery that cuts out a painful and agonizing tumor with a knife as compensation for the pain, healing the wounds, and restoring health."[50]

According to Edwards, the greatest obstacle to self-denial is the false fear caused by the lack of obedience to it. Since self-denial is like surgery that uproots the sinful nature within us, there is some pain involved, but compared to the joy experienced after extracting the roots of sin, the pain is not significant. In this regard, self-denial can be seen as removing the worldly inclinations within us to enjoy greater genuine pleasure. Do you feel exaggerated pain or excessive fear when cutting off anything sinful through self-denial? At this point, if we can draw back the curtains of life, we might witness the desperate roar and fierce struggle of the devil, like a hungry lion trying to devour us (1 Pet. 5:8).

Those involved in the ministry of Teleios Discipleship must lead believers and trainees to confront the vague fears associated with self-denial and guide them to the life lived in self-denial to experience the soul's joy resulting from self-denial. True discipleship training teaches that the myriad fears associated with self-denial cannot compare to one genuine experience of denying oneself. The driving force that enables such self-denial is an understanding deeply rooted in the shepherd's heart and the theology of the cross. I can attest to this through the forty years of my pastoral ministry.

PART 2

The Stem of Teleios: Pastoral Insights from Teleios Discipleship

"The prophesized day of glory for the church has not yet arrived."

Jonathan Edwards

CHAPTER 4

Ecclesiology for Teleios Discipleship Training: Growth of Teleios Disciple and Church Community

A church that has embraced the gospel within Western culture and adorned itself with a heavy accent on individual salvation emphasizes the preciousness of each person. However, the true preciousness of an individual is realized when they are attached to the body of Christ. No matter how important an individual is, a member not attached to the body is no better than dead. Yet, there is still a prevalent tendency to prioritize the individual self over the body of Christ. This tendency has led to a phenomenon where individuals easily leave the church if they are dissatisfied with the people or systems within it. Such behavior is a form of spiritual consumerism, resulting in a weakened sense of community within the church. Extreme emphasis on the importance of an individual, driven by individualism and self-centeredness, inevitably damages the communal nature of the church.

While it is true that the church is constituted by individuals coming together, the church is not merely the sum of its people. The church is both the body of Christ and a being whose existence is marked by being one in Christ as the body (Rom. 12:5). Churches have found themselves in a situation where they are defending against the onslaught of misplaced individualism while holding onto the importance of individuality within the church. The individual's church identity as a walking temple holds significance when connected to the church community where Christ is the head, ensuring its vitality. Overemphasizing individual church identity leads to the elevation of individual glory over the glory of the communal body of Christ, ultimately resulting in being captivated by self-righteousness. The consequence is an excessive individualistic gospel that degenerates into a self-centered faith.

The statement, "You are the church," is accurate. However, it is crucial to reemphasize that the individual is precious when attached to the body. Without being closely connected to the body of Christ, the assurance of an individual's spiritual life cannot be guaranteed. I exist not because of my own sake but because I am a member of the body of Jesus, not the other way around. This priority must not be reversed. It is essential to recognize that some churches have become significantly weakened due to an overly individualistic view of the church and an emphasis on the doctrine of one person and one soul. We must heed Jesus's words again: "I am the vine; you are the branches. Whoever abides in me and I in him, he it is that bears much fruit, for apart from me you can do nothing" (John 15:5).

Healthy Ecclesiology Determines Healthy Pastoral Ministry

When asked, "What is the church?" pastors respond with a variety of answers. Some say it is "a place of worship," others, "a place of education and nurturing," or "a place to heal and comfort the wounded." Still others will argue that it is "a place to implement social justice" or "a place that sends saints to heaven." The answers provide clues as to what the pastor's ecclesiology entails.

If pastoral ministry is metaphorically compared to a tree, the ecclesiology serves as the root, the discipleship as the stem, and the specific discipleship training as the fruit. The reason for using the metaphor of a tree for ministry is it is evident that the abundant fruit of ministry emerges from the solid roots of ministry. We tend to focus on the visible outcomes of our ministry by asking, "What kind of fruit are we bearing?" and "How big or sizable is the fruit?" Yet, we often neglect the invisible parts, the roots. If one stakes one's life on healthy ecclesiology, the path of ministry opens up to a new horizon. If pastors genuinely desire a ministry that remains steadfast even in the face of rough storms, they must firmly grasp a biblical ecclesiology that has modern-day relevance. Pastors should consistently assess whether their current ministry concerns itself with the roots, stem, or fruit.

Closed Churches, Open Churches, and the Emergence of Teleios

Graduates of denomination-affiliated theological seminaries at times face difficulties they had never imagined. Being trapped within one's church tradition makes it challenging to leverage the strengths of other denominations or associations. This can lead to a risk where the dynamism and energy of the church cannot be fully realized and falls prey to the danger of the ministry losing its vitality.

The era of the Fourth Industrial Revolution, where artificial intelligence and virtual reality become commonplace, demands fundamental changes and shifts in attitude for twenty-first-century pastors engaged in sharing and delivering the message. The conventional pastoral "field manuals" from the past can no longer handle the complex and multidimensional demands of the current era. Moreover, it is undeniable that the harsher storms of the secular world make real-life pastoral ministry difficult to withstand the severe weather of the world using only the outer garments of the pastor's denomination or seminary distinctive.

In the current circumstances, it is essential to integrate the strengths of various forms of ministry organizations outside the church for churches to thrive, for pulpits to stand strong, and for pastors and believers to navigate their paths. Refusing to embrace diverse strengths beyond one's own church tradition and solely basing the ministry endeavors on the pastor's preferences, ultimately limits the richness that believers can experience.

How can we integrate the strengths of various churches? Here is an illustration. For all churches, the ordination ceremony in which elders, deacons, and pastors are appointed is a significant time of celebration. If a church combines the solemnity of traditional churches with the anointing of charismatic gifts from contemporary churches, those ordaining members will develop a deeper and fresher self-awareness as servants of the body of Christ. Other members in attendance will also contemplate their calling as servant leaders more profoundly, realizing that their role is not just a position but a result of grace. Certainly, engaging in interdenominational collaboration is not an easy task. Criticisms may arise from individuals who find comfort within their doctrinal and theological perspectives.

In my early days in ministry, I made efforts to embrace the strengths of both traditional churches and mission organizations. Traditional churches had sound doctrine but lacked nurturing strategy, while mission organizations had dreams, visions, and missions but lacked theological training. While serving in college ministry, I dedicated myself to incorporating the strengths of good spiritual traditions in churches and the nurturing and mission strengths of mission organizations into the church. The development of Teleios theology originated from such efforts. Theology of Teleios acts as a compass capable of navigating through any challenges of today's rapidly changing society, while simultaneously forging a gospel anvil that reshapes the wounds and pains of the world with a missional heart.

Changing Your Paradigm for Proper Ecclesiology

My perception of the church has undergone many shifts throughout different stages of faith. During my adolescence, I thought of the local church as a place to worship God. The importance of attending Sunday service for worship was paramount. Whenever I saw a church building, there was an instinctive sense of camaraderie, an inexplicable excitement welling up inside me. In my college years, I began to see the church as an entity that exists to train believers. I began to believe that a church that does not train disciples is failing. I was deeply immersed in the discipleship training models presented by mission organizations and college campus ministries. This was a season when I believed the discipleship training model I encountered in college ministry was all there was to the disciple-making strategy. At that time, my passion for one-on-one discipleship training was intense; I was full of youthful vigor. I often stayed up late at night discussing the direction of the church and college ministries and actively engaged with my mentor, Pastor Oak Han-heum. Those long conversations became the foundation for my ecclesiological framework. Through these interactions and reflections, my preconceived notions about discipleship were at times dismantled and other times expanded.

The solidification of my ecclesiology that now serves as the backbone of my ministry happened when I started my pastoral ministry in the United States. The conviction that "the local church is the community of God's people called from the world, at the same time disciples of Christ sent to the world" became a fundamental definition of the church. The fervor for this truth captured my heart and influenced my entire ministry. The church on earth is a community of God's people privileged to be called out from the world, entrusted with the mission of being Christ's disciples sent into the world. If we only emphasize the privilege of being God's people, we will praise God and rejoice in our salvation; yet we will fail to see the other side of the duality. There is a reason why the Lord has left His people in the world—to send us back into the world (John 20:21). The church does not exist only to disciple people, but it exists to reproduce disciples (disciple-making church). Furthermore, this concept evolved and established itself as a "disciple-making mission church" where trained disciples engage in missional life.

Today, pastors of the church stand on various forms of ecclesiology. Being confined by a rigid ecclesiological perspective cannot effectively handle the present challenges of the world. To be armed with a proper ecclesiology, there needs to be a paradigm shift. Changing our paradigm is driven by the desire to faithfully seek how the people of God can enjoy a fuller communion with the Lord.

Originally, Peter, who was Jesus's chief disciple, seemed to have been the natural fit for foreign missions, but it was entrusted to Paul. This was because Peter, who grew up in Galilee, faced difficulty breaking free from the societal and cultural frameworks of Jewish thinking. This is vividly seen in Acts 10, where Peter is confined by legalistic thoughts regarding food. In contrast, in Acts 16, when Paul attempted to preach the gospel in the region of Asia, the Lord, through the vision of a Macedonian man, said, "Come over to Macedonia and help us" (Acts 16:9). Paul immediately obeyed, following what the Lord had commanded through the vision rather than his preconceptions. Ministers, like Paul, need to open their minds, change their paradigms, and abandon narrow and one-sided ecclesiology for the advancement of the gospel. If the paradigm of thought is not expanded, the vessel of ministry will remain limited, unable to serve as a conduit for the grace of God. Only when one is ready to discard the limitations imposed by a single set of close-minded ecclesiology is one ready to commit to discipleship training ministry.

Ecclesiology Leading the Post-COVID Era

Ecclesiology played a pivotal role as the foundation for the Reformation. If there had not been theological discussions about ecclesiology, the Reformation might not have happened. Alister McGrath summarizes this by stating, "If the first generation of reformers wrestled with the issue of grace, the second generation shifted the focus to church-related issues. Those who broke away from the mainstream teachings of the Catholic Church over the issue of grace found themselves needing to establish a consistent ecclesiology to justify such separation and provide a foundation for the new Christian churches emerging in various cities in Western Europe."[1] Just as the establishment of ecclesiology was crucial for the church to transcend the challenges of its time during the Reformation, the importance of proper ecclesiology is ever greater for the church in the post-pandemic world.

During COVID-19, many churches were compelled to adapt to online worship and forbidden from meeting in person. During this time, one of the cornerstones that kept the church alive and ministry thriving was a biblical understanding of healthy ecclesiology. A healthy ecclesiology, or a biblical ecclesiology, will play a more significant role in the gospel advancement in the post-pandemic era. A robust ecclesiology will prove to be critical to the church's standing. Without it, local churches may lose the meaning of community amid various plausible justifications that seek to replace the essence of the church. It will eventually jeopardize the momentum to move forward. This emphasizes the importance of a pastor's full grasp of the proper ecclesiology and a firm understanding of the church, as they will be crucial in determining the survival of ministry in the post-pandemic world.

Historical Understanding for a Healthy Ecclesiology: Household as Church and Church as Home

The Reformation was God's intervention to correct the distorted doctrine of salvation in Catholicism. Reformers shouted for a focus on the subject matter of soteriology. However, as the Reformation's soteriology contrasted with Catholicism, there was an expectation that other theological topics would undergo significant reform as well.

One such area was ecclesiology. During the fourth century, the church moved away from homes to physical buildings. From the fourth to the sixteenth century, churches were constructed in more elaborate buildings, and the Christian community acquired an identity closely tied to the building. While reformers revolutionized soteriology, their understanding of ecclesiology remained influenced by Catholicism. The traditional Catholic view of the church as a building, in addition to the paradigm of the church as a community gathering in a building, persisted.

The church is, first and foremost, a community of people and an organism before it is a physical place or an organization. Viewing the church merely as a place or a community that sits in a building for worship and fellowship is not biblical, without considering it as a "home." For early believers in the New Testament period, the Christian community was a family, and the family was the church—there was no dichotomy between the family and the church. Thus, for early Christians, the church was not a place they went to but a gathering they participated in. The early church did not have a church that inherently separated from the home. The apostle Paul considered the family and the church synonymous. The church was the family, and the family was the church. In the early Jerusalem church, homes were used for meetings, community formation, fellowship, prayer, teaching, and communion.[2]

Unfortunately, starting from the fourth century, as the church began to separate from the home, the perception that the church was a "place to go" became widespread. Post-Reformation ecclesiology also supported this idea. The Reformers defined and described the purpose of the church in three ways: worship for God, nurturing for believers, and evangelism for the world.[3]

For a healthy ecclesiology, it is essential to place the family at the center of pastoral philosophy and completely integrate the church into the home just as the early church did. Although some may say, "I am the church, and the church is where I walk," they may attend the worship that happens in a church building, but the church disappears in their minds as they step out of the church doors. This separation between the family and the church in faith results in the proliferation of worldly principles for life. Therefore, twenty-first-century pastoral philosophy must return to the model of the early church, focusing on the family and making necessary adjustments from the perspectives that are rooted in the Reformation era.

The Secret to Paul's Wholehearted Ministry: Ecclesiology Absolutely Depended Upon Jesus

Ecclesiology is like a blueprint in our spiritual walk. In order for a building to be flawlessly constructed, a detailed blueprint is a must. In this way, Ephesians is a part of the Bible that serves as a blueprint for ecclesiology. In Ephesians, Paul exhorts this way, "I therefore, a prisoner for the Lord, urge you to walk in a manner worthy of the calling to which you have been called" (Eph. 4:1). Objectively speaking, Paul was more like a "prisoner" in the Roman custody than considered "a prisoner for the Lord." Yet he is adamant: he is not just a prisoner but a prisoner "for the Lord."

Paul was able to make this confession because of an earth-shattering lesson he received from the Lord. On the way to Damascus in pursuit of further persecution, Paul—then Saul—falls to the ground after hearing a thunderous voice calling him out. What were the words he heard? "Saul, Saul, why are you persecuting me?" (Acts 9:4). Paul had never persecuted Jesus in person. He had never met or even seen Jesus in the flesh. When Paul heard these words on the road to Damascus, it would have given him both a shock and an awakening. Paul would have intuitively come to learn that persecuting God's people equated to persecuting Jesus Himself. This offered Paul an interoceptive awareness and embodied understanding of the church as a living organism that is inseparably connected to Jesus.

When Paul says the church is "his body" (Eph. 1:23), and Christ is the "head of the body, the church" (Col. 1:18), he is reporting the truth he experientially acquired. The reason he was able to wholeheartedly give his all for the gospel, for the saints, and for Jesus was because he possessed an ecclesiology that was founded upon this organic connection between the body and the head.

Paul expresses his ministry as "a drink offering upon the sacrificial offering of your faith" (Phil. 2:17). In this confession contains firm grips with his ecclesiology that Christ is the head, the church is the body, and the saints are its members. Just as the drink offering was poured onto the altar of sacrifice, Paul vowed to pour out his life, even to the point of relinquishing his body, as a sacrifice and for service on the altar. He taught that "likewise [we] also should be glad and rejoice" with him (Phil. 2:18). This joy runs in the same vein when we read the epitaph of Rubye Rachel Kendrick, an American missionary who came to Korea about nineteen hundred years after Paul uttered those words. Kendrick's tombstone bears the inscription, "If I had a thousand lives, Korea should have them all." When one fully grasps the truth that the church is the body of Christ, saints are members, and Christ is the head of the body, one cannot tumble into faulty ministry.

What Would Happen If You Were Tested on Ecclesiology? After the church I planted in Southern California began to grow and thrive, a pastor in the local area who heard about the church approached me and asked, "How can I have success with church planting? How can a church experience growth?" At that moment, I posed a question back to that pastor, "Should I give you a politically correct answer, or should I tell you the truth?" with a grin. If I were to respond diplomatically, it would involve stating something along the lines of the "grace of God" or ultimately the "sovereignty of God." However, the pastor wanted a specific, practical answer. I asked, "Can you, who wish to start a church plant, confidently write a four-to five-page, or even up to ten pages, statement on ecclesiology, all on your own without relying on other reference materials or sources? Do you have that depth of understanding of what a church is at this moment?" As pastors, regardless of the storms that may assail our ministry, we must be ready to carry out a ministry that firmly holds onto the essence and vitality without any turbulence. A well-defined ecclesiology and our preparedness to articulate that are keys to true revival of a church.

Teleios Discipleship Training and Revival

Terms like *Jesus*, *gospel*, *church*, *Holy Spirit*, *faith*, *mission*, *truth*, *salvation*, and *Bible* are key words that make up the backbone of Christianity. Without any of these words, we will not see a genuine representation of Christianity. They are core terms that make up who we are. However, these are words that cults and heretics love to use.

While these words themselves are noble, glorious, and saturated with the fragrance of Jesus, Satan's cunning, persistent, and tenacious strategy lies behind this misuse of the terms. By contaminating the most important key words of Christianity, Satan aims to undermine the essence of the gospel, obscuring the true nature of the gospel to hinder people from believing in Jesus. When these words are negatively portrayed and attacked in the media, it is fitting for believers to think, *Ah, Satan is stirring up and acting out again*, and approach the situation with a heart of discernment, proceeding to the place of prayer.

Nevertheless, there is a word that is forgotten or misunderstood not only in cults or heretical groups, nor secular media, but also within the realm of Christianity. It is the word *revival*. There has never been a time in any generation where this desperately urgent word, *revival*, is neglected or dismissed like it is today.

Why is the word *revival* alienated from believers in this way? There is undoubtedly the fierce opposition of Satan again. From Satan's perspective, the revival of the church is the most detested phenomenon, and it is only natural that Satan would resist it vehemently (2 Cor. 11:3). Regardless, revival is the core of genuine discipleship training. Revival is not merely a lukewarm person becoming passionate again. The essence of revival is depicted in Acts 3, where a man unable to walk rises in the name of Jesus of Nazareth, not only walking but also "leaping and praising God" (v. 8). That is the crux of revival.

Teleios Discipleship training reactivates people who have been discouraged by the harsh storms of the world, ensnared by the temptations of the world, or, like the Laodicean church members, are lukewarm to rise again in the name of Jesus. It is revitalizing their walk with the vitality of Jesus's blood pulsating in their hearts, returning them to the Lord with fire burning in their hearts through the power of His Word.

We must reclaim the word *revival* from the clutches of the enemy. Charles Grandison Finney, who led the Second Great Awakening movement in the first half of the nineteenth century in the United States, wrote about the reason we do not readily experience revival: "Do you know why you do not experience revival? It is for one reason: you do not want revival. You do not pray for it, desire it, or make any effort for it."[4]

We must clearly understand Charles Finney's words. Some may argue that surely everyone wants revival and Finney's assessment is harsh. However, Finney is pointing out that there is a significant difference between thinking you want revival and genuinely desiring and living for one. If you genuinely desire revival, you must pray for it and long for it. Revival does not come to those who do not pray for it and do not long for it.[5] Teleios Discipleship seeks to lift those who have fallen, rekindle the lukewarm, and transform them into true laborers for the kingdom of God. This is the revival that Teleios Discipleship training pursues.

Traditional Ecclesiology Trapped in Inward Focus

Throughout history, the image of the church has undergone various stages in relation to society, politics, and culture. The early church from the first to the fourth century possessed untamed spiritual vitality and the purity of the gospel, engaging in a holy battle to evangelize the world. This resulted in Ephesus opening its doors, Philippi raising the banner, and the surrender of the Roman Empire as Emperor Theodosius embraced Christianity as the state religion of the Roman Empire in AD 392.

As Christianity became the state religion of the Roman Empire, the political power of the secular emperor and the church became entwined. From this point until the Reformation, the medieval period spanned a thousand years during which the church played a central role in politics, society, and culture. In Europe, churches spread in all directions and were erected next to town squares and city halls. However, as the church began to align with politics and began enjoying political power, it rapidly secularized. In the early medieval period, the church had a conciliatory image, collaborating with secular political power. In the late medieval period, the church assumed an image of an entity operating with political power with a strong assimilation into the world.

As the church rapidly succumbed to secularization and corruption, reformers were essentially declaring, "This is not the true image of the church. We must restore the true image of the church. To achieve this, the church, which has become conformed to the world by joining hands with the world, must now release its grip. A holy separation must take place." Reformers presented the following three symbols as indicators of the true image of the church: Is the Word being proclaimed correctly? Are sacraments being properly administered? Is church discipline being carried out appropriately? These became the symbols of the true church brought about by the Reformation.

A Severed Church and the Trap of Inward Focus

As the influence of the Protestant Reformation extended more than four hundred to five hundred years, a new problem emerged: the inwardness or internal focus of the church. While it was good for the church to maintain the purity of the gospel through a sacred distinction and separation from the world, the consequences of a church that distanced itself from the world became evident over the course of several centuries. The church's energy for ministry became concentrated inward, leading to the phenomenon of "inward focus" for the church's ministry. As a result, the mission of proclaiming the gospel to the world weakened, and the fragmentation of sects that staunchly adhered to their own doctrines intensified. The harsh consequence of this inward focus produced callous indifference when it came to saving lives.

This shift in the church's focus is the blind spot a church shaped by traditionalism has. Their preoccupation with "preservation" often leads to constant disputes and divisions. While emphasizing the importance of Scripture and the sanctity of the church, they easily fall into a pattern of division and opposition. The focus on doctrinal purity and orthodoxy without corresponding actions has resulted in a tendency to split over minor differences, undermining the church's ability to engage in missions. Consequently, the church's essential purposes of saving souls, global evangelization, and the fulfillment of its mission as salt and light in the world have become more challenging to achieve.

Problems Caused by the Inward Focus of the Church. The decisive problem brought about by the church's inwardness is that the church's power becomes confined to internal matters and the power of the gospel fails to go outward. As a result, doctrinal differences and variations in faith practices clash, and worldly ideologies infiltrate the church, creating internal conflicts and bombing one another. The energy of the church should not lead to internal bombings but rather to a missional explosion.

When the church cannot extend its influence beyond its confines, its power and ability to convey the gospel inevitably weaken. Churches that fail to engage the outside world not only experience internal bombings but also inevitably witness the incapacitation of laypeople and the authoritative problems of ministers. These churches end up preserving their traditionalism. When churches cling to traditionalism, they lose the capacity to fully represent and participate in the mission of the church.

How to Overcome the Inward Focus of the Church. How will the church overcome the issues caused by the inward focus? The answer is found in the historical background of Christianity. In response to the teachings of the Roman Catholic Church, which had deviated from the Scriptures, the Reformers established the five "solas." Even today, pastors following Reformed theology cherish the five solas—Sola Scriptura (Scripture alone), Solus Christus (Christ alone), Sola Gratia (Grace alone), Sola Fide (Faith alone), and Soli Deo Gloria (To God alone be the glory)—as precious tenets of the church's valuable tradition. These five solas have played a pivotal role in differentiating the church from the world and safeguarding the gospel.

However, as the church held onto the five solas, there was a lamentable omission of another crucial sola of the Scriptures. The five solas are scriptural, but they are not the entirety of the Scriptures. Yet, a significant number of believers, and even pastors, regard these five as if they constitute the entire Bible. To be clear, these solas present critical corrections from the doctrinal errors. However, to fulfill what God commands for His church and body, at least two more solas must not be overlooked: Sola Missio (Mission alone) and Solus Spiritus (Spirit alone). Both are indispensable solas for obediently fulfilling God's mission for the twenty-first-century church.

Overcoming the church's inwardness is possible only through a missional life anointed by the Spirit. This approach secures the identity of the church as those sent into the world and paves the way for Teleios Discipleship training to flourish. Furthermore, it is necessary to restore the combative view of the church that the early Christian church possessed in the first centuries. The path to restoring a combative view of the church lies in regaining a strong apostolic consciousness imbued with the awareness of the identity of God's people as the ones called from the world to be sent into the world with a mission.

"Vision 2033-50" and Overcoming Inward Focus. The way to lift the ship buried in the sandy shoreline is not through strength. When the ocean tide comes in, the ship floats and rises out of the sand. To lift the stiff and weakened church, the tide of mission must come in. One must ignite the fire of the mission in the frozen engine of the church.

Many believe that the declining birth rate resulting in an inevitable population decrease is unavoidable. Hence, they project a continued decrease in the number of church members, expecting the natural decline of the church. This pessimism seems to be more saturated among those who consider themselves intellectuals, naively siding with those who believe in a secularized liberal view of the church.

However, these claims and predictions are only calculated based on the logic of the world; at no point are those ideas drenched in the blood shed by Jesus for the church. The prevailing atmosphere is content with maintaining the current state of the church. How can this be the outlook of the church for which the Lord shed His blood?

It must not be so. I examined the history of the church by looking at how the early church grew. The early church grew by 40–50 percent every ten years.[6] In the fourth century, fifteen million people in the Roman Empire believed in Jesus. Here, I see the "Vision 2033-50" reaching 50 percent of the Korean population by the year 2033 which marks two thousand years after Jesus's incarnation. Currently, Korea's birth rate is about 0.7, and Seoul is 0.53. In light of this, those who claim to be the intellectuals within the church shake their heads and call it an absurdity. However, the final verdict does not lie in human hands. God's work surpasses human understanding. "Oh, the depth of the riches and wisdom and knowledge of God! How unsearchable are his judgments and how inscrutable his ways! 'For who has known the mind of the Lord, or who has been his counselor?'" (Rom. 11:33–34). I think of the Korean church after the reunification of the two Koreas. The numbers "2033-50" embrace not only those in South Korea but also North Korean compatriots. If the inward focus of the church brings an internal explosion of energy, the way to heal and recover the right channel of focus is through the missional explosion. "Vision 2033-50" will lead the Korean church once again as the vanguard of global missions through a missionary explosion. How will your church contribute to the global mission and overcome inward focus? What vision do you have?

Power-Driven Ecclesiology, Ecclesiology of Mighty Nation

Many have opinions about what a church should or should not be. However, my experience as a pastor's son who had started a church plant in an underprivileged neighborhood, having stood at the forefront of university student revival, and later having planted a thriving immigrant church called SaRang Community Church in Southern California, I have developed an ecclesiology—or a perspective on what the church should be—through personal and ministry experiences, forged especially during challenging times.

I call this perspective the "Power-Driven Ecclesiology." The core of Power-Driven ecclesiology is found in 1 Corinthians 4:20, which states, "For the kingdom of God does not consist in talk but in power." This aligns with the true essence of those mentioned in 1 Corinthians 4:1 as "servants of Christ and stewards of the mysteries of God." The reality of the Corinthian church compared to the modern church that is now standing after more than two thousand years is not significantly different. In both cases, those who speak the loudest often take the forefront, emphasizing narrow traditions, shallow doctrines, or their version of faith.

However, the kingdom of God is a spiritual kingdom that is established not primarily through words but through the power of God. The national strength of God's kingdom is based on Leviticus 26:8, which says, "Five of you shall chase a hundred, and a hundred of you shall chase ten thousand." The kingdom of God does not consist of a panic-stricken army. Instead, it is a nation where valiant warriors contend against the devil "to the point of shedding your blood" (Heb. 12:4). One must not misunderstand these warriors as individuals armed with worldly armor. God called the timid Gideon a "mighty warrior" (Judg. 6:12 HCSB). When facing storms and the rough waves of the secular world, it may be intimidating, but by fixing our gaze on the greater God who stands behind it all, we become a force that the world cannot withstand. Teleios Discipleship training involves stewarding the power of God for the church and seeing the church be a nation where mighty warriors for the kingdom will be raised.

The Verse That Propelled Me to Disciple-Making Pastoral Ministry

During my college days, I was strongly influenced by discipleship training conducted by campus ministries. At that time, Navigators only disciple-trained those who were willing to serve within their ministry upon the completion of their training period. For that workers, who could have stayed in the church, ended up serving in these ministry organizations. Yet, I had the opportunity to be trained under a Navigators leader who offered personal mentorship, even when he knew that I would return to my church and not end up in their leadership roles. Thanks to this invitation, I was able to go through the Studies in Christian Living (SCL), Designed For Discipleship (DFD).[7] Then the training included the Personal Inductive Bible Study (PBS) course.[8] I progressed in their curriculum to be ready to serve in campus ministry and lead discipleship training.

Looking back, I was heavily armed with a doctrinal preparedness to commit to discipleship training at that time. I was prepared as a drill sergeant for training. It was during such a period that I met Pastor Oak Han-heum, my mentor and the founding pastor of my church. We began to seriously contemplate the issue of whether local churches could train believers as disciples after the model of campus ministries. Through numerous discussions with Pastor Oak, I opened my eyes to the possibility of a discipleship training model adapted from campus ministries for the body of Christ in the local church. Yet, the model we began to envision looked different from the usual emphasis placed on indoctrination by the campus ministries. It was during this time that I gained the conviction that discipleship training within the church was not only possible but I was assured that this was a pillar that would propel me to pastoral ministry. Since then, whenever I found time, I dedicated myself to making discipleship training not only for parachurch ministries but also for the church, in the church, and by the church, by continuously meditating on 2 Timothy 2:2: "And what you have heard from me in the presence of many witnesses entrust to faithful men, who will be able to teach others also."

Paul wrote this letter from a Roman prison, anticipating his imminent execution. Sadly, some of his fellow workers abandoned him in difficult circumstances (2 Tim. 4:10). In the face of such a crisis, Paul strongly urged Timothy to carry out the task of establishing churches with unwavering devotion. Paul's earnest plea is encapsulated in 2 Timothy 2:2.

We must examine the three key aspects contained in this verse. First, there is "hearing." "What you have heard from me" is summarized in 2 Timothy 1:13–14: "Follow the pattern of the sound words that you have heard from me, in the faith and love that are in Christ Jesus. By the Holy Spirit who dwells within us, guard the good deposit entrusted to you." What did Timothy hear from Paul? It was all of the sound teachings about faith in Christ Jesus and all those proper actions of faith fitting to this spiritual teaching.

Second, there is "entrustment." Timothy is entrusted with what he received from Paul to "faithful men," not just individuals with high positions in the church but those who, through their character and life, demonstrate the power of the gospel. By entrusting them with the gospel, Timothy is enabling them to teach and live out the gospel in the church. The term *entrust* carries the sense of a "deposit," indicating a weighty responsibility. Paul is implying a significant responsibility that follows.

This verse led me to the conclusion that there is no reason why discipleship training and nurturing processes should remain only in the context of campus ministries and not be contextualized in the church. I concluded that the fact that the apostle Paul, rather than being a representative of a mission organization, instructs Pastor Timothy to raise and verify people for the church evidences this mission. Furthermore, the essential elements required for the proper establishment of God's church—the gospel of Jesus Christ, validation through witnesses, and reproduction through entrustment, as shown in 2 Timothy 2:2—perfectly align with the content and methods of discipleship training. In sum, based on these principles and methods, Paul's urging to Pastor Timothy to conduct discipleship training in the church and not just campus ministries forms the core belief that I hold with unwavering conviction. Whether in the body of Christ or outside on the campuses, the call is the same: we are to teach the entirety of the gospel of Jesus Christ to those who are committed to following Him, validate their commitment in the presence of witnesses, and entrust this gospel again to those who demonstrate the commitment so that the cycle of the entrustment of the gospel will start.

Beyond Theology Textbooks: Ecclesiology Emerging from Discipleship Training

Discipleship training without a church is like a loaded gun without bullets. It may seem powerful, but it lacks effectiveness in real life. Teleios Discipleship training involves each believer becoming the church, a process of learning the church. Teleios Discipleship training can be described as "unleashing life beyond the church." To actualize this cause, we must explore what discipleship-driven ecclesiology is and how this Teleios Discipleship training comes to shape that ecclesiology.

Completed Church Versus Church in the Process of Becoming

Theological differences between Catholics and Protestants are evident in their ecclesiology. Catholics view the earthly church as a completed entity, while Protestants see it as a church in the process of becoming a transitional church. The pulpit is not a place for just anyone to walk into without a proper wardrobe from the Catholic perspective. The more significant difference lies in the sacraments. Protestants recognize only two: Communion and baptism. In contrast, Catholics adhere to seven sacraments, including a belief in the transubstantiation in Communion.

This difference reflects the contrasting views between a completed church and the anticipation of the arrival of God's kingdom in a church that is still on the way. The church in the process of becoming places a deeper emphasis on the fervent anticipation of the second coming of Jesus Christ. While Catholics emphasize suffering and the cross, often reflected in their hymns, there is a relatively weaker emphasis on the resurrection or the anticipation of the "Maranatha."

The characteristics of a church in the process of becoming organic and transitional are well illustrated in 1 Thessalonians 1:1 which reads, "Paul, Silvanus, and Timothy, To the church of the Thessalonians in God the Father and the Lord Jesus Christ: Grace to you and peace."[9] This passage articulates three aspects of the church: First, the church is in God the Father; second, the church is in Jesus Christ; and third, the church is in Thessalonica. First, being "in God the Father" implies that the church is not an organization of the world, rejecting the secular way of governing, the mindset, or operational systems. Second, being "in . . . Jesus Christ" signifies a clear distinction from the Old Testament temple. It highlights the character of Jesus Christ and His redemptive work, especially His sacrifice for the church. The church stands firmly and completely with Jesus Christ and matures alongside Him. Third, being in Thessalonica emphasizes the value of a specific, corporeal church in a particular region, regardless of denominations such as Presbyterian, Baptist, or Holiness.

The Church We Should Pursue: A Church That Looks Forward to the Second Coming of Jesus Christ

The earthly church is not perfect; it has flaws and imperfections. Yet, it is simultaneously a holy church, free from any blemish or wrinkle, transformed into a state of holiness without any defects (Eph. 5:27). This fact is crucial because contemporary criticisms of the church tend to be dualistic. Some view the church as a sacred entity, vehemently criticizing even minor issues as if scrutinizing them with a magnifying glass. On the other hand, others, considering the church as part of the world, compromise in the face of inevitable problems and imperfections through the lens of secular humanism.

Both perspectives deviate significantly from the vision of Jesus Christ, who loves and gave Himself for the church (Eph. 5:25). The earthly church, the body of the Lord redeemed by His blood, continues to walk steadfastly toward the perfect embodiment of holiness despite numerous flaws and imperfections. Both the critics of the church's imperfections and those who seek to conceal them fail to embody the intuitive love for the church that every member should possess. These two extreme views would not exist if they sincerely embraced the meaning of the blood of Christ.

In a true blood relationship, it is abnormal to run to secular courts over parental or child misconduct. For instance, if the parents suffer, so do the children; if the children face problems, the parents are equally affected. In genuine love, the family will do all that they can with no reservations, even if it means making sacrifices or enduring suffering if it will alleviate the family member's pain.

As genuine believers, it is unthinkable to add to the corruption of the beauty of the church through falsehood and greed, as if one would intentionally soil the bride's garment with various impurities. The virtue of a bride is purity and cleanliness. Yet, the church sometimes gets comfortable wearing filthy garments, stained by the world's impurities, under the guise of tolerance, love, and forgiveness.

Teleios Discipleship is the training that aims to transform disciples so that they will instinctively cultivate and embody passionate love for the church, the body of Christ. Witnessing any harm to the church's reputation should cause bruises in a disciple's heart. Teleios disciples are those who lose sleep over the pain inflicted on the church and ache to see it beautified. To guide and nurture the believers along the path of embracing and enveloping the church's pain is like parents embracing their children and children wrapping their arms around their parents. Such a mentality is the true manifestation of Teleios Discipleship. Our goal is to condition the disciple's intuition so that devout love for the church becomes their second nature.

The Church on the Way: Looking into Jesus Christ's Heart Through the Seven Churches in Revelation

Among the seven churches mentioned in the Book of Revelation, only two receive praise. However, Jesus Christ did not claim only these two as His own churches. He embraced and loved even the remaining five churches that were lacking, imperfect, and shameful. The love that disciples must harbor for the church entails embracing not only the church worthy of praise but also those who deserve criticism. We signal to the world that we are anticipating the second coming of Jesus Christ—when all will be made right despite any flaws, imperfections, wrinkles, or blemishes that may exist at present.

How can one discern whether they are currently undergoing Teleios Discipleship formation? We must ask the following: Is there a deepening sense of longing for the second coming of Jesus Christ with the hope of the kingdom of heaven? Is there a growing commitment to live with the resilience of faith empowered by the resurrection in the present circumstances? Is one's heart throbbing with anticipation for the glorious, perfect church without any flaws, wrinkles, or blemishes, with an expectation of entering the kingdom of heaven? Is there a profound belief that death is not a dead end of despair but a new door leading to eternal life? If the answer is a clear yes to these questions, then one can affirm the ongoing Teleios Discipleship formation.

From Institutionalized Church to Vital Missional Church!

"The church is a supernatural organism formed by believers united with each other through their connection to the Lord."[10] This statement implies that the church is something that cannot be fully comprehended by the world's standards or values. It represents a society that overcomes social divisions of rich and poor, men and women, young and old; under the unity of one Spirit, one Lord, one faith, and one God the Father. To illustrate, it is common to see in the local body of Christ those individuals with multiple doctoral degrees demonstrating a humble attitude to learn alongside elderlies from rural areas who had limited access to educational opportunities contribute to the church with spiritual virtues and wisdom gained through reading the Bible. The church is that entity where people who have never left their towns pray for missions around the globe.

Organic Church Versus Organizational Church

In 1973, the Billy Graham Crusade and the subsequent EXPLO '74 event took place in Seoul, Korea. While these events indeed have organizational structures in place, it was the dynamism of life, not just organizational power, that made such large-scale events possible. Pastor Kim Joon-gon, who played a significant role in EXPLO '74, traveled across the country to give presentations that aimed to mobilize churches in Korea. During a presentation in Busan, people challenged him with concerns such as "If one million people gather as you say, how will we manage restrooms?" or "Where will they eat?" and even more hypothetical questions like "What do we do if North Korea launches missiles at the gathering, causing a mass casualty event?"

At that moment, a shared understanding emerged as a result of joint prayer. "As far as the restrooms go, let us hold it in as much as we can. As far as the food, we can fast. If North Korea launches missiles, we will launch back the missiles of prayer." During the EXPLO '74 event, significant resources were needed to provide meals for attendees coming from across the country. Over 600 tons of rice, 150 tons of pickled vegetables and shrimp, and 3.6 million loaves of bread were consumed by participants.[11] EXPLO '74 was not an event orchestrated by an organization; it was an event fueled by an organic life force. Such spiritual vitality became the catalyst for the revival that set the Korean church ablaze.

A representative movement demonstrating the organic nature of SaRang Church is the Special Dawn Revival. Despite the absence of conventional leadership roles such as president, secretary, or treasurer, ten thousand to twenty thousand congregants gather every morning for a week—once in the spring and once in the fall. Even amid the challenges of the COVID-19 pandemic, the revival meeting was held adhering to safety guidelines. The display of spiritual life, the indescribable power of prayer, and the restoration of missional zeal erupted without a formal organizational structure, showcasing the potent grace that transcends the need for formal organization.

The Church Is a Tangible Holiness

The statement "The church is a tangible holiness" signifies that the earthly church is rooted in this world, much like the incarnation of Jesus Christ. Criticism toward the church increases when people idealize it as something not belonging to this world but to heaven. The moment the church is idealized, maturity and growth come to a halt. The law of discipleship multiplication disappears.

Many Western churches in the twentieth century lost their dynamic life force and the power of gospel outreach in this manner. People have opinions about what the church should be but without ever engaging in evangelism or short-term missions. Trained individuals who have experienced real-world ministry through spreading the gospel feel a pang of heartache for the love of the church whenever they see people talk about church but never being one. Many contemplate the church on a conceptual level, vaguely describing it as a "house of prayer for all nations," a "spiritual gathering for worship and fellowship," or "not a building but people." However, upon closer inspection, they struggle to articulate the depth of these meanings because they have not genuinely grappled with these ideas themselves in practice.

Consider the statement "The church is not a building but a people." We juxtapose this statement with what we find in Acts 2:43–47, which portrays the image of a healthy church that has just begun. Jewish believers, confirming Jesus Christ as the long-awaited Messiah and gathering as a new community, expressed their faith materially. They used and shared possessions through relief efforts, and, most importantly, engaged in the everyday worship act of breaking bread and communal meals. The early church's "church" was a tangible space represented by material expressions.

It is crucial not to misunderstand the church as merely a place with material expressions. Christian faith and theology are concerned with the sanctification of material things and the sacredness and holiness of the ordinary—such as a pot, commonly used throughout the world, symbolizing the holy utensils in the temple, or inscribing the words "Holy to the Lord" on warhorse bells reserved for the high priest (Zech. 14:20–21). This is the essence of Christian faith and theology.

Meanwhile, "Eradicating sin related to money is the most challenging aspect of repentance from sins. Even after confessing their faith in Christ, the last piece people are hesitant to experience transformation is their wallet."[12] Hence, true repentance involves seeking holiness in the tangible aspects of life. This is what it means for the church to be a tangible holiness. We believe that the church is both a people and a place.[13] A church devoid of real-life situations, material aspects, time and space, and historical moments can never truly be a church. When we use the term *place*, it refers to a concrete, demonstrable, physical space. In this sense, a holy church possesses physical concreteness. Again, the church is confined to an idealized concept from philosophical musings but a real entity. Unfortunately, there is a growing tendency for people to view the church as a conceptual entity, separating it from reality and its spatial character.

The Church Is Born from the Womb of Mission

God's mission originates from the triune nature of the Holy Trinity. It is an extension of God's work infiltrating the space and time of human creation. When the time came, God sent forth His Son Jesus Christ as a missionary to this earth (Gal. 4:4). Jesus, upon His arrival, did not establish schools, synagogues, or temples but rather initiated the formation of a discipleship community—the church. God the Father and Jesus Christ, in sending the Holy Spirit to the church, aided the church in assuming its identity and role as a missionary community.[14] Therefore, the identity of the church is inherently missional from the beginning.[15] Similar to how an unborn child in a mother's womb inherits the parents' DNA, the church, before its birth, received and retained the missional DNA originating from Jesus and the Holy Spirit. Hence, the notion that a church becomes missional through subsequent involvement in missions is a misunderstanding.

What kind of church did the Lord envision on this earth? How did the Lord intend to connect world missions, evangelism, and serving our neighbors? How do these aspects relate to discipleship training? We first examine the missional community of Old Testament Israel. God, the Lord of missions, took the first step in missions by seeking Adam and Eve after they sinned (Gen. 3:9). Instead of waiting for them to come, God sought them with a shepherd's heart. Moreover, with a shepherd's heart, God looked upon the scattered nations after the Tower of Babel incident, found Abraham who was the firstborn of idol worshippers, and sent him on a mission to become the fountainhead of blessing (Gen. 12:1–3).

Abraham was not sent when he was ready; rather, God, whose nature is inherently missional, sent Abraham from the first moment they met. From the moment God called Israel within Abraham, there has been a missional community in the heart of God (Gen. 12:1–3). The purpose of rescuing the enslaved Israel, who had forgotten even the name of their ancestral God in Egypt, was mission. Giving them commandments and inviting them to be a redeemed community, ultimately purposed to save the nations (Exod. 19:5–6).

Similarly, the story of young David facing Goliath is also about mission. Through David, the whole world learned that God was with Israel (1 Sam. 17:46). The incident in the lion's den with Daniel proclaimed to the Persian Empire that Daniel's God was the living God (Dan. 6:26). God's calling is for us to spread His salvation as a light to the nations, reaching to the ends of the earth (Isa. 49:6).

The Church Was Always Missional from the Beginning

Israel's mission was revealed not as a powerful nation with military strength and thriving commerce but as a holy nation. It was to be a priestly nation, leading in service for the salvation of all nations. Moreover, the strategy for Israel to be a missional nation was to become a holy presence, a nation that is "Holy to the Lord" and distinct from the world. Most important, Jesus Christ received "all authority in heaven and on earth" (Matt. 28:18) through the cross and resurrection. This Jesus instructs us to go to the ends of the earth to lead out His people from the world. In this way, the church was designed to be missional from the very beginning of God's heart.

Second Chronicles 6:32–33 records Solomon's famous prayer for the Jerusalem temple. Within this prayer is a request for God to hear the prayers of foreigners who come to this temple, making them realize that God is the God over all. Found within this prayer, Israel was the missional Israel, engaged in the most active missional commitment in her history. Solomon's temple prayer, seeking to hear the prayers of foreigners, finds a deeper and broader meaning in Isaiah 56:7: "My house shall be called a house of prayer for all peoples." God's church is not just a house of prayer; it is a house of prayer for "all peoples."

As SaRang Church began to update its discipleship training curriculum, the biggest change was made in its intentional focus on a missional commitment. Emphasizing the need for more missions or becoming more mission oriented is a misunderstood approach to cultivating a Teleios disciple. The goal is for the church to know that its existence is for missions. Achieving maturity through discipleship training so that they will be able to handle mission work is not the primary emphasis of Teleios Discipleship either. The main purpose is to recognize that discipleship training is missional training as well as a training in evangelism of which results should be evidenced in daily life. Mission, training, witness, and life are not separate; they are all part of being part of God's covenantal relationship with us.

As part of the SaRang Church discipleship training process, everyone involved in the training now participates in a mandatory summer short-term mission. This mission takes them to various countries served by SaRang Church's missionaries and cooperating missionary partners worldwide. These trips take the form of vision trips or volunteer activities in domestic church plants along with various mission organizations. Teleios Discipleship training offers a paradigm where discipleship and mission, evangelism, occur simultaneously. Missions are the training itself. In this regard, Teleios Discipleship is a process of restoring the lost missional DNA to the church.

Apostolic Identity and Prophetic Vision: Writing the Future Resume of the Church

The Remarkable Blessing of the Twenty-First-Century Church: Succession of Apostolic Identity

Traditionally, the church on earth has been defined as the gathering of God's people called from the world. However, over the past half century, the emphasis has shifted to the succession of apostolic calling, rediscovering the significance and mission of laypeople. The church is now not only defined as the people of God called from the world but redefined as those gathered people of God sent into the world.

Regarding the succession of apostolic identity, Pastor Oak Han-heum, drawing from Hans Küng, contended that while the church cannot succeed the apostolic office, it has inherited apostolic calling, and this is affirmed by the work of the Holy Spirit.[16] The core of apostolic calling is the idea that the church on earth is a community founded upon this apostleship with every one of its members partaking in this mission.

What makes the succession of apostolic calling significant in terms of salvation history? In Genesis 3, God, through the proclamation of the primitive gospel, declared that the offspring of the woman will "bruise your head" (v. 15), foretelling the coming of Jesus Christ to the earth. The salvific plan of God to send Jesus into this world for our salvation is weighty, precious, covenantal, and glorious. His sending of us follows the same pattern, as Jesus said, "As the Father has sent me, even so I am sending you" (John 20:21), encapsulating the incredibly weighty glory of salvation, the depth of the covenantal relationship, and hope for the new creation that God's apostolic succession carries.

How Does the Church Inherit the Apostolic Calling? The inheritance of the apostolic calling through the Holy Spirit is not a matter of choice; it is a duty, a mission, and an honor for all saints in the church. To actualize this, dedicated commitment and commissioning are required, as demonstrated by the servants who simply brought water to Jesus before knowing that it would turn into wine (John 2:9).

The first method is through receiving the Word. The difference between Catholicism and Protestantism lies here. Catholics, with their unique ecclesiology, rarely engage in in-depth, consecutive study of the Scriptures as we concentrate on the biblical passages every week. However, because we have the inheritance of apostolic calling through the Word, we take the opportunity to teach and share the Scriptures through Sunday sermons, Bible studies, and small-group studies.

God has given the church the Word and pastors for the succession of apostolic calling. Pastors should be excited about the gracious privilege of relaying the Word to the believers. The fact that pastors can be instruments of God for the ministry that is so dear to God's heart should be truly exhilarating. This is the glorious task that inherits the apostolic calling, and it cannot be anything less than a heartwarming and thrilling mission.

The second way the church inherits apostolic calling is through a recognition of our callings. The mission of pastors, especially in making saints Teleios disciples to transform the world, is like the lifeblood of the church in inheriting apostolic calling. God has already blessed every local church, every earthly church, and the body of Christ with the inheritance of apostolic teachings and ministry. How lamentable would it be if the church severs from the apostolic calling and fails to own the unique callings that God has for every believer due to a lack of the Word or absence of purpose?

To Experience the Blessing of Apostleship, One Must Be Awakened to the Grace of Prophethood

Three aspects are often mentioned when describing the characteristics of the church in systematic theology: unity, catholicity, and holiness.[17]

However, in the twenty-first century, some theologians began to include a fourth characteristic—apostleship.[18] If theologians view apostolic calling to be a calling to succeed, how do theologians view the succession of prophetic ministry in the early church? Are we to perceive it as a role and function similar to that of Old Testament prophets when the apostle Paul mentions the spiritual gift of prophets in Ephesians 4:11, or are we to view it as a broader function necessary for the church's wide-ranging ministry?

Theologian Wayne Grudem explains that the role of Old Testament prophets is carried out by the apostles in the New Testament.[19] Just as Old Testament prophets pronounced God's Word, the apostles represented the authority of the Scriptures. Hence, he acknowledges that the prophetic ministry of the Old Testament seen as preaching of God's Word, in a broader sense, still exists today.[20] Moreover, Gordon D. Fee, a world-renowned evangelical theologian, interprets the individuals mentioned in Ephesians 4:11 more in terms of function than office or gift.[21] He argues that for the church to be united and complete, five essential functions are needed: apostleship, prophethood, evangelism, pastoring, and teaching. No gift exists without a function. While individuals like Old Testament prophets may not exist today, prophethood enables the church to fully function. The crucial question for twenty-first-century ministers is how to use prophethood to make the saints whole.

As someone who personally met prophets, the apostle Paul acknowledged their gift (Acts 21:9–14; 13:1). He affirmed the existence of prophets without denying their existence (1 Cor. 12:28; 14:37). Peter's warning about false prophets and teachers was not a denial of the gifts but an acknowledgment of the presence of prophets among them.

If the church is established "on the foundation of the apostles and prophets" (Eph. 2:20; 2 Pet. 3:2), can prophethood not be a characteristic of the church? Why is there a silence on prophethood while apostolic calling is readily acknowledged? Many churches in the twenty-first century struggle to integrate prophethood into their gospel-centered practices. Avoiding the use of prophetic gifts due to the risks involved is akin to not using fire. The misuse of gifts can occur in two ways: excessive use of the gift or avoiding the use of gifts altogether. We are struggling with both today.

How can apostleship and prophethood achieve balance in pastoral ministry philosophy? Resources or publications on these topics are not always readily available. Perhaps we will find clues as we look at Acts 13. The leadership of the church included individuals with apostolic and prophetic gifts, alongside teachers like Paul and Barnabas. The church in Antioch became a healthy missional church through the good balance of the roles of apostles and prophets. This is a topic we must continue exploring.

Prophethood Is for Mission. "The Spirit is the spirit of the missionary God and the missionary Son, breathing life and power into God's missionary church."[22] The church is established on the cornerstone, Jesus Christ, and the foundation of apostles and prophets (Eph. 2:20). The Holy Spirit leads Gentiles and foreigners to draw near to God the Father (Eph. 2:18). Beginning with the outpouring of the Holy Spirit at Pentecost, the apostleship and prophethood of the church were infused with a missionary DNA. Prophethood holds a place in the heart of missionary activities undertaken by God's people.

The function of Old Testament prophets was to call Israel to return to God and awaken them to a missional life toward other nations. The major and minor prophets of the Old Testament are filled with prophetic sensitivity to missions, wrapped in the shepherd's heart (Isa. 49:6; Joel 2:28; Jonah 4:11). After the resurrection, Jesus, at the center of the church's ministry, instructed the disciples not to depart from Jerusalem until they received power from on high (Luke 24:49) and gave them a prophetic command not to leave (Acts 1:4). This command contains Jesus's missional intention for the church to move from Galilee to Jerusalem and then expand from Jewish Jerusalem to the global region.

Looking at Acts 13, the church in Antioch became a healthy missional church by harmonizing the roles of apostles and prophets. Apostleship provides the driving force forward, and prophethood sets the direction for that path. In this way, the church in Antioch opened the door to a missionary journey toward the global region with the two wheels of apostleship and prophethood.

Writing the Résumé of the Future with Prophethood. Prophethood allows the discernment of the future in the present, providing a holy vision of the future based on a biblical perspective. With it, apostolic calling guides and ensures the fulfillment of that vision. In this regard, Teleios involves integrating prophethood with apostolic calling in a balanced and pastoral manner. Wayne Grudem explains that prophethood is rather than merely a "prediction" of the future, is more about "edification," which enables the church to move toward the future.[23] As discussed, the five functions of the church exist to fulfill the missional purpose in the world. Specifically, the gifts of "evangelists, pastors, and teachers" enable believers to fulfill their present mission (Eph. 4:11 NRSVUE). Similarly, the functions of "apostles and prophets" propel them toward the future mission as a form of edification.[24]

If prophethood is an ability to discern and illuminate the future, bringing it into the present for execution, how can we apply this pastorally? As Paul once confessed, our life journey is a walk between the unknown (Rom. 8:26) and the revealed (Rom. 8:28). Prophethood ensures that our lives stay on the path of God's will, pulling the future into the present and allowing us to write the résumé of the future. However, human thoughts and perspectives are susceptible to the gravitational pull of the world and can go astray. For this reason, one might be tempted to neglect the gift of prophethood, but we have the "safety net of prophethood" where "all things work together for good" (Rom. 8:28).

Those illumined with the prophethood can live out the future-present without being bound by the résumé of the past. How can one bring the future into the present if the world looks bleak? The secret lies in comparing God and reality. Among the twelve spies in Numbers 13–14, only two compared God with reality and wrote the résumé of the future, while the rest compared themselves with reality and failed to write the résumé of the future. Teleios Discipleship trains believers to put God and reality side by side, even in the bleakness of the present, making them capable of writing a brilliant résumé for the future. Peter Drucker said that if something is certain to happen in the future, then even if it has not been experienced yet, it is the "future that has already happened."[25] We are not bound by the résumé of the past but are the people of God who look forward to the splendid fulfillment of his promises in the future.

Even if our current state seems meager, God sees the tremendous potential blessings hidden when the seed of grace is sown. This is the key to Teleios Discipleship. In the miracle of the five loaves and two fish in John 6, the disciples questioned how it could be enough for so many people (John 6:9). Jesus blessed the five loaves and two fish and sowed the seed of grace in the boy's heart. The result was not only feeding the five thousand and more but also the leftover fragments filled twelve baskets (see John 6:13). This is how the disciples write the résumé of the future. The devil may make us look back at our weaknesses and a dubious past. Nevertheless, the Holy Spirit, even when we are small, sees the potential that will happen in the future when we walk with the Lord. This is the key to Teleios Discipleship. When there is strife between disciples among themselves, this is almost always due to the inability to turn away from their past or the past of others in the church.

The Mystery of Teleios Faith: The Glory of the Church

The era of the Fourth Industrial Revolution and the onset of artificial intelligence have dawned. Secularism and atheism are on the rise. The situation surrounding the church has become more challenging and acute, especially after the COVID-19 pandemic. However, I remain firmly convinced that only the church of Jesus Christ can change the world. What is the basis for the hope for change and the remedy that the church offers to the world?

Ephesians declares that Jesus became the "head" of the church (Eph. 1:22; 4:15) and further declares that the church is His "bride" (see Eph. 5:23). Both expressions signify that the church has become the primary focus of our Lord's greatest interest. To the bridegroom, the bride is the most beautiful being in this world, and Jesus sees His body, the church, through such eyes. In this sense, the church is the unique love of Jesus, the place where He poured out His love. The bridegroom automatically assumes the responsibility to protect his bride and make her happy. Jesus similarly has a dream of making His bride, the church, beautiful and holy. Ephesians 5:27 expresses this dream as follows: "So that he might present the church to himself in splendor, without spot or wrinkle or any such thing, that she might be holy and without blemish."

A glorious church is the earnest desire of our Lord for us. Even if the church has various issues, the Lord's yearning for us remains unchanged. God's greatest concern is the church. The center of history is neither the hero nor the people; it is the church. This statement is unrelated to church triumphalism or arrogant imperialism. It emphasizes the fact that Jesus's interest and gaze are fixed on the church, His bride.

How does the church, which receives this attention and care from the Lord, exist on earth in a way that reaches the holy perfection, free from any flaws? The apostle Paul stated in Colossians 1:24 that he fills up in his flesh what is lacking in the afflictions of Christ for the sake of His body, which is the church. Then how does one fill up Christ's remaining afflictions in His body for the church? The answer lies in one word found in verse 27: "glory of this mystery." This mystery aligns with the expression "church . . . in splendor" in Ephesians 5:27. What is the mystery Paul is talking about? It is the "Christ in you," the true mystery of our faith. The genuine mystery of our faith is Jesus Christ within us. The glory of the church is consistently evident to those who know that the real mystery is Christ in them.

A Shabby Yet Glorious Church

In the 1960s and 70s, shortly after the Korean War that devastated the entire Korean peninsula, the Korean church was shabby with little to boast about. My father planted a church on the mountainside near Busan where the poor and needy people ended up. The humble church building my father had secured as a place of worship always leaked when it rained, and it was located next to a large Buddhist temple. Knowing that my father was a pastor, the kids in the neighborhood would throw rocks at me whenever I walked by them, saying, "It's the pastor's kid," and proceeded to curse at me as one of their favorite pastimes.

The church needs to regain such conviction for the church that no matter how little, the church is glorious because of who God is. Even if one's personal life goes well and is having good days, if church life is unstable and challenging, one ends up facing rough challenges of the world in every other aspect. On the other hand, when experiencing the grace of breakthrough and deepening the relationship with the Lord, I have seen countless instances where problems and issues they face in the world melt away like snow under the sun.

Our Lord has always been meek and served humbly. However, when it comes to talking about the church, He declared it fiercely with no reservation. When speaking about Himself and the glory of the church, he did so with a roaring confidence. In Matthew 16:18, Jesus proclaims, "I will build my church, and the gates of hell shall not prevail against it." Immediately after, in chapter 17, Jesus appeared in a glorious form on the Mount of Transfiguration. In Revelation 2, the Lord holds seven golden lampstands and walks among seven stars, indicating that He will personally grip and steer the churches. Imagine what glory He appeared in that scene. Contrasted with His appearance on earth, when He had nowhere to lay His head (Matt. 8:20), Jesus in the vision of Revelations wears a golden sash, and His feet were like refined bronze, glowing in a furnace (Rev. 1:14–17). This symbolizes that He is unstoppable and uncontainable, much like the image of the feet of iron in Nebuchadnezzar's dream. The Lord, though He is gentler and meeker than anyone, displays a power that is stronger than any breaching force of a chariot division. The Lord does not merely stop at observing the church on earth from a distance. Through the Holy Spirit, He empowers the church, supplies purity, and preserves it until the final victory.

The Glory of the Head Is the Glory of the Body

The renowned Western historian Edward Gibbon wrote in *The Decline and Fall of the Roman Empire*, "While the colossal fabric of the Roman Empire was crumbling into pieces by the public force, a pure and humble religion gently insinuated itself into the minds of men, grew up in silence and obscurity, derived new vigor from opposition, and finally erected the triumphant banner of the Cross on the ruins of the Capitolinus."[26] Jesus Christ was the greatest revolutionary. Through humility, meekness, and the way of the cross, He fundamentally transformed both the human spirit and the world.

We read in Ephesians 5:23, "Christ is the head of the church, his body, and is himself its Savior." What is clear is that every member of the body must follow the instructions of the head. The church is a place to hear the command of Christ. Only then can spiritual warfare take place. The ecclesiology presented in Ephesians culminates in spiritual warfare. Victory in battle is guaranteed when there is obedience to the orders of a courageous and strategically astute commander. Spiritual warfare is one of the core topics in ecclesiology. The body must heed the commands of the head. If the body does not listen to the head, it is simply dysfunctional. If the head departs from the body, the body does not become free but dies. Therefore, we must believe that Jesus is the glorious head of the church.

The Hardening of the Church Caused by the Disappearance of the Glory of the Lord

When local churches become spiritually dull, they exhibit a rise and fall similar to secular organizations and institutions. In the beginning, there is a honeymoon phase. When a church grows, people are willing to sacrifice everything without any regrets and become generous with their gifts. However, after fifteen or twenty years, when the church experiences certain growth, bureaucracy inevitably sets in. This stagnation and hardening are threatening to the church. Regarding this, Os Guinness aptly expressed, "No one knows how long it will take, but after a certain period of time, the laughing portrait of the founder will hang in the boardroom of the successor as a holy memorial. In short, bureaucratization turns revolutionary events into everyday tasks and disguises discoveries as institutionalization."[27]

The terrifying aspect of the bureaucratization of the church is that there are no symptoms initially. Once it occurs, recovery is nearly impossible, and the depletion of vitality gradually progresses until only a plastic façade remains. This phenomenon occurs when the church becomes a mere organization, a certain level of stability becomes the goal, and history and tradition begin to form as the highest priority. Then suddenly, various complaints emerge to challenge that stability. Complaints that were seemingly unthinkable in the early stages readily surface during these seemingly stabilized periods. This results from the church becoming bureaucratized and dependent only on organizational structure. The church enters a stage called the "fortress of the mind," where it becomes rigid in its thinking. It starts rejecting what is untraditional, builds factions, and eventually becomes an inaccessible fortress.

Although the history of the church is ancient, the church must always remain youthful. Youthfulness is a sign that the church, as the body of Christ, possesses vitality. To maintain freshness like the evergreen olive tree deeply rooted by the brook, the church should not be submerged in past traditions (Ps. 52:8). Sometimes, it needs to surpass tradition with a clear discernment of the present age. Lloyd-Jones expresses this as the "principle of discontinuity" that avoids being submerged in the tradition. Here, discontinuity means not blindly adhering to the "way things always have been." Gospel-driven disciples, having examined the history of the church, understand how a church that once was a vibrant body filled with the life of "Zoe" can easily become a rigid and practically dead institution. They recognize that this is the greatest danger.[28]

The Church, the Fruit of New Creation, Must Always Be Renewed

The church, the most glorious fruit of new creation, must always be renewed. The God who gave the church, which is like a mother to believers, is the Creator.[29] The first creation was splendid and majestic, but how marvelous is the second creation accomplished through the cross and resurrection of Jesus! How much more beautiful and exalted will be the completion of this new creation in the new heaven and new earth!

The church, created anew through the incarnation of Jesus, thus must be renewed. Without this resolution, how can we, the members of the body of Christ, be renewed day by day? The Holy Spirit sent by Jesus is the One who renews. The fallen world is always being renewed by the Spirit of the Lord. In this sense, the old ways stand in contrast with the work of the Spirit, who always renews. The Holy Spirit sent by Jesus is the renewing God. In this way, complacency and stagnancy are opposites to the ministry of the Holy Spirit.

The ecclesiology according to Teleios Discipleship is marked by the commitment that the church is to be renewed every day through the Holy Spirit. It does not refer to the outward appearance of worship, preaching, prayer, and praise. It is the anointing of the Holy Spirit that makes all of them new and fresh. In this regard, the most important concern and task for pastors, ministers, and lay leaders should be, "How can we renew the church as the body of the Lord?" The renewal of the church by the work of the Spirit is different from distorted reform or renewal as a tool for one's own purposes. Teleios disciples seek the renewal of the Holy Spirit.

What Does a Church Full of Believers Awakened by Teleios Discipleship Training Look Like?

SaRang Church has been committed to discipleship training for now a generation. As a result, there has been much awareness and knowledge about the role of lay believers within the church. The expression "lay believers as the principal agents of the church" has now become a popular phrase among those in Korea. Lay believers are not a specific group or individual within the church. The lay believer, sought by the Teleios disciple, refers to all those believers who have received God's calling, awakened with a sense of mission, and sent into the world.

Lay Believers, the Nation of the People, and the Kingdom of God

Activating the laity to become laborers of God's kingdom and all areas of the church is the solid framework of healthy pastoral ministry and discipleship training. Starting from Jesus's Great Commission to make disciples of all nations (Matt. 28:19–20), through the awakening of the universal priesthood through the Reformation in the Middle Ages, lay believers have been reaffirmed as the "principal agents" in the church.

Regarding the way discipleship training has activated the role of lay believers as the principal agents of the church in Korea, it is necessary to consider the historical context of Korea. Without understanding how Christianity transformed the country from a "kingdom of kings and nobles" to a "nation of the people," or how the deeply ingrained influence of Confucianism in their unconsciousness was overcome, it is difficult to properly appreciate the true meaning of lay believers becoming the principal agents of the church.

In medieval times, Korea was known as Goryeo, a country of nobles based on Buddhist ideology. Following the collapse of Goryeo, the Joseon dynasty was erected in the Korean peninsula also as a country of nobles but this time based on Confucianism. As Confucianism took root for more than five hundred years, the rigid hierarchy of scholars, farmers, artisans, and merchants became as firm as a rock. As a result, the average people were marginalized, lacking autonomous power. Looking at historical records, there were regional differences, but generally, until the early eighteenth century, commoners and slaves accounted for more than 80 percent of the population. Especially, the ratio of slaves reached 30 percent. Although the ratio of slaves sharply decreased from the late nineteenth century to the twentieth century, the consciousness of anti-classism was deeply rooted in the minds of the people.[30]

The incident that shook the anti-class consciousness from its roots was the March 1st Movement. The March 1st Movement, which resisted Japanese occupation, was a movement led by Christians. At that time, the church occupied 70 percent of the nationwide March 1st Movement centers. Within forty days of the March 1st Movement, the Provisional Government of the Republic of Korea was established in Shanghai. Article 7 of the Shanghai Provisional Government's Constitution states that the Republic of Korea was founded "according to the will of God."[31] It is a surprising and amazing declaration. The goal of the Provisional Government, rooted in the March 1st Movement where the people took the main stage, was to establish the kingdom of God. And in 1948, the Republic of Korea became the first "nation of the people" as the people became the sovereign subjects of Korea.

The nation "of the people" originated from the spirit of the kingdom of God, which does not allow any discrimination in class. This opened the way for lay believers to fulfill their role as the subjects of the church, dedicating themselves to service. The Christian-based March 1st Movement became the driving force behind the establishment of the Provisional Government that advocated building the kingdom of God, and thirty years later, in 1948, the first session of the National Assembly of the Republic of Korea began with the prayer of Pastor Lee Yoon-young. This acted as the spiritual DNA of the Korean church, allowing lay believers to play their role as the principal agents of the church and as members, turning Korea's national religion into a holy asset within one hundred years of the gospel entering the country.

Four Privileges of Lay Believers with Priestly Consciousness

First Peter 2:9 highlights the universal priesthood mentioned in the New Testament as a representative biblical basis for the awakening of lay believers as the principal agents of the church. In the Old Testament era, the priesthood was limited to the descendants of Aaron from the tribe of Levi. Until the medieval period, or arguably until half a century ago, the role of mediating between God and people was assumed by pastors, and the believers did not challenge this hierarchy. However, the Bible teaches that all saints who are saved and redeemed by the blood of Jesus Christ have the privilege to approach God like kings, functioning as priests, regardless of time and space. The privilege of the universal priesthood includes the right to approach God, offer spiritual sacrifices, bear witness to the Word, and intercede.[32] All laypeople have the right to exercise this access as Christ's disciples. So, what privileges are bestowed upon believers?

First, Teleios Discipleship training is truly empowering for saints, emphasizing the fact that they can directly approach God through His Word and prayer, anytime and anywhere. This training teaches and ingrains the profound gratitude and excitement of this privilege.

Second, all saints have the privilege of offering themselves as a spiritual sacrifice to God for the sake of their brothers and neighbors. In the Old Testament, sacrifices were expected to be without blemish, pure, and the best of what was available. Today, we are presented as pure and unblemished spiritual offerings through the blood of Jesus—a righteous existence. Teleios Discipleship emphasizes the need for a proper holy consciousness, which includes living by faith (Heb. 11:4), obedience (1 Sam. 15:22), righteousness (Mal. 3:3), and thanksgiving (Ps. 50:14). It further instructs about the blessings received when offering oneself as a spiritual sacrifice.

One of these two is becoming a spiritual sacrifice can bring about a transformation in family, colleagues, and neighbors. Changing those bound by sin and the gravity pull of the world is practically challenging. The most effective way to transform them is by becoming a sacrifice ourselves. Furthermore, as the second of the two, being a spiritual sacrifice can serve as a source of strength for those who groan in affliction, pain, and distress.

In that era, slaves were in a more wretched condition than ordinary livestock.[33] However, Paul speaks joyfully to those considered as breathing beasts, and the Thessalonian believers received the joy of the Holy Spirit even amid great tribulation (1 Thess. 1:6). The reason is that Paul, who proclaimed the message, lived a life offered as a sacrifice (Phil. 2:17). By first offering himself as a sacrifice, Paul's life connected with all those associated with him, and joy overflowed.

Third, proclaiming the cosmic authority of God, the Creator of heaven and earth, as a priestly king like Christ, delivering the message of eternal life, is not a privilege granted to a select few but a privilege and purpose for all saints. The challenge lies in not considering it an obligation but failing to regard it as a privilege. However, George Eldon Ladd pointed out that the ultimate triumph of the church must wait until the task of proclaiming the gospel of the kingdom of God is fulfilled. He emphasized that there is no greater hope for the church and saints than this. Ladd poses a poignant question, "Do you long for the coming of the Lord?"[34] Living as a priestly king today means hoping for the Lord's coming daily.

Fourth, saints have the privilege of offering intercession, as the universal priesthood of the believers involves offering prayers to God for brothers, sisters, neighbors, ministers, and pastors. In this regard, saints can intercede for ministers and pastors as well. An anecdote about Abraham Kuyper's church is a helpful illustration in this regard. Kuyper confesses his own experience of renewal through the members he was ministering to while pastoring in a rural church. One day after he was finished preaching, he found some parishioners staying back and praying. These parishioners were praying for their young pastor, Kuyper, who lacked nothing except regeneration.[35] The person who was "regenerated" was none other than Abraham Kuyper himself.

Intercessory prayer is both a privilege for saints and evidence of Teleios Discipleship training. It is also a clear indicator of what true disciple training ultimately pursues—the ministry of life. Through the years of discipleship training, I have discovered a distinct truth concerning the type of leadership that was produced as a result of discipleship training. Though they were all trained under the same regiment, there was a stark difference when they were commissioned as small-group leaders. A leader who sows the seed with tears for their small-group members is much richer in the fruit, compared to a leader with abundant biblical knowledge but filled with cynicism. Commitment to willing and joyous intercessory prayer as a privilege made all the difference in the world.

Laity Enjoying the Blessing of a Kingly Priest

When God said to the Israelites, "You shall be to me a kingdom of priests and a holy nation" (Exod. 19:6), the Israelites were truly destitute. Only two or three months had passed since they escaped centuries of slavery in Egypt, yet the Israelites could not easily throw off the slave mentality. The wicked nature that made them want to return to Egypt persisted whenever troubles arose. Although they had escaped the status of slaves, their outer appearance still reflected the tattered garments of former slaves. To these seemingly insignificant people, God spoke these resounding words, "You are a kingdom of priests."

Our current state as kingly priests resembles that of the Israelites. Like them, we are still subject to the power of sin in the world, displaying a pitiful image that cries, "Who will deliver me from this body of death?" (Rom. 7:24). Nevertheless, God calls us "a kingdom of priests" for a reason. It is because within us, as children of the King of kings and as disciples of Jesus, who came from the seed of the King and the seed of the Priest, we carry the same royal destiny of living as priests. Despite our current humble appearance, all saints are born as kingly priests and must live with the holy destiny that comes with it.

How Can We Train for the Responsibility, Perspective, and Capacity of a Kingly Priest? In both the East and the West, special education is provided for the crown prince who will inherit the throne to equip him with the ability to govern the country and instill a contemporary perspective. In the East, the children of kings were taught classics, calligraphy, and history. By teaching and learning classics, calligraphy, and history properly, even an ordinary person can acquire the sense of responsibility and capacity to lead a country.

If teaching classics to a person properly readies a former nonprince to fulfill the responsibilities of a king, likewise pastors, by teaching the living Word of God, can nurture believers into kingly priests with privileges, responsibilities, and a mission in the kingdom of God. In this regard, the role of pastors in teaching and proclaiming the Bible is critical.

To teach believers properly, pastors should not only have the heart of a teacher but also the heart of a father and the compassion of a shepherd (1 Cor. 4:15). Teaching and memorizing the Bible properly are not only a blessing for the children but also the best way to live a spiritual life. "If I had to choose only one thing among all the training for spiritual life, I would choose Bible memorization."[36] Believers should also be obliged to memorize the Bible. Doing so will ultimately revive believers with the living Word in decisive moments of their lives.

Laity Participating in Spiritual Reproduction

One of the areas that laypeople have been significantly awakened to regarding their role is the task of making disciples and sending them out. Previously, disciple-making was considered to be a duty given to pastors or professional ministers. Laypeople now realize that spiritual reproduction, making disciples and sending them out while serving the souls of others, is a mission of their own.

How is spiritual reproduction possible in the church? How do laypeople dedicate time to teach and train others with the Word and then send them out? Of course, it is not easy for those with full-time jobs to engage in these tasks like full-time ministers. However, contrary to the popular notion, laypeople play a crucial role in spiritual reproduction in a disciple-making church. From being a Sunday school teacher to a small-group leader, ordinary believers can actively participate in spiritual reproduction. For example, one of the most important roles of a small-group leader is to discover, develop, and dispatch their small-group members as disciples and leaders. While small-group meetings may only happen once a week, the time spent praying for small-group members' discipleship takes place throughout the week, providing opportunities for lay-driven disciple-making. Even without dedicated training sessions, laypeople can engage in spiritual reproduction through intercessory prayer and loving service along with a variety of other means to impact their lives.

Spiritual Reproduction Must Begin at Home

According to Teleios Discipleship, spiritual reproduction begins at home. The core of spiritual reproduction does not stop at merely making disciples and sending them out. Spiritual reproduction is concerned with inheriting the faith to the next generation. Even if spiritual reproduction saves the souls of many through disciple-making in the present, if faith does not pass on to the next generation, its significance is inevitably diminished. The true pinnacle of spiritual reproduction happens when parents' faith continues to the faith of their children, grandchildren, and the next generations. No matter how well a minister trains disciples or how well a disciple is trained, there is nothing more regrettable than to see them failing to reproduce faith to their children at home.

Establishing SaRang Church in Teleios: Three Foundations

Special Dawn Revival Rally: A Scene That Instills the Disposition of Teleios in the Church and Believers

The Special Dawn Revival Rally originated from an inspiration that struck like lightning one early morning. While ministering in Southern California and commuting long distances to Calvin Theological Seminary in Michigan, I had a moment of realization that "spiritual blessings transcend the limitations of the flesh." This thought became a holy flame that elevated my ministry to a new dimension. From the time of ministering at SaRang Community Church in Southern California, I launched the Special Dawn Revival Rally meetings, and this ministry continued without skipping a beat even after I assumed the senior pastor position at SaRang Church in Seoul.

After concluding my ministry at SaRang Community Church in Southern California, I returned to Korea in August 2003. When I began as the senior pastor at SaRang Church, with this new church community in Seoul, I immediately began the early morning prayer meetings at 5 a.m. every morning. The prayer meetings began in a church annex initially, involving myself, the newly appointed senior pastor, and those who simply wanted to come together with the same hearts for the church. However, the fervor of prayer that was ignited by these hearts began to get intensified. As the fire spread, more and more started to come out in the early morning to join me in prayer, and we had to move the meeting location to the main sanctuary to accommodate the growing fervor of prayer. The unplanned Special Dawn Revival was birthed this way. What morphed from an ordinary prayer meeting into the first Special Dawn Revival Rally at SaRang Church lasted for forty-seven days. The Special Dawn Revival Rally has been an ongoing history of God's work, reaching the twenty-first season in 2023.

The early morning of the Special Dawn Revival is a time when the dew of heavenly grace descends upon our spirits. The blessings received during Special Dawn become a reservoir of life and a source of spiritual blessings, like the combined effects of early and late rains, revitalizing believers and the church. The spring Special Dawn Revival Rally starts in March or April and meets for a week. The fall Special Dawn Revival is held in October or November. Special Dawn Revival serves as a communal demonstration of the biblical exhortation, "Pray without ceasing" (1 Thess. 5:17), acting as a fortification that protects the believers and the church. The fiery prayer in Special Dawn Revival is closely related to the soil cultivated through disciple-making. As the soil is well prepared to receive the Word through discipleship training, the fire of prayer naturally descends and burns brightly through the ministry of the Holy Spirit.

Special Dawn Revival Rally: Custom-Tailored Scene of the Holy Spirit's Personal Ministry

As I lead the Special Dawn Revival Rally, there is a profound and clear conviction that has accumulated over time and with each season. Special Dawn Revival Rally is a field where the personal ministry of the Holy Spirit works in a customized manner according to the needs of each believer. There is no predetermined set order in the Special Dawn Revival Rally; preaching, prayer, and praise naturally flow.

Participating in the Special Dawn Revival Rally in the early hours of the morning can be seen as voluntarily engaging in "discomfort" in light of God's grace. Each person has unique circumstances and prayer topics. However, the Holy Spirit personally provides tailored blessings according to each person's needs. Special Dawn Revival Rally is a place of healing. When the diverse prayers of believers who carry each of their burdens and difficulties of life burst forth as a fountain in the early morning, it envelops SaRang Church and flows back to replenish individuals and families.

Special Dawn Revival Rally is a field that transforms the church and believers into the culture of Teleios. It is a concentrated time of intense preaching, prayer, and spiritual praise, allowing the body of the Lord, the church, and the individuals within it to become more like the Lord.

Special Dawn Revival Rally is a time when maturity is engraved in a tree ring of the soul. Everyone wishes to live their lives without regret, and the Special Dawn Revival Rally can be considered the most powerful spiritual tool for believers to live their lives without regrets, facing life's challenges head-on. Attending the Special Revival Dawn Rally for one or two years, our souls will be engraved with the commitment to prayer, to the Word, and to praise. Unconsciously, a sturdy age of faith will be established, serving as a strong foundation to withstand any storms in life.

Special Dawn Revival Rally is also a time to sow the seed of spiritual homecoming to children. Every believing parent wishes for their children to live faith when they go out into the world. When the time comes for children to leave their parents and navigate the challenging path of life, many challenges pull them to stray from their faith. In moments of difficulty or temptations in their life's journey, children will recall the time spent in the Special Dawn Revival Rally with their parents—the moments of blessings, the memories of the presence of God shared as a family and answered prayers.

Special Dawn Revival Rally invites all believers to one pulpit, one gathering, and one unique experience. It connects every corner of the church under the umbrella of grace to avoid missing the easily overlooked blind spots of blessings in a large church. From Sunday school to the elderly, Special Dawn Revival Rally ushers them into a time of anointing and equips them as God's army (2 Chron. 14:13).

How Does the Special Dawn Revival Rally Lead the Community's Teleios Faith?

One of the greatest blessings enjoyed through the Special Dawn Revival Rally is preventive pastoral care. It happens as the Special Dawn

Revival Rally leads the church community to Teleios maturity. It is evident that through the Special Dawn Revival Rally, the wounds and personal issues of believers are miraculously healed and resolved. To be certain, prevention is more important than healing in pastoral care. Once a disease sets in, it requires more energy to return to health. Special Dawn Revival Rally acts as a powerful autopilot device, launching the faith of believers into a new horizon. It gives them the space to be assured that the faith entering orbit will not deviate but will continue the trajectory of grace.

The Special Dawn Revival also has an online testimony platform, where believers post their testimonies in a dedicated online space referred to as the Blessings Board. It serves as a holy communication platform leading the community to wholeness. When anyone wants to know where the testimonies of the living God are, the only place they have to look is the online board. Thousands of posts are filled with the excitement and joy of believers. Those who write about their inspiration from the Special Dawn Revival Rally and those who read the posts become one in spirit, creating a spiritual river that builds SaRang Church. When facing difficulties due to challenges from the world, reading posts on the Blessings Board becomes a source of renewed strength, allowing individuals to rise above the issues with a new heart. Even though believers may not meet face-to-face, communicating spiritually through the board fosters communal healing and contributes to the health of the community.

In sum, I see that the Special Dawn Revival Rally is a new way the Holy Spirit cultivates a healthy community. It is a special time of intercessory prayer when believers gather together in the presence of the Holy Spirit, offering prayers for one another, the church's body, and the nation and global church. In this way, the Special Dawn Revival Rally strengthens healthy communal life. Therefore, the consistent practice of the Special Dawn Revival Rally in the church reinforces community health. Through this time, Teleios of communal faith is secured more powerfully.

Upper Room Leaders Meeting: A Deep Well for Bearing the Fruit of Teleios in Believers and the Church

SaRang Church holds a small-group leaders' meeting called the Upper Room Leaders Meeting every Tuesday. Upper Room Leaders Meeting is a lifelong education program designed for male and female small-group leaders who have Teleios Discipleship training and are leading small groups in my church. This meeting allows all our Upper Room (small group) leaders, who serve as a means to continue cultivating Teleios dispositions, keeping them from falling into spiritual dormancy and averting the potential dangers of becoming complacent. It can be considered SaRang Church's secret weapon to always maintain the spiritual vitality of the entire church.[37]

More than anything, the Tuesday Upper Room Leaders Meeting is a place where small-group leaders align their hearts and minds with the senior pastor's pastoral philosophy and reaffirm the motivation to serve their small groups. The vitality of the community depends on the spiritual strength of its members. Robust and healthy spiritual strength prevents the community from deviating from its orbit. Solid spiritual strength determines healthy centrifugal force. Enriching the community and bearing the fruit are some of the results that result from the dedication of a committed few.

Time to Be Aligned with the Senior Pastor's Pastoral Philosophy. The time spent in the Upper Room Leaders Meeting is the heartbeat that invigorates the church more than any other meeting or community gathering within the church. It is the heart that allows the senior pastor's pastoral philosophy to flow through the church's veins. Therefore, I pour as much effort into preparing for the Upper Room Leaders Meeting as I do to prepare for sermons.

When the church faced difficulties and needed recovery, the small-group leaders through the Upper Room Leaders Meeting, aligned themselves with the senior pastor's heart and direction. Thus, the heartbeat of the local church as a community of life is closely tied to the energy and health of the Upper Room Leaders Meeting.

The Tuesday Upper Room Leaders Meeting is a time when small-group leaders gather to prepare the small groups they will lead for the week, as they sit under the teaching of the senior pastor. Upper Room small-group leaders who guide evening small groups or male Upper Room leaders prepare for their small group by watching a recorded video on this day. However, the Upper Room Leaders Meeting is not just a time to prepare for weekly small-group meetings. It is a time to align with the senior pastor's pastoral philosophy. During this time, the senior pastor's pastoral philosophy is shared in the small groups throughout the church, creating a spiritual posture that blesses the entire church to be surrendered to God.

In the Upper Room Leaders Meeting, the roles, responsibilities, and blessings received through ministry are emphasized to small-group leaders to the extent that they become engraved in their minds. This emphasis aims to instill a strong sense of mission consciousness, recognizing how precious the ministry of serving souls entrusted to small-group leaders is. From the moment a person believes in Jesus, the seed of a mission is sown in every believer. However, whether that sown seed grows depends significantly on the senior pastor's recognition of its importance.

Time to Establish Upper Room Leaders as Missionaries of Spiritual Reproduction. Upper Room Leaders Meeting is also a time when the concept of a universal priesthood is realized. In reality, it is challenging for all members of the church to establish and live a priestly life, in service of the souls around them. However, the Upper Room Leaders Meeting can be considered a field where this task is practically implemented in the context of life. It is a training ground where Upper Room leaders are prepared and trained to participate in spiritual reproduction.

Upper Room Leaders Meeting is the heart of the church. It is because when a small-group leader is healthy and vibrant, the small-group members can be healthy and vibrant. In this sense, leading the Tuesday Upper Room Leaders Meeting for the senior pastor is a spiritually burdened yet sacred time filled with great expectations. I, together with my small-group leaders, eagerly anticipate the nourishment of the Word, as we gather together with warm and joyful hearts on Tuesday mornings. Through the preparation for small groups that takes place through Upper Room Leaders Meeting, ordinary leaders can handle the ministry of the Word with faithfulness and confidence.

The Upper Room Leaders Meeting is an opportunity for individual leaders to grow and be armed with the Word. Upper Room leaders cover the main text of the small-group materials at least four times. Before the Upper Room Leaders Meeting on Tuesdays, they preview the materials for the first time; then for the second time, they learn the text through the meeting; for the third time, they organize the small-group content before the actual small-group meeting; and finally, for the fourth time, they lead the small-group meetings sharing with others what they have gained over the other three times of engagement with the text. In this way, they acquire a faith that becomes more whole in the presence of the Word than anyone else. Upper Room leaders are particularly careful not to think of themselves as simply learning to teach others. Just as when clergy depart from grace, they are susceptible to hypocrisy, the small-group leaders are always reminded to maintain a posture of learning the Word to be spiritually healthy and upright before teaching others.

Time to Prepare for the Future of the Church. Upper Room Leaders Meeting is a place where visions about the future of the church are shared. It is not uncommon for ministers to use the platform to tell stories of the past as they reminisce about their heroic achievements. However, there was an event that established how I must use the platform at the Upper Room Leaders Meeting.

When I became the senior pastor of SaRang Church, I remember Pastor Oak Han-Heum leading the last Upper Room Leaders Meeting as the founding pastor. He had led the Upper Room Leaders Meeting for more than twenty-five years from its inception. The last session could well be a time when he could have reflected on and shared many nostalgic and moving stories. However, Pastor Oak focused more time on encouraging and praying for the leaders to become even more firmly rooted in the Word than reflecting on his past achievements. I realized then and again that the Upper Room Leaders Meeting is a dedicated place for preparing the future of both believers and the church.

In the Upper Room Leaders Meeting, Upper Room leaders not only experience the richness of the Word and experience transformation through prayer, but they also become good shepherds who care for members of their small groups entrusted with the perspective of shepherding.

Before delving into the small-group materials in the Upper Room Leaders Meeting, there is a time for prayer for the church members. It is a united intercessory prayer for those who are in extremely desperate situations and require urgent intervention from God. It is a time of wholehearted prayer for church members and small-group members to feel a sense of community as members of the body of the Lord.

When I lead the Upper Room Leaders Meeting, I lead as if I am leading a revival rally, praying that the leaders' hearts will be stirred anew. This is because preparing the soil of the heart is a critical first step to receiving the Word, so that the Word may take deep root and bear much fruit in time. It is a time that recharges small-group leaders with a sense of mission and repositions the members of the church on the track of faith, serving as the deep well that supplies nutrients to bear the fruit of the church's Teleios maturity.

"Called to Awaken the Laity": Discipleship Training Leadership Seminar for the Teleios of Believers and the Church

SaRang Church's "Called to Awaken the Laity" is a spiritual platform for the Teleios of believers and the church. "Called to Awakening the Laity" is a seminar that was launched in 1986 to introduce and equip the local church discipleship training to the churches and church leaders worldwide. Known as the CAL Seminar, it has been ongoing for over forty years, exceeding 120 occurrences, and now is established as a seminar on a global scale. Although numerous seminars appear and disappear in the world, the fact that SaRang can offer CAL Seminars without ceasing for decades is only the testimony of God's grace.

Vibrant Scenes of the Discipleship Training Leaders Seminar. Participating pastors learn about the spirit and practical aspects of discipleship training through the CAL Seminar, which consists of tracks, namely keynote lectures, small-group leadership methods, on-site observation, and hands-on training. In the following, I briefly introduce these four tracks of the CAL seminar:

Teleios Discipleship and Other Keynote Lectures Track. The Keynote Lectures track instills a strong conviction in the necessity of training lay believers, providing a time to shift paradigms in pastoral philosophy, strategy, and methods. Particularly, the Teleios Discipleship lecture, held as the first-day keynote session since March 2014, focuses on how Christ's disciples should be formed. It emphasizes the urgency of transforming a disciple-making church into a disciple-making missional church that brings the whole world to the Lord.

Inductive Small-Group Bible Study and Small-Group Leadership Methods Track. The small-group leadership methods sessions introduce methodologies for leading small groups, how to run successful small-group ministries bent on making disciples, and the theory of small groups. It delivers systematic lectures on the environment and nature of small groups, small groups and its leadership, inductive personal Bible study, and inductive small-group Bible study. These teachings aim to explain why the small group is an optimal environment for Teleios Discipleship to take place and various leadership methods in navigating through small-group ministry.

On-Site Observation Track. One notable feature of the CAL Seminar is that participants not only attend lectures that deal with principles and theories but also actively participate in and observe SaRang Church's real-life small groups. Moreover, delegates of the seminar attend actual discipleship training meetings, the Upper Room Leaders Meeting, and the Upper Room small-group meetings. Through these three on-site observation tracks, participants can directly witness the training environments that have shaped SaRang Church. This allows the participants to witness the fruit Teleios Discipleship training has produced in SaRang Church over the years in the front seat.

Hands-On Training Track. The distinctive aspect that sets the CAL Seminar apart is its emphasis on practical training. It goes beyond passively hearing about a theory. Instead, participants are invited to actively participate in practicing the theories and realities learned during the week in actual SaRang small groups. This hands-on approach ensures that delegates gain results beyond the level of knowledge transfer.

Engaging with the Global Church with the Heart of a Debtor: The Globalization of Discipleship Training. The CAL Seminar has become a field for the globalization of discipleship training, hosting seminars directly in Ethiopia, Ghana, Brazil, China, and Taiwan. At the same time, CAL Seminar consistently hosts participants from around the world on all continents. The concept of "globalization of discipleship training," now familiar to SaRang Church believers, was first introduced in the *Disciple Journal* in January 2011, defining it as "providing a global standard platform for the dissemination of the gospel." Pastor Oak Han-heum had already discussed the globalization of discipleship training as early as 2005.[38]

Taking discipleship training to the global scene will be thoroughly developed and completed on the basis of a mutual relationship. Though we generously plan to share what we have accrued over the years, it is fundamentally driven by the debtor's mindset to spur one another on as co-laborers in the kingdom. The internationalization of discipleship training is poised to equip the Chinese church to serve as a gateway for the global mission, hindering the southward expansion of Islam in Africa through churches in Ghana and Ethiopia, leading Christian growth in Brazil, countering the decline of European churches, and fostering spiritual growth in Southeast Asian churches amid the influence of Islamic authority. There is a synergy that can be expected when we understand that the Korean church possesses a "missionary spirit" that sends missionaries worldwide. Combined with the "martyrdom spirit" of the North Korean church and the "global spirit" of

Korean Christian diasporas scattered worldwide, the globalization of discipleship training has the potential to create tremendous synergy and practical impact for the church everywhere.

CHAPTER 5

Pneumatology for Teleios Discipleship Training: Rediscovery of the Holy Spirit from the Perspective of Teleios Discipleship

Breaking the Shell of Traditional Faith and Opening Eyes to the Ministry of the Holy Spirit

I was born into a family that has believed in Jesus for four generations. My father recited the Twelve Articles of Faith before leading worship, every time we worshipped both at home and at the church. I still appreciate this as a part of the nice traditions of conservative faith that Korean churches possess. However, ministries immersed in such traditions readily emphasize the Word and doctrines but demonstrate a tendency not to focus on the fullness of or the charismatic ministry of the Holy Spirit.

It is not uncommon for conservative churches or pastors to neglect the power or the anointing of the Holy Spirit. To illustrate, John Calvin's *Institutes of the Christian Religion* is considered the most significant book by Calvinists, perhaps next to the Bible. In the 1541 French edition, the expression "power of the Holy Spirit" appears about twenty times, with little emphasis on or explanation of the ministry of the anointing of the Holy Spirit that Pentecostals and charismatics value. Considering the need to correct the errors of Catholicism and return to the truth of the Bible at that time, one can assume that John Calvin thoughtfully focused on writing about the ministry of the Word as a higher priority. In such a tradition, the expression "power of the Holy Spirit" was mainly used to describe the illumination of the Word, the power to control the instincts and greed of the flesh, and to experience the grace of the sacraments. Therefore, for someone like me, who grew up in a conservative denomination, it seems natural not to have properly heard, understood, and experienced the anointing or the public ministry of the power of the Holy Spirit.

However, an event occurred to me that shattered the framework of my conservative reservation about the Holy Spirit. This event became a starting point for me to rediscover the Holy Spirit, the ministry of the Holy Spirit, and to open the door of thought to a balanced spirituality—a historical turning point of my faith and convictions. In 1976, more than thirty college students from Naesoodong Church, where I was leading the college ministry, went to a retreat at Yesuwon in Gangwon Province. There I met Rev. Dae-Cheon Deok, and I experienced the peeling away of layers of accumulated coverings of my practice of faith shrouded by traditions.

This one day we were supposed to have an outdoor meeting, but it rained. Rev. Dae-Cheon Deok stood up and said, "Let us pray that rain will stop for the glory of God." He proceeded to pray, and the rain stopped. What shocked me at that moment was not the stop of the rain as a result of a prayer. It was the way he prayed—the prayer that completely relied on the Holy Spirit without limits or restrictions. Until then I had always prayed, but it seemed that there were preset criteria within me that limited how God would answer my prayers. Yet, Rev. Dae-Cheon Deok's boldness in seeking the rain would stop for the sake of God's work shattered the limits that I had set up for my prayers. It usurped my qualitative understanding of prayer, bringing about a change in my spiritual paradigm. It was a time to experience that there could be no limits or restrictions in prayers when relying on the Holy Spirit. Until then, I had the knowledge to teach others about the Holy Spirit, but I had not known or experienced the Holy Spirit to that degree.

The power and anointing of the Holy Spirit are a stream of grace that flows through the Bible. Therefore, becoming a Teleios disciple for Jesus demands the discussion and treatment of this subject. Why does the Holy Spirit come like pouring water in the last days? It is not for us to live with the power of the Holy Spirit as if we have some badge to wear, wielding the power as if we have the jurisdiction. To be clear, such people—those who acted like they had the right to use the power—too existed even in the early church, and thus the apostle Paul emphasizes the topic of love after talking about the power of the Holy Spirit. At any rate, we must remember that the reason the Holy Spirit performs the ministry of anointing is rooted in the shepherd's heart to help the weak. As we receive the power of the Holy Spirit, we receive the power to help, comfort, and build up one another with the shepherd's heart. To be reminded of this purpose, we must engrave these words in our hearts, "If I speak in the tongues of men and of angels, but have not love, I am a noisy gong or a clanging cymbal" (1 Cor. 13:1).

The Holy Spirit and the Charismatic Movement Seen from the Perspective of Teleios Discipleship

Artificial intelligence is not only replacing human labor but also extending into the intellectual domain. Artificial intelligence will soon dominate even the spiritual realm. In the dawning of the highly scientific and sophisticated era, how should one view the Pentecostal movement and the charismatic movement, particularly from the perspective of Teleios Discipleship? Looking at the history of Protestantism, after the Reformation, there was a period of intense theological debate with Catholicism, where a solid doctrine on soteriology was crucial and was the focus. As a result, the charismatic and miraculous works of the Holy Spirit were not emphasized as much in the theological figures like Calvin and Luther. Luther and Calvin personally believed in cessations, the idea that spiritual gifts such as praying in tongues and miraculous works had ceased.[1] Protestant reformers opposed charismatic believers even more strongly than the Catholic Church did.[2]

Yet, a significant shift in this perspective occurred when the Reformation was well over four centuries ago. One of the more prominent movements in the twentieth century in the evangelical world was the Pentecostal charismatic movement. The reason the twentieth-century evangelical churches refocused on this movement is because they realized from their pastoral experiences that it was nearly impossible to undertake the journey of Teleios faith if the dynamic works of the Holy Spirit were excluded. In this sense, a fervent longing for Teleios maturity that God intended for his children was the essential reason that propelled the charismatic movement at the grassroots level. Pentecostal charismatics attached the set of wings called "enthusiasm" to the doctrinally centered body of the church.[3]

Then, how does the Pentecostal charismatic movement add "enthusiasm" to Teleios Discipleship? First, the contribution is found in the process of internal sanctification. The process of saints being sanctified completely is a collaboration between the Word (John 17:17) and the Holy Spirit (1 Pet. 1:2). In this way, the charismatic movement is closely related to the pursuit of Teleios in faith. "The charismatic movement is a stimulant sent to mobilize the entire church to pursue a higher level of perfection than most Christians know today."[4]

Second, the Pentecostal charismatic movement has become a holy means by which saints and the church fulfill God's perfect will by focusing on evangelism and mission. The movement informs the identity of all saints are ministers as those who received God's calling for evangelism and mission.[5] They believe the Holy Spirit grants the same gifts given to the early church for evangelism and mission to the church of this generation.

When one describes the charismatic movement as a "stimulant sent by God to mobilize the entire church for a higher level of perfection"[6] one understands why we should not overlook the charismatic movement based on doctrinal or denominational differences. Consequently, receiving the charismatic gifts of the Holy Spirit is not merely an optional choice for those in pursuit of Teleios in discipleship; it is a mandatory obligation and a privilege of saints to enjoy the Teleios Discipleship God desires.

The Framework of Pneumatology Seen from Teleios Discipleship, Holy Spirit That Enables Revelation-Dependent Contemplation

Pneumatology is the backbone of Teleios Discipleship. Teleios without the Holy Spirit does not exist. So, what is the framework of pneumatology from the perspective of Teleios Discipleship? We look to the disciples for the answer. Though they had experienced numerous miracles, the cross, and even the resurrection, the twelve disciples could not change their paradigm of faith. This is because they had not yet experienced the Holy Spirit. They returned to fishing at the Sea of Tiberias because they had not yet experienced the Holy Spirit. Therefore, receiving the power and anointing of the Holy Spirit coming from above is crucial.

Just as one must go to deep waters to catch fish or enter the mountains and valleys to dig for wild ginseng, if one desires to encounter the Holy Spirit and receive the anointing of the Holy Spirit, one must seek a place filled with the revelation of the Holy Spirit. There are two places for this. The first place is the Bible, filled not only with the revelation of the Holy Spirit but recorded solely by the revelation of the Holy Spirit. Revelation-dependent contemplation means judging and reasoning based on the words given through the revelation of the Holy Spirit. At the same time, the true interpretation of the Bible is only possible with the help of the inner testimony of the Holy Spirit, given by the illumination and the revelation of the Holy Spirit. Romans 8:16 beautifully illustrates the role of the Holy Spirit as an inner witness confirming the truth of God's revelation in the believer's spirit. The pneumatology of Teleios Discipleship is firmly based on revelation-dependent contemplation. Seeking or experiencing the Holy Spirit through anything other than the overflowing blessings from the Bible, saturated with the Holy Spirit, is not the mainstream of Teleios Discipleship training.

There is a misunderstanding among not a small group of people about the fullness of the Holy Spirit. Some focus only on the evidence of the Holy Spirit, such as fire falling from heaven, speaking in tongues, and healing of diseases. While these are indeed manifestations of the Holy Spirit's work, there are more vivid instances of the evidence of the fullness of the Holy Spirit in other various ways. For example, many intellectuals who believe in Jesus also experience a total paradigm shift in their worldview in their reading of the Scripture. A notable figure who received the anointing of the Holy Spirit through revelation-dependent contemplation and had a major transformation is none other than St. Augustine. He was deeply involved in Manichaeism in his youth but had an intellectually transformative experience while reading the Scriptures one day that converted him. This is a clear example of his intellect receiving the baptism of the Holy Spirit. This is what we mean when we talk about the "Holy Spirit who assists in revelation-dependent contemplation."

The second place is the church community filled with the presence of the Holy Spirit (1 Cor. 3:16). In the Old Testament, God's Shechinah glory dwelled in the temple Solomon built with materials from the land (2 Chron. 7:1–3). The space capable of containing the glory of God was a temple visible to the human eye as well. However, in the New Testament era, the identity of the biblical church is not a stationary building but a dynamic community filled with the power of the Holy Spirit. Performances of charismatic gifts outside the boundaries of the church community are not healthy. Just as the Bible is essential for building Teleios disciples, the ministry of the Holy Spirit in the community is definite for establishing Teleios disciples.

In the early church, the Holy Spirit came when the community gathered. At the same location in Jerusalem, the Holy Spirit descended upon a community of 120 members who gathered to pray at the same time and changed them completely (Acts 1:15). Although these 120 people could have prayed individually at their homes, the Holy Spirit came when they were gathered together. When the Holy Spirit was poured out on the Gentiles, it happened in a community where several people had gathered (Acts 10:44–48). Likewise, in the church in Antioch, the Holy Spirit came when the five leaders gathered to worship and pray together (Acts 13:1–3). The event when the Holy Spirit came upon the community of Antioch, a simple local church, marked the historical birth of the first missionary church.

The Personality and Power of the Holy Spirit Are the Same in Essence

Just as the Holy Spirit accompanied Jesus in His incarnational ministry, the Holy Spirit has been helping the church establish Teleios Discipleship since the day of Pentecost. The Holy Spirit's arrival on Pentecost gave birth to the Jerusalem church. Following this, Paul makes the celestial proclamation that the "church is the body of Christ" (1 Cor. 12:27). This is a declaration that leads to the confession that all churches inherit the apostolic calling; while acknowledging that since the church is the body of Christ, it can rightfully be referred to as the second incarnation of Jesus.

Pneumatology Based on the Shepherd's Heart

When dealing with pneumatology in ministry, there is a trend to treat the "power of the Holy Spirit" and the "personality of the Holy Spirit" as separate entities. Traditional denominations emphasize the personality of the Holy Spirit, while charismatic denominations prioritize the power of the Holy Spirit. The problem lies in considering them being as mutually exclusive. R. A. Torrey explained, “Some people consider only the work of the Holy Spirit important, while others almost ignore the work and focus only on the Word.”[7] This requires an exercise of discernment, to ensure that there is a balance in the gifts of the Spirit and the fruits of the Spirit in a believer. For this reason, James Packer called leaning toward one side “spiritual misjudgment.”[8]

Pneumatology, as viewed from the perspective of Teleios Discipleship based on the shepherd’s heart, does not see these two aspects as mutually exclusive but as intimately related, like two sides of a coin. In some ways, the dualistic pneumatology that has been popularized in Korea that distinguishes between personality and power can trace the reason for this confusion from Confucian influence. Confucianism, which flows through the veins of the Joseon era, evolved as Neo-Confucianism in Korea. It focused on conceptual studies that deal with the metaphysical essence of all things and emphasized the pursuit of celestial principles and order. With this bent, it lost its practical functionality to solve real-world issues. In reaction to this, Yangmingism emerged, emphasizing the unity of knowledge and action; rejecting the truthfulness of all that cannot be actualized. A sharp dichotomy that sets the person and the power of the Holy Spirit separate from each other, as well as dismissal of the reality of the Spirit’s power, is not too far from an error reminiscent of Neo-Confucianism.

We need to broaden the spectrum of ministry. While there are strengths in traditional denominations, we must look beyond denominational distinctives to discover what is more beneficial for fulfilling God’s command. We must learn to transcend each other’s boundaries by looking at the world from God’s perspective. Pneumatology based on the shepherd’s heart integrates principles and practices into a holy pragmatism. In it there is no room for the dichotomy of knowledge and action, between the power of the Holy Spirit and the personal fruit of the Holy Spirit. After all, this dichotomy is not consistent with the ministry of the Holy Spirit who always works to unite rather than divide. The pneumatology of Teleios Discipleship, pursued by holiness, emphasizes 100 percent the personal ministry of the Holy

Spirit and 100 percent the powerful ministry of the Holy Spirit in a balanced manner.

The Teleios from the Holy Spirit as Seen Through Elijah

I believe the conflict and discord in pneumatology that we have discussed so far can be attributed to two vantage points. They arise because one either sees the Holy Spirit only through a New Testament lens or fails to perceive the multifaceted nature of the Holy Spirit. To comprehensively understand pneumatology, we need to examine the depictions of the Holy Spirit in the Old Testament as well.

When the Holy Spirit nurtures a Teleios Discipleship in one individual, He intervenes in a specific manner according to the condition and the circumstances of each soul. Elijah serves as a role model who simultaneously demonstrates how the personality and power of the Holy Spirit can be ministered in a person. We commonly view Elijah as the "prophet of power" who defeated 850 prophets of Baal and Asherah on Mount Carmel. However, before being the "prophet of power," Elijah was the "prophet of service." Elijah took refuge in the house of a Zarephath widow endangered by drought, ensuring that her provisions did not run out. Moreover, through his heartfelt prayer he revived the widow's son who fell ill and died. As a part of his service, Elijah cared for a marginalized and vulnerable life, and in this we discover the personal ministry of the Holy Spirit. The New Testament describes the Holy Spirit as the one who assists our weakness (Rom. 8:26), revives our lives (Rom. 8:11), and abides with us (John 14:17). This aligns with Elijah's role in helping the unnoticed Zarephath widow, reviving the widow's son, and remaining together until the end of the drought.

On the other hand, in 1 Kings 18, Elijah forcefully revealed the power of the Holy Spirit. In a spiritual battle against the idolatrous King Ahab and 850 prophets of Baal on Mount Carmel, Elijah, with a jar, prayed to make fire fall from heaven, annihilating the prophets of Baal. Through his prayer, Elijah ended the three-and-a-half-year drought, finally bringing rain to Israel. Although Elijah's demeanor in the house of the Zarephath widow and his appearance in the spiritual battle on Mount Carmel differed significantly, both were magnificent works of the Holy Spirit. When Elijah became exhausted and wanted to die, God called him to Mount Horeb, the same mountain where God had given him a mission to the nations. This process reveals the work of the Holy Spirit in giving him a mission.

Through Elijah, we see the complete set of ministries of the Holy Spirit, demonstrating both the personal and the powerful aspects. In Elijah's life, we see the personal work of the Holy Spirit that is gently providing, caring for a lowly person like the Zarephath widow and bringing healing to a son. We also see the powerful side that brings immediate rain and fire to judge false prophets with incomparable might. This completeness in duality shows us what ministry of the Holy Spirit we should pursue today. To raise a Teleios disciple, the apostle Paul carefully followed the work of the Holy Spirit, emphasizing the power of the Holy Spirit when necessary and the personality of the Holy Spirit when needed. Paul commanded the Ephesian church to be filled with the Holy Spirit amid a serious spiritual battle, wielding the powerful sword of the Spirit—the power of the Holy Spirit. However, in the Philippi church, he emphasized the joy in the person of the Holy Spirit. Toward the Galatian church, he encouraged them to bear the personal fruit of the Holy Spirit. Sensitively responding to the work of the Holy Spirit and harmoniously balancing and integrating the personality and power—this is key to Teleios Discipleship training.

The Work of the Holy Spirit and Discipleship: The Refining Fire of the Holy Spirit and the Formation of Saints

Discipleship is sovereignly initiated by the Holy Spirit and led by the Holy Spirit. Yet, the word *training* in discipleship training inherently implies "effort, diligence, and striving." Thus, this aspect has not been without conflicts in light of our sinful nature that remains. This tension has even extended to Western Christian history, involving the clash between Jonathan Edwards's understanding of revival by "the absolute sovereignty of God" and Charles Finney's "revival involving human effort."[9]

Discipleship is akin to being refined by fire by the Holy Spirit. When a blacksmith refines iron, he heats it, forges it on the anvil, reheats it, and tempers it, then shapes it into the desired form. We are heated in the fire of trials in the grip of the Holy Spirit, struck on the anvil of life, and refined to be molded into the form desired by God. Therefore, the refining work of the Holy Spirit and the formation of saints can be seen not as a clash but as a sacred complement in discipleship. Let me illustrate some ministry examples for the refining work of the Holy Spirit and the formation of saints.

Cheonggye Mountain Prayer Meeting, Altar Prayer Meeting: The True Way to Love the Saints with the Shepherd's Heart in the Era of Artificial Intelligence

SaRang Church holds a mountainside prayer meeting on Cheonggye Mountain every year after the Independence Day service. It is a gathering of thousands of saints who climb the mountain to listen to the preaching of the Word and fervently pray. Mountain prayer is a unique practice in Korean Christianity. Just a generation ago, the valleys of the mountains in Korea echoed with the sound of prayers. However, somewhere along the line, the sound of prayer from the mountains became faint. The rocks that used to resound with the knees of prayer are now covered with moss and surrounded by vegetation.

The Cheonggye Mountain Prayer Meeting is not aimed at a nostalgic return to a past revival. It is a strategic and powerful place of God breaking through this era with the power of the Holy Spirit. Some argue that mountain prayer is not relevant in an era where the world is moving at hyper-speed and artificial intelligence like ChatGPT is shaping the world. I disagree. Even with artificial intelligence dominating the world, now is the best time for us to advance to the place of prayer. The Spirit of God cannot indwell in artificial intelligence and the love of God cannot fill artificial intelligence. Establishing the kingdom of God on this earth is a blessing given only to those in whom the Spirit of God dwells.

Mountains have always been a place where the power of God descends. Abraham met the Lord Jireh on Mount Moriah. Moses ascended Mount Sinai to receive God's commandments. Elijah experienced God answering with fire on Mount Carmel. Peter witnessed God's glory on the Mount of Transfiguration. Jesus prayed with tears on the Mount of Olives and bore the cross on Mount Calvary to save the world.

The prayer in the mountains is not something we have to wait to physically ascend to be involved. SaRang Church holds a mountainside prayer meeting every Saturday morning, named the Saturday Vision Early Morning Prayer Meeting. We may not be physically in the mountains, but we gather with the same fervency to seek the help of the Holy Spirit for individuals, neighbors, society, and the nation, praying wholeheartedly together.

The purpose of approaching God through prayer is one aspect, but there is also the goal of creating a praying disposition in saints so that they may have the ability to respond to any situation with prayer. It is commonly said that you are what you eat, you are what you love, and what you possess is your status. The true nature of a human being is revealed in moments of crisis. The mountain prayer meeting is a training that shapes the saints' disposition to prostrate themselves before God with a holy instinct in times of life crisis. It is conducted from the pulpit with the pastor's sincere desire for the saints to truly love one another, to desire to live as genuine people of God, and to become people who cry out to God in moments of crisis.

The Staff of Prayer: A Blessed Symbol of Revival's Substance

The bible offers symbols in the scenes of the remarkable miracles of God. We also have a symbolic item for prayer, dreaming of revival: It is the staff—or rod—of prayer. It is meant to resemble the ones Moses and Jacob held in their hands. The staff of prayer is not some type of a holy article but a symbol of prayer for revival. We stand against considering the prayer staff itself as a sacramental element or a charm.[10] Anything we possess cannot become a protective charm on its own. Even the printed Bible, while it should be highly regarded, is not a protective charm. Only when we receive the Word and embody it in our lives, does it become an enactment of God's living Word within us.

The staff of prayer symbolizes the grabbing of the tail of a snake as Moses did in front of Egyptian sorcerers and striking a rock. Generally, to catch a snake, you need to subdue it from the head. Catching the tail may lead to the risk of being bitten by the snake. However, God commanded Moses to grab the tail of a snake, and Moses obeyed. Moses, with his staff, parted the Red Sea, making way for salvation, and struck a rock, providing water. While the world may mock striking a rock with an egg, the staff of prayer is about having that audacious faith that we have faith that one can break the rock.

The world continues to impose life according to worldly wisdom. However, living by the world's common sense, one cannot expect to part the Red Sea or bring forth water from a rock. The staff of prayer readies one's determination to approach God with a prayer so bold that they would be led to cling to God for life. It encapsulates the earnestness of saints expecting God's help to part the Red Sea and bring forth water from a rock. It is a reminder that we can boldly approach God with lifelong prayers. The power lies not in the staff of prayer itself but in God, who sees the earnestness of the saints through the staff of prayer.

The staff that we use at SaRang Church has a unique serial number. The number is connected to the names and phone numbers of the members of the church. Why is that so? As we are familiar, the internet has changed the world; and one of the ways it has changed our world is that it allows for anonymity when expressing the darkest desires and deep anger as a weapon. Yet, when one hides behind anonymity, one cannot take the position of a true disciple, especially when praying for genuine revival. By connecting real names to the staff's serial number, no one can hide behind the crowd.

While we talk about the causes for revival and numerous histories of revival, genuinely yearning for "revival to happen at least once in my lifetime" happens in an entirely different dimension. Experiencing revival at least once in our individual lives and living as fervent messengers of grace from that revival are the substance contained in the staff of prayer. The desire to pass on faith to the younger generation is embedded in the staff of prayer as well. Jacob, who was familiar with the schemes and ways of the world, was refined in God's hands and ultimately became Israel, relying on the staff's head to worship God (Heb. 11:21). The staff of prayer will be a testament to the children of what their parents' faith was like. It will serve as a tangible record of faith, inspiring the continuation of prayer and faith in the next generation.

Discipleship Training in the Language Found in the Fullness of the Holy Spirit

We need to be humble when it comes to claiming an authoritative position on pneumatology. However, such a posture should not stop us from asking bold questions such as this: If the essence of ministry is to make a person Teleios, how do we connect the fullness of the Holy Spirit with discipleship training?

The original form of the verb "to be filled" in Ephesians 5:18 and Acts 6:5 is 'πληροῦσθε' (*plērousthe*), and the root is 'πληρόω' (*plēroo*). This word fundamentally implies personal fullness.[11] Personal fullness is a "long-term filling," a process that takes time. Just as the moon does not become full overnight to become a full moon but takes a certain amount of time, so does the long-term filling. However, in Acts 4, when the crowd boldly proclaimed God's word, a different term was used. The term used in this context is 'πίμπλημι' (*pimplēmi*) in Greek.

Acts 4 narrates the situation where Peter and John were persecuted by the Sanhedrin and imprisoned, facing a circumstance where there seems to be no way to survive. Healing must happen now; power needs to be received; boldness is required right now. Therefore, in this context and situation, the filling of the Holy Spirit is described as a "short-term filling," or an "immediate filling." If "πληρόω" requires time to be filled, "πίμπλημι" is a special, temporary filling for a specific ministry, given immediately. So the former is long-term and internal filling, while the latter is short-term and external filling. In sum, the former is personal fullness, while the latter is ministry-specific fullness.

Depending on the tradition, some churches emphasize ministry-specific filling, while others emphasize personal fullness. The crucial issue in light of this difference is not to determine which tendency one follows. Rather, it is to realize what is lacking in me and make efforts to fill one's own deficiencies.

The Fullness of the Holy Spirit Must Be Evident as an Overflow in Ministry

We always seek the fullness of the Holy Spirit. However, why can we not readily experience the ministry of the Spirit? It is because we often interpret the fullness of the Spirit literally as if something must physically fill us like water. Yet, this is not the filling of the Holy Spirit described in the Bible. The Bible consistently portrays the fullness of the Spirit as springing forth and overflowing whenever it speaks of the Spirit.

The concept of "overflowing" is also an inherent property of the triune God. God is called the "the fountain of living waters" (Jer. 2:13). Jesus said, "The water that I will give him will become in him a spring of water welling up to eternal life" (John 4:14), and the Holy Spirit is expressed as "rivers of living water" (John 7:38–39). Andrew Murray insightfully described the overflowing of the triune God, stating, "God is a spring of pure love and blessing, always overflowing. Christ is like a reservoir of grace that reveals God's fullness, and the Holy Spirit is like a river of living water flowing underneath God's throne and the Lamb."[12]

Our spiritual life becomes a tragedy when it ends as an accumulation of one's own self. True resolution of one's issues in life takes place when the rivers of the Spirit's living water begin to overflow in me, connecting with others and bringing about mutual transformation in them. This is the paradox of faith. The most powerful evidence of the fullness of the Holy Spirit is not only in the overflow but also in becoming a conduit for the overflow to be transmitted as a channel of grace. When the Spirit works, that person becomes a river of living water, a conduit of grace. Even a repentant thief, though the time lived in repentance may have been short, became a channel of blessing to numerous souls.[13]

Many people think that once their problems are resolved, other people's problems will be solved. However, the Spirit is contrary—when the rivers of living water flow from me to heal others, only then am I truly healed. This is the fullness of the Spirit that Teleios Discipleship pursues.

What is the overflow of the Spirit? "No one can possess God's Spirit and confine it only to themselves. The Spirit does not stay where it is but flows out. If there is no outflow, then God is not there."[14] This corresponds to the meaning of Isaiah 35:6–7, "For waters break forth in the wilderness, and streams in the desert; the burning sand shall become a pool, and the thirsty ground springs of water; in the haunt of jackals, where they lie down, the grass shall become reeds and rushes."

The Accumulation of Anointing Determines the Ministry

What distinguishes between those who operate with power and those who do not? The key lies in the accumulation of anointing. This determines the thickness and depth of the ministry. The solidity of ministry is the weight and depth of the pastoral ministry. The deeper the ministry, the less it is shaken by storms within and outside the church.

This is my advice for junior pastors: "Speak with unwavering faith, starting with yourself the speaker. This is not limited to preaching but includes everything spoken and extended from the pulpit. For example, even if you sing one praise song, sing it with an anointing, sing it with wholeheartedness. Sing it not once or twice, but ten times, twenty times, before you rise to the pulpit. Confess the lyrics; embody it as your own, fully believing in it. When leading praise, singing according to a predetermined order and singing it as your confession spontaneously are two entirely different matters. Whatever you communicate, do so because you believe every word of the preached Word or lyrics of praise—let those truths be embodied and believed in you."

This is an experiential truth in ministry. I probably have sung the hymn, "Tho' Your Heart May Be Heavy," at least a thousand times. During seven years of ministry at Yongsan Railroad Hospital in my college ministry, I sang this song by the hospice bedside every week. It is not about the number of times I sang this song but about the accumulation of anointing in the hymn. When singing such a hymn, even if only once, a holy resonance occurs in people's souls, grace flows from the heart, and God's work becomes present. Singing even a hundred times, standing on the pulpit saturated with the anointing of the Spirit, the congregation will begin to sense it spiritually.

Cynicism is prevalent even within the church. The atheistic and anti-Christian cultural influences seep into the church. As a result, even the pulpit is becoming cold. The path of the pulpit must be paved with the accumulation of the Spirit's anointing. When this accumulates on the pulpit, at some point, the spiritual threshold will open wide. The day will surely come when the overflow of the "cup of blessings" from your pulpit takes place (1 Cor. 10:16) through the downpour anointing of the river.

The Portrait of the Holy Spirit Based on the Shepherd's Heart

The Holy Spirit Who Provides Order, Structure, and Direction

In central California, there is a medieval castle called Hearst Castle. One of Hearst's hobbies was collecting paintings. One day, while looking at a catalog, Hearst thought, *Ah! I want to buy this painting*, but he could not acquire it. Later, he found out the reason he was unable to purchase it was that the painting had been sitting in his art collection at home all along. He was searching for it without knowing it was already in his possession.

We are no different from Hearst. Through the merit of Jesus's blood, we have received God's forgiveness and acceptance. The Holy Spirit has enlightened our eyes to believe in this incredible truth (Eph. 1:18). This is a great treasure. Yet, do we not often put this treasure in one corner of our hearts and search for it in the wrong places?

In the opening of Genesis it says, "The earth was without form and void, and darkness was over the face of the deep. And the Spirit of God was hovering over the face of the waters" (Gen. 1:2). The expression "hovering" invokes an image of an eagle soaring high, watching over the chicks in its nest on a cliff. The Holy Spirit, from the first moment of creation, demonstrated love and concern for the world being formed as a sovereign and powerful one. The Holy Spirit revealed and acted upon His love and concern for the world being formed. The Holy Spirit created an ordered world from a formless, chaotic, empty, and dark state. Even when life is disorderly, full of chaos, emptiness, and even darkness, the Holy Spirit hovers over, bestowing grace. Then the intended creative order of God is established.

In light of this, Alistair McGrath described the works of the Holy Spirit providing order, structure, and direction to God's children as "the formative energy that gives life and direction to humanity" and "providing direction and momentum to the life of faith, like the wind filling the sail of a ship."[15] Spurgeon similarly remarked that "the Spirit works to change the direction of fallen people in a sudden instant toward Christ" and said what the Spirit does essentially carries out is the "renewal operation that renovates the heart anew."[16]

This shows why we must rely thoroughly on the Holy Spirit when undergoing discipleship training. We must strive to resemble Jesus, but it is ultimately the Holy Spirit that provides direction and momentum to our lives. It is the work of the Holy Spirit to orchestrate the renewal of our heart, turning our stubborn heart chained by the world and reorienting it toward Christ in freedom. Without the powerful work of the Holy Spirit, how can we detach the stalwart impurities remaining in our spirits like barnacles? Therefore, if there is no substantial change in our old habits after discipleship, it is evidence that it was not a discipleship relying on the Holy Spirit providing order, structure, and direction.

The Holy Spirit Who Raises the Shipwrecked Life Again

We may have the wrong idea that if the Holy Spirit is in my life, I will miss out on life. It may feel like the Holy Spirit is using or exploiting me. However, the reality is entirely different. When the Holy Spirit comes and completely dominates me, it is not a loss. Instead, my character and life become wholly filled with the influence of the Holy Spirit (2 Cor. 3:17; Gal. 5:22–23; Eph. 5:18). When the Holy Spirit comes and completely dominates me, it is like the road to Zion is opening before me, springs of water bursting forth in the desert, and being given a roadway in the wilderness. When the Holy Spirit comes and dominates my thoughts and takes my life over, my ministry will abundantly enjoy spiritual blessings like a spring that is welling up every day.

In life there are times when we face hardships. We might unexpectedly land in unfamiliar places. In life, there are moments when the ship called life gets shipwrecked. The way to move the shipwrecked boat in the right direction is not to go down into the mud and try to lift the boat. There is only one way for the boat in the mud to rise. It is when the tide of grace, the flood of blessings comes through the overflowing work of the Holy Spirit, to make the ship afloat. Discipleship training inspires believers to daily plead for the fullness of the Holy Spirit, that He alone would dominate our thoughts and use our lives without limitations for His purpose. Discipleship training after the Teleios of a believer trains them to invite the Holy Spirit to completely master us and to embody that reality. Discipleship is something that cannot be done with human thoughts, arguments, or strength. It is solely the ministry enabled by the river of living water flowing through the fullness of the Spirit.

The Holy Spirit Who Liberates Us from the Weakness of Fallen Nature

Many believers desire the fullness of the Holy Spirit and seek the gifts of the Spirit, but they often struggle to take the first step because they overlook the fact that it all begins with dependence on the blood of the Lamb. The starting point of prayer for the fullness of the Holy Spirit should be, "We rely on the power of the blood of the Lamb. We desire the power of the blood of the Lamb to work among us."

In the ups and downs of past ministries, the turning points that gave me breakthroughs occurred when there was wholehearted dependence on the blood of the Lamb. This is precisely when the gravity of the Holy Spirit works, not the gravity of the world. Fragile, a piece of thin paper is full of weaknesses. However, the moment you attach it to a thick steel plate, no storm can tear it apart. A nail sinks when put into water. However, when you put the nail on a thick wooden board, it floats. This is what the Holy Spirit's intercession looks like. We overcome when we are attached to Him. When we depend on the blood of Jesus, the Holy Spirit will liberate us from the weaknesses bound to our fallen nature (2 Cor. 3:17).

There is a vivid expression of the way the power of the Holy Spirit liberates us from the bondage of weakness and chains of frailty: "If a drop of joy from the Holy Spirit falls into hell, it will swallow up all the pains of hell."[17] No matter how thick the rope of weaknesses and frailty bind us, when the Holy Spirit flows within us, He will set us free like Samson, who broke the ropes that bound him by the Spirit of the Lord. If any disciples still find themselves entangled in the wounds and weaknesses of the past, it may be time to reevaluate whether the training process truly involves dependence on the Holy Spirit.

When Jesus began His earthly ministry, He proclaimed the words from Isaiah 61:1 (Luke 4:16–19). From His pronouncement, we must take note of the meaning of freedom. This freedom is not the freedom to do as we please but the freedom to let God work through us according to the will of the Holy Spirit. When under the law, it was an obligation, but when under the law of the life-giving Spirit, we move by the freedom given by the Spirit.

The Holy Spirit liberates us from our weaknesses and frailties so that he may freely work in and through us. Therefore, if you truly desire freedom from weaknesses, it is essential to cling more to the key to freedom, which is secured by willingly depending on the Holy Spirit and seeking His help as the priority.

The Holy Spirit Who Melts, Molds, Fills, and Uses Us

Teleios Discipleship is training that teaches the melting of the heart as a priority. Melting is both the beginning and the result of the work of the Holy Spirit. David Brainerd, known as the father of Indian missions, wrote in his diary about a day when the power of the Holy Spirit was strongly felt, "Powerful authority accompanied holy truth. . . . There was no rough passion, only sweet and humble melting."[18] The reason the melting of the heart is important is because the true substance of one's inner being is revealed in this process. When gold ore is melted, everything else is burned away, leaving only gold. Putting our nature into the crucible of the Holy Spirit likewise reveals only the true substance. Even after trusting in Jesus, some believers still harbor sharp cruelty, malevolence, and hard hearts. However, when one receives the new spirit, the "heart of stone" is removed, and He gives a "heart of flesh" (Ezek. 36:26). Through Teleios Discipleship, the Holy Spirit melts and purifies us in the fullness of His refining fire, leaving only the essence fitting for His purpose and glory.

Teleios Discipleship endeavors to open the door for the Spirit to mold us into the likeness of Christ. Why should the Holy Spirit mold us? We often pray for God's power to break the devil's stronghold. We seek God's gift of spiritual tools to oppose the devil. However, the most powerful weapon we have is being molded into Christ's likeness through the Holy Spirit.[19] Therefore, we must continually pray for the Holy Spirit to mold us.

We must recognize that molding us into Christ's likeness involves a supernatural process that requires a high level of precision. "God's ongoing work of molding us into that of Christ's nature within us is supernatural."[20] When we properly realize this, we can truly look at the work of the Holy Spirit with a new perspective. We delightfully obey His leading with an attitude of gratitude and expectation. The process of producing masterpieces like Michaelangelo's *Pieta* from marble involves not only the breaking of the marble but also the dedicated devotion of the sculptor who carves and shapes the marble with perfect precision.

The Holy Spirit Who Abolishes All Differences Yet Uses Personalities

When Bible writers want to convey a special truth to Bible readers, they sometimes retell an event from a different angle. Representative examples include the creation account in Genesis 1 and 2 and the Holy Spirit's descent on the Gentile household in Acts 10 and 11. While Peter was preaching at Cornelius's house, the Holy Spirit was poured out on all the Gentiles gathered there, similar to what happened at the Pentecost in Jerusalem (Acts 11:15). The fact that the same Spirit that came upon everyone in the upper room in Mark also came upon all the Gentiles gathered at Cornelius's house symbolically shows the Holy Spirit works to abolishes all differences.

One of the most important pieces of evidence of Teleios Discipleship at work is seen through the overcoming of all differences among believers. Gathering people with similar social classes, similar economic levels, and similar lifestyles is a form of homogenous social community frequently seen in the world. However, this is not the image of a Teleios disciple. "Barnabas, Simeon who was called Niger, Lucius of Cyrene, Manaen a lifelong friend of Herod the tetrarch, and Saul" (Acts 13:1). These are the names mentioned in Acts 13, which deals with the sending of Paul and Barnabas by the Antioch church. Simon who was called Niger refers to a person from Africa. Manaen was part of a royal family. Saul was an orthodox Jew who also was a social elite. All these five had completely different backgrounds. Nevertheless, with the Holy Spirit's presence, they overcame all differences.

The abolition of such differences has its roots in the abolition of legalism. The apostle Paul thoroughly declares the abolition of legalism in Colossians 2:20–23. The Holy Spirit speaks of the abolition of all differences, such as race, gender, and social class. God had not created or established these in the first place (Eph. 4). Why do we need to break down differences and discrimination that stem from legalism? It is because such differences and discrimination do not fit with our status before God. The existence of differences and discrimination within and outside the church we still find today is a residue of legalism.[21] The process of Teleios Discipleship is to eliminate the residue of legalism through the unity of the Holy Spirit. If even after the training process, one still maintains an exclusive and discriminatory attitude, one cannot be on the path to arriving at Teleios Discipleship.

The Holy Spirit Who Works Through the Relationship Marked by Obedience and Dependence

The true blessings of Christianity are given through the relationship marked by obedience and dependence. The ultimate source of these blessings can be found in Jesus alone. The great blessings that Jesus has given us—the blessing of salvation, the blessing of eternal life, the blessing of becoming children of God, and the blessing of enjoying the kingdom of heaven forever after leaving this earth—all come from obedience and dependence. If Jesus had not perfectly obeyed God in Gethsemane and if He had not fully depended on God the Father on the cross, we would not have been able to receive the great and glorious blessings that descended from heaven through the cross of Jesus.

However, such a relationship is something we cannot accomplish with our strength. Our Teleios obedience is given through the help of the Holy Spirit, but at the same time when we obey, God gives us the Holy Spirit (Acts 5:32). Furthermore, to fulfill God's mission as His children, we must completely depend on the Holy Spirit. The apostle Paul ministered with "words not taught by human wisdom but taught by the Spirit" (1 Cor. 2:13) and "in demonstration of the Spirit and of power" (1 Cor. 2:4).

As we continue to learn the relationship marked by obedience and dependence, we must ask, "How can we participate in God's infinite resources, a blessing so vast—like an endless horizon without an end in sight?" We can make that blessing ours when our will is continuously being aligned with God's will. In this way, we can enjoy "who has blessed us in Christ with every spiritual blessing in the heavenly places" (Eph. 1:3). Teleios Discipleship is about establishing a relationship marked by obedience and dependence on God through the ministry of the Holy Spirit, no matter what circumstances or challenges we face.

CHAPTER 6

Pastoral Theology for Teleios Discipleship Training: The Character of a Pastor Pursuing Teleios Maturity

A pastor engaged in Teleios Discipleship training must always carry three essential questions in their heart for the sake of a healthy pastoral ministry. First, one must ask, "Is it theologically sound?" This involves questioning whether it has been validated through the ecclesiastical traditions and orthodoxy. Second, "Is it pastorally genuine?" Even if there are no issues of orthodoxy, it is crucial to inquire whether there is a vibrant power of life that will be beneficial in shepherding the people in the pastoral field. In other words, one must not compromise the pastoral field to danger just because an idea seems theologically sound. Third, "Is it missional suitable for this contemporary ministry context?" Even if the minister nurtures the congregation well, if they remain within the church walls, it may end up as an incomplete ministry, unable to properly advance God's kingdom.

No figure in the entire Bible epitomizes the ideal pastor as much as Paul. He was an apostle, a missionary, the author of numerous epistles, and, above all, a pastor. He understood the urgency of protecting and nurturing the church. He knew the importance of pastoral ministry more than anyone else. His letters were written not just for the sake of sophisticated theological discussion but to correct, at times to rebuke, or other times to encourage the body of Christ.

The reason Paul could be a great pastor was his keen awareness of the events in the community of believers.[1] Paul did not claim that disciple-making was possible solely through preaching the gospel. He includes, "Teaching everyone with all wisdom" (Col. 1:28–29) as part of a disciple-making strategy. Hence, "teaching well" is a crucial condition for becoming a good pastor along with preaching.[2] To teach well, the help of the Holy Spirit is paramount (John 14:26). The one working with power within us is the Holy Spirit. At the same time, the one putting in maximum effort to utilize the talents and gifts given to me is me. So, when Paul introduced himself as "Paul, an apostle of Christ Jesus" (Col. 1:1), he was emphasizing that his teaching came from above. It demonstrates where the authority of pastoral teaching originates from. In what follows, I aim to examine Paul as a pastor to explain that the pastor's character is crucial for a Teleios pastoral ministry.

The Character of a Teleios Pastor

Reawakening to Pastoral Ministry by Inquiring the Essence

When you throw yourself entirely into pursuing the real essence of ministry, the new horizon of pastoral ministry opens. In my younger days, a friend suggested visiting a Bible study hosted by a mission organization in Sinchon. With a light heart, I knocked on the door of the Bible study group. I can never forget the question I received during the first session: "Brother Junghyun, what do you think is the most fruitful life?" I did not know what to say—the inquiry itself had never crossed my mind. When I faced this question, it made me ponder deeply. Eventually, I realized that the most fruitful life is the one characterized as being the most valuable, and the most valuable life is one invested for eternity.

The personal value of one soul is eternal. When I met my mentor, Pastor Oak Han-heum, most young people with a spiritual fervor joined mission organizations or campus ministries rather than getting plugged into a local church. Yet, I dedicated myself to integrating the dynamics of campus ministries into local churches, dedicating myself to the internalization of parachurch dynamics in the local church context. Looking back, it was a significant event that determined the course of my pastoral life.

Embarking on Spiritual Reproduction as the Backbone of Ministry

I, along with three brothers in Christ, launched a college ministry at Naesoodong church with two mottos. The first was to engage in spiritual reproduction with a spirit of discipleship training, and the second was to preach the gospel "in season and out of season" (2 Tim. 4:2). The college ministry at Naesoodong, inspired by the motto of living a life as "witnesses" as Jesus did, grew to constitute 30 percent of the attendance at the adult Sunday service.

After serving in the college ministry at Naesoodong for seven to eight years, I went abroad for studies in the United States. Following this, I began ministering in the college ministry at a church in Los Angeles, where Pastor Kim Dong-myeong and Mrs. Ahn Yi-suk were serving as senior pastors. At that time, the college ministry had a considerable size, consisting of around thirty university students. This was a sizable group given the number of Korean international students in the area at that time. At first, the group lacked an understanding of campus ministry, the concept of nurturing, and ideas about small-group ministry. Moreover, there was little motivation or enthusiasm. Without hesitation, I gathered a few college students for intensive discipleship training. As they were nurtured and trained, they were promptly commissioned as small-group leaders. Members were held accountable daily for their spiritual disciplines at each member's campus. A significant revival became visible, evidenced by 120 students attending the winter retreat six months after I assumed leadership.

The revival in the college ministry was not due to any human charm or charisma. Looking back, the materials and training tools used at that time were not exceptional either. It was the dynamic power of discipleship training itself that nurtured people, and this led those trained individuals to nurture others in a continuous cycle. Spiritual reproduction occurred naturally. With the conviction that this was the essence of ministry, I started SaRang Community Church in Southern California in 1988, with less than a year of preparation. There were so many different events, stories, and testimonies of ministries that were birthed as a result. All the ministries grew substantially at the church and through the church.

No matter how many different ministries rose or developed, the conclusion was one, and my passion was singular—total commitment to the essence of ministry: making disciples. When life is devoted to the essence of discipleship training, God will most definitely open new doors and new horizons for ministry. Placing the highest value on God, God's Word, and the eternal nature of one soul, is what makes people come back to life and communities thrive.

Leading the Believers to Teleios by Transforming the Competitive Paradigm into a Serving Paradigm

In a capitalist society, there is a tendency to reward those who climb over others with the victory trophy. Despite being aware of the harm caused by a competitive paradigm, we find ourselves riding on the back of the tiger of a winner-takes-all mentality. People in the capitalism-driven society are racing all the time, unconsciously believing that they might fall behind and will be cast aside the moment they fall off that tiger.

The Bible speaks about the outcome of a competitive framework: "But if you bite and devour one another, watch out that you are not consumed by one another" (Gal. 5:15). How can we break this chain and tread the path of shepherding where everyone can live in harmony?

Practicing Christian service in a reality that considers competition as the foundation of social culture is no easy task. Living the life of Paul who willingly made himself a slave to all (1 Cor. 9:19) is equally challenging. However, this is the path of a disciple. How can we replace the notion of "mutual suspicion" with "mutual service" and "competition" with "collaboration" in our ministries and spiritual walks?[3] Even Paul was concerned with this sentiment when he lists names causing division through competition in his letter to the Philippians (Phil. 4:2). In today's context, resorting to legal actions over internal church issues and causing significant harm to the body of Christ through slander among individuals within the church are the scenes that find their root in the competitive framework. This has deeply infiltrated the church due to the influence of the culture.

How can we transform the competitive paradigm into a serving paradigm? While everyone acknowledges the need for Christian service instead of competition within the church, merely knowing this fact is not enough to take the necessary steps forward. Serving enabled by ethical motivations or a conscience of faith cannot be the ultimate solution due to the inherent weakness of sinful human nature. To transition from a competitive paradigm to a serving paradigm, it is imperative to adopt a mission paradigm rooted in a sense of calling. What is the Christian mission? It is risking one's life and throwing themselves into God's calling. What is the goal? It is articulated in the first principle of discipleship training: being sent into the world as Jesus commissions us.

For holistic pastoral care and Teleios Discipleship training, one must open their eyes to the missional way of thinking. The mission of the church is a genuine one when it knows no limits. There should be no limits to proclaiming the gospel and serving others. This is because the fields of evangelism and service are uncharted territories of infinite potential. The mission paradigm is the optimal way to enhance the capacity of believers. For that reason, Teleios Discipleship aims to increase capacity—capacity in pastoral ministry, ministry work, faith, and Christian service. It is the pastor's duty in Teleios Discipleship training to help individuals have increased capacity to find their rightful places of calling. While there may be various reasons for the failure of King Saul, the core issue was a lack of capacity. Increasing the capacity of a believer through the mission paradigm purports to instill in believers an "incarnational mission consciousness," cultivating a sense of service and making their hearts beat for it.[4]

The Three Capacities Required to Cultivate Teleios Disciples

First is the leader's capacity called character. It is common knowledge that becoming a good leader or even meeting one is crucial for character development. So, what makes a good leader? Is it someone with both abilities and leadership skills? The leader's capacity for character is proportional to their clear understanding of the gospel. A leader's capacity for character grows when one opens their eyes to the definition and purpose of the gospel. A person with the gospel should rightfully mature. This is the meaning behind the apostle Paul's wish for the Ephesian believers to reach "to the measure of the stature of the fullness of Christ" (Eph. 4:13). With an accurate self-awareness of the gospel, individuals do not fixate on right or wrong but rather open their eyes and hearts to the principles of grace and mercy. When one's eyes are opened to the shepherd's heart, the leader's character capacity and, subsequently, the vessel of faith expand.

Second is the capacity of the church. The church's capacity refers to the size of the vessel that can own God's mission, not the numerical size of the church. Even if a minister has developed character capacity through a clear understanding of the gospel, the vessel of the church must be prepared. Otherwise, comprehensive spiritual formation for the congregation is not possible. The core of the church's capacity will be ascertained by whether the church moves by duty or by mission. In other words, we must ask, "Does the church operate based on its reliance on positions or organizational skills, or does it move through the ministry of life, driven by a sense of mission?" Additionally, "How many numbers of people move not because of their positions at church but by mission?" The church's capacity is determined accordingly.

One of the reasons the church grows weak is because we have created a system where elders assess pastors and pastors evaluate church committees. While administration is an essential aspect of ministry, more critical for the vibrancy of the church is for elders to step up as individuals driven by a sense of mission, and for pastors to collaborate with elders to help them thrive in their ministries more effectively. When elders and pastors evaluate each other instead of joining hands with a sense of mission, church discord arises, and the glory of God is greatly obscured. Pastors and elders should both take on the role of a shepherd in their hearts, where the pastor assumes leadership, and the elder takes responsibility for ministry.

Third, it is the capacity for understanding new social culture. When a church grows to a certain extent, it inevitably encounters a stage of maintaining the status quo, a period of stagnation. The way to break through this stagnation is to lean into the capacity to have an increased discernment of new cultures. In other words, there must be a paradigm shift in how the church should navigate through the new world. Fundamental principles cannot change, but new wineskin must be used to better chart the future with a greater understanding of the cultural trends and sentiments of the era. This is also the responsibility we bear as the church. The church must take the leading role in guiding society and culture into the rule of Christ, who is sovereign overall. This is important because when we can analyze the world through the biblical perspective, we can confront anti-Christian societal and cultural phenomena with a gospel-centered combativeness.

Through the Sermon on the Mount, Jesus changed the concept of blessings. In Matthew 20, Jesus provided a new definition of greatness, completely reversing the perception of power. Moreover, Jesus personally washed the disciples' feet, causing a seismic shift in their souls regarding service. Consequently, the disciples' capacity for truth significantly increased as a result. If Jesus's disciples had not experienced the paradigm shift Jesus intended, and if they had not undergone a true change in consciousness and an increase in their capacity for understanding the times, they would not have been able to combat the anti-Christian threats of the culture in the brutal persecutions from the world in the early days of the church.

Abundant Spirituality Leads Believers to Teleios

If there is leakage in ministry—those blind spots created by pastoral oversight and negligence in ministry, neither the church nor the believers can properly stand. The zeal of ministry cannot manifest as the fruit of ministry. What makes spiritual leakage terrifying is, as Oswald Chambers puts it, one ends up losing the vision of God when spiritual leakage goes unchecked.[5] Pastors would likely already be aware of this fact.

I have a creed of faith that I have taken as the compass for the direction of my ministry: "Do not worry about what has already been decided for me; instead, put my life on what I can do better." This changed the direction of my pastoral ministry. However, among younger ministers, there are still those who, despite cognitively recognizing that one cannot break away from the decided past, cling to the past outcomes. Still others are obsessed with it. To address this, it is necessary to approach it with a redemptive perspective that begins to look beyond what is visible, being set free from the veil of what is seen. It is essential to understand that there is a pull from Satan to divert one's gaze from an irreversible past. The power of the gospel does not bind itself to the past. Again, Christians should not waste their lives on what has already been decided but should put their lives on what they can do better.

The reason we should not waste our lives on what has already been decided and put our lives on what we can do better lies in the awareness of God's sovereign providence. The past has already been refined within God's sovereign providence and carved as a stepping stone for the present and future. Therefore, a minister's continued attachment to the past is nothing but a manifestation of unbelief in God's sovereign providence.

If the pastor's focus is always on the past, believers cannot move forward from past issues. We should always think, *What can I do better?*

Everyone in Christ possesses the freedom to be more like Him and love Him more, all this for the sake of family and neighbors. Loving the Lord more makes the heart earnest, and with an earnest heart, our entire attitude becomes fresher, more creative, and more innovative. In that way, pastors and believers can engage in ministry without leakage and lead a life without leakage. This is the path to Teleios pastoral care and Teleios Discipleship.

Tune Your Ministry to God's Time for Leak-Free Pastoral Ministry. If there is anything crucial for leak-free pastoral ministry, it is aligning the time of ministry with God's time. When God's timetable and the timing of pastoral ministry are out of sync, achieving desired fruits becomes challenging no matter how hard one tries. Looking back, I have discovered a principle that instinctively awakened me to tune the time of ministry with God's time. The principle is to view all ministry and pastoral schedules from the perspective of *Anno Domini*.

We are all under God's calendar—meaning that we are under God's sovereign rule. The world's calendar focuses on how much pleasure one can derive from this world. However, God's calendar is focused on our living most valuably and meaningfully during the given time on earth. Those who live by the world's calendar are like slaves running toward death with no way to escape. Those who live by God's calendar can walk toward the day we will meet God face-to-face day by day and live within God's eternal timeline. The world's calendar says, "We were born to die," but God's calendar emphasizes, "We were born for eternal life." The world's calendar describes our brief life between two lines on a tombstone. However, God's calendar says we are beings recorded in God's Book of Life. The world's calendar advises us to grasp and enjoy passing time, but God's calendar encourages us to hold onto the given mission and live in the joy of that calling.

The "Finish and Start" of Ministry for Ever-Fresh Pastoral Ministry. Does the rhythm of your ministry operate with a "finish and start" mentality or a "start and finish" mentality? Keeping the ministry fresh every day is a primary concern for all pastors. Most ministries follow a pattern of "start and finish." How can we send the believers who attended

Sunday worship back into the world, not just physically but with a holy excitement for the gospel in their hearts? I pondered on how to engage in a dynamic and fresh ministry that over and over again revitalizes believers. Through an agonizing search involving a pastor's heart, I realized the key to keeping the ministry fresh every day is to restructure the rhythm of ministry from "start to finish" to "finish and start."

Ministry must be done weekly but conclude with an exciting "finish" and an anticipated "start." Although it seems to be at a standstill, it can be likened to the state of an engine right before accelerating. "Finish and start!"—this is the secret of the pastoral ministry that kept my ministry fresh every week for the past forty years. For ministry to bear fruit and have a lasting impact, it must have a sense of delight. The moment ministry is considered labor or an obligation, the momentum of ministry starts to weaken. Make a week the cycle of ministry and finish it with a fresh and joyful conclusion on Saturday morning. Yet, Saturday's early morning prayer meeting is not just a conclusion but an exciting anticipation to start back again the joyful ministry of Sunday morning.

The reason we adopt this new pattern and rhythm for ministry is because of the change in time that Jesus's earthly ministry accomplished. Jesus transformed the time of ministry into a feast. If the Old Testament emphasized "finish" as rest after labor, the New Testament emphasized "start" after the rest as the first day of the week. Generally, Monday is still considered the beginning of the week from a worldly perspective. But in Christianity, the day of Jesus's resurrection, Sunday or the Lord's Day, is the beginning. However, even the church has failed to make the Lord's Day a real starting point in the lives of believers. For Sunday to become a true starting point in the lives of believers, the ministry of the church needs to be transformed. Sunday is not a day of rest but a day filled with joy, a day full of excitement that can lead the new week. Therefore, all ministries of the church should be realigned with the rhythm of "finish and start." If you want to start Sunday with strength and joy, wrap up your weekly ministry with anticipation for a new day on Saturday mornings, not on Wednesdays or Fridays. Then you will be able to start Sunday morning ministry that is fresh, joyful, and full of excitement. This way, every Lord's Day becomes a feast and a joy. In the ministry of "finish and start," sacred delight is guaranteed.

Overflowing Ministry That Protects the Pastorate. During ministry, everyone encounters situations where there seems to be no way out. When facing circumstances with no visible openings on any side, why do some ministers give up while others rise? Every time I faced situations like this, my father shared with me the words from Isaiah 40:27–31, "They who wait for the Lord shall renew their strength," repeatedly and persistently. Every time he shared these words, I responded, "Father, you are saying this because you don't know what I am going through." However, later in life when I was faced with adversities or struggles, those words from Isaiah became a living word, raising me from the pit. The phrase in verse 28, "There is no limit to his understanding" (CSB) deeply resonated with me. It became the foundation for the central theme of my ministry, which is characterized as being "overflowing."

Overflowing ministry always begins with expectations of God's guidance, relying on the belief that God's new paths will open no matter what the circumstances. It is a ministry that relies on God's "limitless understanding." An overflowing minister, with an expectation and faith in God's unfailing guidance, cannot view situations negatively or be paralyzed by wounds. When I faced significant difficulties during the construction of the church at our current site, many people thought I could not rise again. However, what ultimately became the starting point for a new horizon in ministry was solely the sacred expectation of God who has "no limit to his understanding" burning in my heart.

Overflowing ministry originates from the word deeply embedded in the heart that becomes a source and a stream within the minister. It leads to an outpouring of creative ministry without regrets or lingering aftereffects. Additionally, overflowing ministry guides pastors into spiritual ecstasy. It does not emanate from within a ministry, but rather, it bursts forth from the promise of the Word engraved in the heart through the work of the Holy Spirit. An overflowed minister confesses, "What an amazing blessing! I am completely satisfied and incredibly happy just because I have an overflowing ministry entrusted to me from morning to night."[6] An overflowing minister cannot hide the spiritual joy pouring out through the power of the Holy Spirit, even amid internal and external challenges.

Preemptive Strike in Ministry for the Protection of Believers in Spiritual Battles. The concept of preemptive strike against the enemy is evident in the Old Testament, notably through the Israelites conquering the new land of Canaan. In the New Testament, it is used in a missionary context, emphasizing the establishment of God's kingdom in dark territories tainted by sin and under Satan's dominion. Missions involve bringing the gospel to regions and people ensnared by Satan. The Bible refers to this as God's "divine power to destroy strongholds" (2 Cor. 10:4).

Preemptive strike in ministry is the supreme tactic for protecting and safeguarding believers. The pastor's utmost concern is to guard the believers from the attacks of the enemy and temptations of the world. To achieve this, the pastor must teach and guide believers, akin to the way the boundary set by the blood on the doorpost at Passover delivered the people of God. Likewise, pastors have the responsibility to protect the believers by guiding them to live under the power of the blood shed by Jesus on the cross. It involves the work of anointing the doorposts and lintels of believers' lives with the blood as it was done during the Passover.

However, preventative ministry, ensuring believers do not step beyond the boundary of the blood, should not be passively understood. There is a tendency within Christianity to adopt a passive and defensive attitude, perceiving God as a mere passive and defensive being. On the contrary, it is always God who initiates the preemptive strike in the spiritual battles surrounding our existence.[7]

The Bible teaches tolerance, unity, and coexistence for both believers within the church and nonbelievers. Despite these teachings, the gospel also demands the preservation of the purity of the message and the integrity of faith. Paul instructed believers to live in harmony with everyone as much as possible. However, in Galatians 1:6–10, Paul seems to be contradicting his own teachings, taken to be the most cynical and harsh in the entire New Testament. It is no wonder then this passage is considered "one of Paul's most combative expressions and a form of Paul's preemptive assault."[8] What Paul is concerned about here is protective and preventive pastoral care. He aims to preserve the saints within the boundaries of the gospel as well as to teach that no attack is too little when it comes to the preservation of the purity of the gospel.

Pastors must not only teach passive attitudes to believers but also instill the concept of proactive spiritual attack. It must be done so that it does not remain in a defensive sense but actively infiltrating areas and territories enslaved by Satan for the sake of gospel-driven restoration. They must teach the believers that preemptive strikes against the evil ones are the way to apply the blood of Jesus to their doorposts, a way to keep them preventively protected against attacks from the world. Whether it is through rising from bed to pray or actively seeking God's wisdom to open new doors in their daily faith life, these actions must be considered proactive spiritual attacks.[9] It is a preemptive attack against the enemy when a believer cognitively trusts the wisdom of the Lord to freshly and creatively serve the Lord in a new way.[10] The concept of preemptive force and spiritual warfare may create a holy stir in a believer's life. Yet, pastors must work to consistently refresh the spiritual walks of the believers while keeping the gospel intact in its purity. Pastors must work to help the saints break free from lukewarm or powerless faith and journey toward a vibrant and energetic faith.

Ministry That Chooses the Tree of Life. If the pastor's heart is the lifeblood that keeps the ministry alive, then the ministry that chooses the tree of life is evidence that the pastor's heart is being translated into action. If the pastor's heart is the backbone of the ministry, it must manifest externally. As for me, this is seen in the ministry that chooses the tree of life.

The story of Adam choosing the tree that reveals good and evil in the garden of Eden is a historical event; but spiritually, it is an ongoing narrative for us today. We still stand before the tree that reveals good and evil, just like Adam. Choosing the tree that reveals good and evil means choosing commandments and the law. Commandments determine what is right and wrong. The law serves to make us aware of our sins and transgressions, leading us to Christ as a schoolmaster (Gal. 3:24). However, we are no longer under a guardian-tutor since we have believed in Jesus (Gal. 3:25). The law can only participate in the ministry of life when it serves the gospel. The fractures we witness today in church meetings, among believers, and in individual lives are often the result of choosing the tree that reveals good and evil—a legalistic mindset still operating under the law. No matter how intense our spiritual experience may be or how many terminal degrees we hold in biblical studies, growth is impossible if our eyes are not opened with this perspective.

The tree of life, initiated in Genesis 2, passes through Ezekiel 47 and culminates in Revelation 22, the last chapter of the Bible. The path of the tree of life, blocked by Adam's fall, was reopened through the redemption of the cross. Choosing the tree of good and evil is a personal decision—choosing to put what is right for me, my style, and my benefit before anything else. However, choosing the tree of life is a decision centered on the Lord. Choosing the tree of life transforms death into life, allows the fallen to rise again, and liberates from one's weaknesses. In essence, choosing the tree of life is a life lived in the "mainstream of grace."

Teleios Discipleship training involves training believers to choose the tree of life. This training must be experiential. In marital conflicts, church meeting disputes, and life's crossroads, it must help disciples choose the tree of life. This training works to accumulate in their mind and body the result that is distinguished by the types of trees they choose. Teach them to choose the tree of life.

Balanced Spirituality Leads Ministry to Teleios

If the pastor's heart is the backbone of a Teleios Discipleship, then a Teleios disciple, formed by this backbone, will inevitably manifest a balanced spirituality. The reason the churches around the world still struggle with the issue of heresy today is rooted in distorted spirituality, or even treating spirituality as a personal achievement. Even atheism produces a type of spirituality. Such a spirituality endows spiritual elements to human agents or even machines. These are all results of a misguided direction.

Decoding and opening the path to healthy spirituality, free from impurity, lie in the heart of a shepherd with balanced spirituality. The reason we focus on balanced spirituality is that it forms the foundation of biblical ecclesiology and, above all, leads to a missional life based on the heart of a shepherd.

Healthy Spirituality Cannot Solely Rely on the Spiritual Dimension. For pastors to possess a robust spirituality that withstands the currents of secularism and breaks through the times, there must be intellectual support. There is a tendency to view spirituality only in the spiritual realm, emphasizing prayer and meditation. However, healthy spirituality cannot be established solely on the spiritual dimension; it requires the backing of intellect.[11] A spirituality devoid of intellectual support cannot yield the fruits of a substantial ministry.

On the other hand, the reason we should focus on balanced spirituality is that spiritual imbalance leads to the stagnation of faith. "One common cause of spiritual stagnation is not realizing that the Christian life should be comprehensive and balanced. Losing balance is the primary cause of confusion, inconsistency, and unrest in the Christian life."[12]

Discerning for Ministerial Spirituality, Personal Spirituality, and Balanced Spirituality: Five Criteria. The two axes of balanced spirituality, that is also based on the shepherd's heart, are ministerial spirituality and personal spirituality. If ministerial spirituality is external, personal spirituality is internal. When these two spiritual aspects are not balanced, a calamity can occur where meditation occurs without movement or movement without deep meditation or reflection. Let us examine an example of imbalance in the church.

In the past two thousand years of Christian history, there have been eight streams of spirituality.[13] These include spirituality each emphasizing either meditation, holiness, the Holy Spirit, social justice, the Word, sacraments, training, and communal life. Each stream has its own excellent historical, theological, and pastoral background, but there is a risk of losing balance by being overly absorbed in a specific outlook of spirituality.

First, emphasizing only *meditation* can lead to neglecting the real world. While one can experience intimacy with God through meditation in a monastery, there is a risk of falling into an escapist faith. Second, emphasizing *holiness* alone can lead to insensitivity to God's grace. Being sensitive to sin and striving not to fall into it is commendable, but it can result in wearing the garments of holiness while neglecting the robe of grace. Third, emphasizing the *Holy Spirit and His gifts* may lead to forgetting the Giver of the gifts. Overemphasizing the gifts may eventually lead to the dangerous misconception of acting as the one bestowing the gifts. Additionally, there is a risk of an inversion where one thinks they are directing the Holy Spirit rather than being led by Him.

Fourth, emphasizing *social justice* alone may weaken the power of the gospel. Many admirable individuals give of themselves and accompany those in need, particularly the disadvantaged. However, focusing too much on visible physical challenges while neglecting the unseen issues of the soul can result in losing the life-changing power of the gospel. Fifth, emphasizing only the *Word* may weaken the operational power of the Holy Spirit. Churches that predominantly emphasize the Word, fellowship, and theology often find it challenging to gather mass amounts of people. While we understand that Jesus nurtured and focused on twelve disciples through His teachings, we must also remember that Jesus also fed the hunger of thousands. People gather where there is spiritual life because of their innate desire to live spiritually.

Sixth, focusing solely on *sacraments* may lead to overlooking the meaning and purpose embedded in them, resulting in formalistic and ritualistic practices. Consequently, participants in the sacraments may dwell on the superficial spirituality of the rituals, losing touch with their original significance. Seventh, emphasizing *training* alone may cause missing out on the joy the Lord has given. If training becomes the sole purpose, joy in walking with the Lord may be neglected. Ultimately, this may lead to a dry and critical believer. Eighth, emphasizing *communal life* alone may lead to losing one's individuality and unique identity. When individual lives fade, so does the sense of community. Throughout history, vibrant communities have been the ones where individual lives also shine.

Each of the mentioned aspects of spirituality is biblical, faith oriented, pastoral, and edifying. However, without embracing balanced spirituality without consideration of one's ministry context and end up showing bias toward one aspect while neglecting others, one cannot live the abundant life the Holy Spirit imparts. Balanced spirituality marks the life Jesus intended to share with us when He came to this earth.

Over the years of ministry, I have come to realize that the criterion for evaluating ministry is determined by whether there is the power of "life" or not. Moreover, I have observed that life bears fruit where there is a shepherd's heart, as the Bible consistently emphasizes that the ultimate concern of a true shepherd lies in the life of the sheep.

There are five distinct criteria for discerning balanced spirituality centered on life. Do you love God? Do you love the Bible? Do you love the church? Do you love the gospel? And do you love souls? If you can clearly answer yes to these five questions, then it is likely to be moving in balanced spirituality. If, in any case, one claims to love God but hates their brother, claims to know God but does not keep His commandments, one cannot claim to have a balanced spirituality (1 John 4:20). If one claims to love the church but is blinded to the glory of the church, claims to love the gospel but shows no footsteps in spreading it, or claims to love souls but condemns others under the banner of justice or righteousness, then it cannot be a result of balanced spirituality (John 2:4).

Creative Future Strategies for Teleios Pastoral Ministry

To Become a Teleios Disciple-Making Pastor, One Must Elevate the Standards of Ministry

Merely desiring Teleios Discipleship training does not automatically make everyone a suitable trainer. One of the qualities required for pastors aiming at comprehensive discipleship training is vision—to put it narrowly, and perspective—to put it broadly. To see farther out, one must ascend to a higher point. No matter how good one's eyesight is, it is impossible to see the panoramic view from the mountain peak while standing at its base. This explains why the level of ministry is crucial. Members of the church usually cannot see beyond what the pastor sees. Pastors must elevate the standards of ministry.

Even though the pastoral field may be local, the perspective of ministry must be oriented toward a global standard. This way, the congregation's eyes can envision the world that God dreams of rather than the world Satan desires, even while in the sanctuary. The pulpit should direct them to view the world from the mountaintop. Pastors should read not only books on current trends and delve into works that address the primary sources shaping those trends. Occasionally, pastors should attend concerts and exhibitions by masterful artists. This ensures that pastors do not get trapped or biased by specific ideologies or thoughts, enabling them to survey the church and ministry with a perspective of global standards and elevate the congregation to the image of Teleios on their journey.

What Is the Global Standard of the Gospel? The foundation of the global standard of the gospel lies in the biblical perspective that Jesus's command to make disciples of all nations is mandated to all believers at the starting point of their faith journey.

The global standard of the gospel allows one to see how their lives are called to save the lost all over the world, not confined to a specific era or region. This must be the pivot and the anchor that shift their attention from their inner comfort zones to the heart set on the globe. Achieving this mindset requires shattering the exclusively closed mindset. It involves holding onto the gospel as an absolute truth with one hand while embracing the inclusive nature of the gospel that invites all to salvation.[14] The grace of the gospel is for all, and the power of the gospel must fall on everyone. Pastors pursuing Teleios Discipleship training must not be sheltered in their own denominational or regional bubbles or take comfort in religious exclusiveness that confines them.[15]

For instance, at the root of the conflicts Korean society is experiencing right now lies narrow-minded ethnocentrism, prideful Confucianism, and superstitious regionalism. With such distorted hearts, it is impossible to serve the world with the gospel. To establish the kingdom of God with the gospel of the cross, one must be ready to reach out a hand even to an enemy—if it is for the kingdom. This is the global standard of the gospel. We find this commitment in Isaiah 19:24–25,"In that day Israel will be the third with Egypt and Assyria, a blessing in the midst of the earth, whom the Lord of hosts has blessed, saying, 'Blessed be Egypt my people, and Assyria the work of my hands, and Israel my inheritance.'"

In the history of Israel, Egypt enslaved the Israelites, and Assyria was the nation that sought to annihilate them. However, God declares that Egypt and Assyria will be a blessing to Israel and the world. This may seem incomprehensible to human reasoning or emotions. It is a statement that can only be embraced from the perspective of the gospel, God's salvific work, and a global perspective. The global standard of the gospel is about applying the gospel to all regions and people.

Fundamental Principles for Teleios Pastoral Ministry

Discipleship training is a training focused on the members of the church, the believers. In the pursuit of holistic pastoral ministry and discipleship training, the pastor needs to adhere to four principles: spiritual, lifestyle, social, and ethnic principles.

First, faith must be conservative. Conservatism, in this context, means preserving the orthodox theology of the two-thousand-year history of the church. It involves adhering to the core of Christian doctrines such as the Christology of the first century, the soteriology of the sixteenth-century Reformation, and the ecclesiology that has been the foundation of the church as the body of Christ for nearly two thousand years. Being conservative implies safeguarding the truth of God in a tumultuous world, unwavering in any circumstance.

Second, life must be progressive. Here, progressiveness does not refer to the political leftism. It means pursuing progress through giving one's best in the context of life. It involves asking questions like, "Can I do that a little better? Can I think more deeply for the sake of the Lord? Can I practice the love of my neighbor a little better? Can I reach a higher level of excellence?"

Third, society needs to be reforming. Social reform means the transformation of society into holiness based on the gospel. The reforming of society is directly linked to the healthy revival of the church. John Stott welcomed the mention of social reform when Charles Finney, a revivalist and evangelist, talked about revival. "The church's significant mission is to reform the world. Confessing Christianity itself is a confession of a commitment to do what is best for the overall reform of the world." It is not surprising that people who repented through Charles Finney's gospel preaching led the antislavery movement.[16]

Fourth, race must be healed. All nations, especially the ones that have experienced the tragedy of intra-ethnic conflict or are still struggling with ideological disputes, need healing. The nation's future direction will follow in the direction of the tears of prayer flow. As we pray, the healing of the nation will take place as a consequence. Praying for the healing of the nation will move mountains and bring healing to individual problems as well.

Considering these four principles as the foundations of faith and pastoral principles, our faith will experience a spiritual delight that focuses more on its fundamentals. This is the essence of Teleios pastoral ministry and Teleios Discipleship training.

Face the Challenges of the Times with Asymmetric Strategies

We find ourselves surrounded by three powerful adversaries: the audacious current of postmodernity, the unprecedented idolization of science and technology driven by the Fourth Industrial Revolution, and the unplanned threats of disaster of a contactless daily life that could be caused by events like the COVID-19 pandemic. The unwelcome guest in the form of the COVID-19 pandemic has brought more challenges to the churches than ever before. Contactless worship, an unimaginable event in the history of Christianity, has subtly changed the conscious structure of believers. It will be challenging for some churches to restore the number of Sunday attendees to the pre-COVID-19 level. Some argue that those who have not attended church for over six months may need to hear the gospel again.

We Need Creative Asymmetric Strategies for Ministry. Pastoral work has become increasingly more challenging today. In my youth, there was no internet in the digital world, and social media did not exist as it does now. Yet in this day and age, people of all ages spend hours and hours engrossed in the time of this enticing world. How can we resist or restrain the shimmering jewels of such a world?

To reverse and overturn such an appetite, the depth and ability of dedication that ministers must pour out to ministry should be much stronger than in previous generations. Antagonistic currents against Christianity are gaining strength over time. Their arrogance and momentum are like that of Goliath. What the church needs now is not swords and spears but David's sling—an asymmetric strategy that transcends the conventional rules of war. An asymmetric strategy is a strategy for weak forces to win against strong adversaries.

The Bible provides numerous examples of creative asymmetric strategies. Particularly, the story of Gideon's three hundred warriors in Judges 7 is a representative case. The Midianite coalition in Judges 7 consisted of 135,000 troops, while Israel had only Gideon's three hundred warriors. It was an imbalanced situation that could not have even been considered a battle, for it was severely one-sided. However, this perspective only looks at war from a worldly point of view, evaluating it in terms of the superiority of swords and spears. God led the people of God to fight against the enemies using a unique asymmetric strategy, namely torches and trumpets. Furthermore, when the Israelites faced the strategic threat of the evil Haman, Esther advanced with determination accompanied by fasting. She confessed, "If I perish, I perish" (Esther 4:16). This became a powerful asymmetric strategy that delivered the Jewish people.

Throughout history, there have been events that changed the course of world history with asymmetric strategies. One such event is Admiral Yi Sun-sin's Battle of Myeongnyang in Korean history. This decisive and amazing victory was won by fighting the fleet after a fleet of invading Japanese Navy with only twelve ships. In an era that evaluated the outcome of battles based on the number of ships and soldiers, Admiral Yi employed terrain and tidal currents to approach warfare with a complete asymmetric strategy. In the case of the United States, Lincoln's hastily assembled Union Army suffered consecutive defeats against the South's General Robert E. Lee armed with military strategy and overwhelming battle equipment during the early stages of the Civil War. However, one day in the middle of the war, Lincoln issued the Emancipation Proclamation, declaring the liberation of slaves. The war between the North and South, which started due to differences in views on the federal system, suddenly shifted to a confrontation between justice and injustice. The Incheon Landing Operation during the Korean War in 1950 is another example as well.

To confront a world opposing God, we must fight not with power but with a creative asymmetric strategy rooted in the gospel. What the church needs now is a spiritually asymmetric strategy that reverses the situation in an instant like Lincoln's Emancipation Proclamation. This is not easy, as we are rigid and bound by the inertia of fixed attitudes and a reality-focused mindset. What the church needs now is a deliberate strategy that does not settle and is coupled with flexibility that is mindful of the value of the souls we are serving.

If you think about it, asymmetric strategy is Satan's exclusive strategy, for he knows the outcome of this war. Knowing also that his final defeat and the day of judgment are imminent, Satan understands well that he cannot beat God. Therefore, Satan, like a roaring lion, will strive to do whatever it takes to reverse the tide, attacking more relentlessly and preparing to ambush unexpectedly at unforeseen times and places like a guerilla.

To combat Satan, we must counter him with a more creative and well-equipped asymmetric strategy. We need to dream of an asymmetric strategy armed with greater faith. Is the ultimate goal of discipleship training merely to achieve a certain status in the world but to completely overturn the world with the gospel? Teleios Discipleship training reminds believers that we gladly rely entirely on God's asymmetric strategy. We must not end our lives regretting that we did not dream bigger for the kingdom of God.

Disciple-Making Pastors Must Embrace Four Principles to Build a Resilient Foundation for the New Future

Disciple-making pastors must embrace the next four principles to build a resilient foundation for the new future of ministry. First, they must strengthen their grasp of basic tenets of faith. In the era of the Fourth Industrial Revolution, intertwined with advanced science and technology, "golden idols" of Babylon will be erected everywhere (Dan. 3:1). Leveraging social transformation, they will impose entirely different ideologies from biblical standards. Noncompliance will lead to the oppression of churches and believers in the name of "public opinion" and "national unity and stability." Moreover, crafty temptations, disguised idolatry, and the virtue of political reconciliation will be employed to induce apostasy. Religious pluralism will rise to attack the uniqueness of Jesus, and believers will constantly be challenged to compromise with the world.

Second, disciple-making pastors must regard their mission highly. The mission is more precious than life itself. Since becoming the senior pastor at SaRang Church, there are number of missions I embraced as an outworking of my philosophy of pastoral ministry. Some of them are "gospel-driven reunification of Koreas without shedding blood," "ministry bridging the gap between older and younger generations," "globalization of the Korean church," "completion of East Asian missions," and "advance of the gospel for the revival of European churches." Korean Christians stepping up to repay the debt of love incurred by Western churches in the past hundred years over the next century is another important mission for Korean Christians. Even in the ashes of the Korean War in 1950, Koreans witnessed a miracle on the Han River—becoming the only nation among newly independent nations post-World War II to transition from a beneficiary to an aid donor. Considering the amount of missionary-sending capacity of the Korean church, one can argue that Korean Christians' spiritual strength now surpasses that of Russia, China, and Japan. When the church esteems the mission of the kingdom and considers it more valuable than life itself, a new path of mission will open. Any church committed to breathing in and out a commitment to its mission will come to change the spiritual landscape of the world.

Third, disciple-making pastors must nurture the next generation to confront the spirit of the times. Every parent in the church should consider it a privilege to teach their children the gospel that cost the blood of Christ. Specifically, they must approach and teach their children with a missionary mindset to avoid repercussions in child-rearing. Many parents express their pride in raising their children well according to worldly standards. Yet, behind the curtains of their homes, there are not a few who regret their child-rearing choices. Teaching children to embrace a missionary life is engraving the identity that continuously rings the sound, "I am a child of God" like an alarm in their hearts.

Fourth, disciple-making pastors must instill an end-time consciousness in the next generation, leading them to look forward to the Lord's return. The current visible world inundates us with visual pleasures that leave no room to catch our breath. It keeps us focused on the present, making it challenging to even think about life in five years, ten years, or even decades later. A missional life results from an active consciousness of end time, leading believers to look beyond the visible reality to anticipate the delight of heaven and the Second Coming. If there is no life after the end and life is confined to this world alone, then Christians are the most pitiable among all people (1 Cor. 15:19).

If You Wish to Dream of the Future in Ministry Again, Seek a New Heart, a New Spirit, and a New Body

Ministry can only survive when a minister focuses on the heavenly reward. It is a journey that cannot be sustained by concentrating solely on what meets the eye. "I walk this path alone. I have to walk it alone. No one can walk it for me. I walk this path alone." The lyrics of this Korean praise song carry the sentiment that one must bear when traversing the path of ministry.

For a minister to dream of a future in ministry, the minister must ask whether there is sufficient mental fortitude to endure it before he or she sees any light of day. After transitioning out of my ministry in North America, I assumed leadership as the second senior pastor of Seoul SaRang Church in 2003. Strangely, I was not afraid of this weighty burden. God had undeservedly granted me an unusual amount of courage and grace over my ministry through the years. He had also allowed abundant fruit, so I was not overly anxious. However, the problem lay within my heart. After planting a church on my own and leading it for sixteen years, it was a journey that started very humbly and the one that led me to be a senior pastor of a megachurch. I had my share of joys and sorrows, ups and downs. Week after week, I discipleship-trained people in multiple small groups, sharing laughter and tears several times a week. Many spiritual companions and comrades in faith went through the journey together with me. My former church was a place where all my energy, love, service, vision, and calling, as well as sweat, tears, and blood were poured out. I did not know if I could start all over again in Seoul.

That was when I suddenly felt afraid. I did not know if I had what it takes to love this new church. So I prayed prostrate before the Lord, "God, give me evidence that I can start again." While reading Ezekiel 36, I received an immense blessing from the words promising a new heart, a new spirit, and a new body. With that promise in my heart, I started my post. The first step I took was to gather my lay leaders at Seoul SaRang Church for a two-day retreat. God surely came through, and we were united in hearts, soaked in His blessings. That retreat then led to spontaneous early morning prayers that gathered thousands at 5 a.m. every morning to pray and ended up lasting for forty-seven days straight. It marked the moment that God's promise was being fulfilled. "New heart, new spirit, and new body," was the answer to my prayer but also a significant testimony that God was creating the community anew.

Disciple-Making Pastors Embrace the Value of Guarding the Heart

What is discipleship training? In a word, it is heart training. What kind of heart training is it? It is the training of the heart so that this heart will be the heart of a servant of Christ. This heart does the will of God (Eph. 6:6) and fears the Lord alone (Col. 3:22). So why train the heart as a servant of Christ, doing the will of God and fearing the Lord? It is to win more people (1 Cor. 9:19). While the world trains the heart to enhance one's personality and become a mature person, discipleship training is solely about training the heart as a servant of Christ, to fulfill Christ's will, fear the Lord, and, through this, to win souls. This kind of heart training is vividly portrayed in the Old Testament. Moses became the meekest person on earth through

God's training of Moses's heart (Num. 12:3). The root of his meekness was his heart (Num. 11:12), and this heart ultimately saved the Israelites (Exod. 32:32).

Discipleship training is the practice of redirecting the heart so that the heart, which unconsciously lived in attachment to money, power, and pleasure, turns back to the true God. It is training to break free from spiritual stagnation and to advance toward the prize called Christ through transformation.

Guarding the heart in theory and practice can be like night and day. In a valley of the shadow of death, guarding the heart is the key to either making or breaking both ministry and personal life. Guarding the heart was a matter of life and death for Jesus as well: "My soul is very sorrowful, even to death" (Mark 14:34). This deeply agonized Jesus, in human nature facing crucifixion, carrying the burden of the world's sins.

A pastor needs to grasp and guard a restless heart, but it may be even more critical to guard oneself from a wayward heart. When Proverbs 4:23 says, "Keep your heart with all vigilance," not only does this command include guarding against the heart departing from God and keeping the heart gate firmly guarded, but it also speaks of protecting oneself from the whims of the heart. Guarding the heart can then become a source of joy beyond duty.

So, how do you guard the heart? The heart is not neutral; it will be filled with something without ceasing. Nature abhors a vacuum, and so does the heart. If the hearts of believers are not filled with God's truth, these hearts will be filled with the lies of the devil. Pastors, therefore, must strive to minister to fill the hearts of believers with God's truth, even if it comes down to just one verse. For this purpose, Paul wished that the hearts of the Colossians would be filled with "the knowledge of his will in all spiritual wisdom and understanding" (Col. 1:9). This reflects the heart of a shepherd.

A Person After My Own Heart

The apostle Paul went to a place called Pisidian Antioch to proclaim the gospel. To substantiate the message, Paul spoke about David, saying, "I have found in David the son of Jesse a man after my heart, who will do all my will" (Acts 13:22). This passage becomes more alive and meaningful as pastoral experience deepens and the shepherd gains more experience in tending the flock. "A person after God's own heart" can be considered the baseline of faith that marks a genuine life in the Lord for both pastor and believers. Discipleship training is the practice of transforming the entirety of oneself to align with the heart of God, relying on the atonement of Jesus's blood for those who were inherently incompatible with God due to sin.

Perhaps no figure wrestled with God as fiercely as David on the theme of guarding the heart. David lived an intense life, excelling in many areas. He was a skilled warrior, an excellent poet, a natural leader and had a remarkable artistic soul and a natural leader. Numerous psalms were composed through him, and significant progress in the history of God's revelation unfolded. He was also a flawed human. He fell into conspiracies and experienced numerous human tragedies. The last verse evaluating David's life in 1 Chronicles 29:28 states, "Then he died at a good age, full of days, riches, and honor." It does not mean he did well and prospered materially. Rather, it means his end was beautiful, and he finished well. In other words, David was becoming more Teleios over time, reaching the level of shalom in God.

Comparatively, Moses's life was adorned with miracles. He walked through the Red Sea on dry land and witnessed the miracles of God who personally led his people with pillars of cloud and fire. Joshua was no exception to a miracle, either. He prayed, "Sun, stand still at Gibeon" (Josh. 10:12), and God granted his request.

However, the character whose life is most extensively covered in the Bible is David. His life is recorded in more than sixty chapters from 1 Samuel to 2 Samuel. He also wrote seventy-three psalms.[17] Yet, when examining David's life, few events can be called miracles. While some may argue that defeating Goliath with a slingshot was a miracle, it is also possible to hit the mark with much practice without involving a supernatural intervention. Still, the greatest miracle that happened in David's life was guarding his heart.

David guarded his heart amid extreme loneliness and solitude compared to his brothers. He had to endure loneliness while tending sheep through the night. To become a Teleios shepherd, one must guard the heart. Guarding one's heart is impossible with a neutral or indifferent attitude toward external circumstances.

The reason we must guard our hearts is that "it is the place where God and people meet."[18] The devil, who knows this fact best, attempts all kinds of schemes like threats or temptations to occupy the hearts of saints by any means necessary. Guarding the heart is like rescuing the soul from a burning house. The command in Proverbs 4:23 (NIV), "Above all else, guard your heart" is an exhortation to establish a holy fence around the source of life.[19] We see Paul's cry in Romans 7 as a holy outcry, urging the believers to guard the heart. It is also the groaning of every minister today who seeks to minister faithfully.

A Firm Sense of Mission Is the Gateway to Guarding the Heart

David guarded his heart through numerous trials, successes, glory, shame, reproach, and grace—all because of the sense of mission rooted within him. David became the king of the tribe of Judah at the age of thirty and the king of all twelve tribes of Israel (2 Sam. 5:4–5) seven years later at the age of thirty-seven. It was almost twenty years after his anointing that this kingship was realized. Guarding his heart for nearly two decades was undoubtedly challenging. During this period, David experienced betrayal, sometimes feigned madness, and shed tears in the presence of spectators. All these events and more could easily have led him to despair. But through it all, the strength that empowered David to guard his heart was the identity of being a person with a mission: "I am the one anointed for a purpose."

Those who possess a sense of mission exhibit certain characteristics. One of those characteristics is not harboring a double heart. Many pastors may struggle with uncertainty about whether they can guard themselves against Satan's temptations and threats. Before succumbing to such fears, one should examine whether they truly have a sense of mission that they value more than life itself. Think of Jonathan Edwards: Not only is he an exemplary pastor, but he was also someone who unwaveringly guarded his heart by writing seventy resolutions and reading them once a week.[20]

Having a sense of mission instinctively increases the capacity of our faith. More than forty years ago, a group of college students, who were then poor and destitute, gathered for an inauguration ceremony for leadership in the college ministry. They made resolutions with extraordinary determination. "I vow today not to live for myself but to serve other souls with the Word. Whether I am a pastor, a missionary, or a professional, I will be someone who serves other souls with the Word wherever God sends me." These students wrote out their own unique commitments and made the pledge. Yet in one voice, they proclaimed, "We are disciples of Jesus to the ends of the earth until the end of the world. This life we live once will soon pass away. All that we do for Christ will only be everlasting." This declaration shouted with a confession-like fervor, preserved these leaders through the stormy youth. It is the power that brought us to where we are today.

The Secret of Ministry That Guarded the Pastor's Heart Throughout a Lifetime

Paul wrote in Colossians 1:27 (NIV) from his imprisonment in Colossae, "The glorious riches of this mystery, which is Christ in you, the hope of glory." This mystery, hidden for ages and generations, has now been revealed to his saints. About forty years ago, these words clashed with my life experience. At that time, life was tougher than I could handle. The social and political landscape was tumultuous and confusing as well, and the difficulties of serving the members of the college group who were smarter and more capable juniors and seniors were so overwhelming and exhausting that I just wanted to give up the ministry altogether.

It was then that these words resonated like a heavenly loudspeaker: "The glorious riches of this mystery, which is Christ in you, the hope of glory." I realized that the secret of faithful and resilient ministry was not about their qualifications but solely about Christ in the person. The moment these words collided and resonated in me, my heart surged, feeling as if it would burst. My heart confession contained in the lyrics of a praise song, "I will love and serve You, my Lord Jesus, who gave me life," broke through the barriers of my limitations.

The Three Dimensions of "This Mystery." The moment I grasped these words, there was an exhilarating joy in discovering this spiritual gold mine. We need to see the following three dimensions of this: First, Christ lives within me (Gal. 2:20); second, the living Christ within me is a mystery the world cannot know or dare to understand (Col. 1:27); and third, Christ being a mystery is the greatest hope of glory in human life (Col. 1:27). As I held onto these words, I comprehended the following: Now, everything of God is in Jesus, and everything in Jesus is within me. The living Christ within me becomes the hope of glory for the rest of my life.

Realizing this mystery, I started to overcome the fatigue and challenges in my ministry. Around this time, a slogan that has driven my ministry burst forth: "Grace transcends the limitations of the flesh." When you understand that everything of God is in Jesus, and everything of Jesus is within you, you become sweetly broken. But at the same time, anointing and power come down from above to fill you. When I discovered the truth of this mystery, my soul was awakened, all that was hardened in me melted, and areas of my life tainted by sin began to wash away. Then Christ in me began to do a new work. My ministry exploded dramatically. There was such an outpouring of grace and blessings that all I could do was to marvel, "This is what boundless ministry looks like."

When Jesus Christ Becomes the Mystery of Ministry, You Come to Desire Worship and Love the Church Intensely. As you begin to see

Jesus Christ as the "glorious mystery" of ministry, you come to see the same phenomenon unfolded in the two-thousand-year history of the church. First, you worship and adore God. It is not just any worship. Colossians 1:18 refers to Jesus as "the head of the body, the church," revealing that He has become preeminent in all things. People begin to open their eyes to see God the Creator directly, hence worshipping God genuinely as the pure bride of Christ. One's social status recedes to the background to a point of meaninglessness. Instead, awareness of oneself as bearing the image of God comes to the fore. Worship becomes the top priority of life. Public worship is not the only priority, but personal worship and daily worship also become foundational to their lives.

Second, you start to love the church, the body of Christ. "Now I rejoice in what I am suffering for you, and I fill up in my flesh what is still lacking in regard to Christ's afflictions, for the sake of his body, which is the church" (Col. 1:24 NIV). When Jesus Christ within you becomes a mystery, a determination arises in you to bear the remaining afflictions of Christ for His body with the rest of your life. Filling up what is lacking regarding Christ's affliction means that all that Jesus was committed to during His earthly ministry will be precisely what we will be committed to. Genuine discipleship that aims to instill Teleios maturity resolves to make Jesus Christ their "glorious mystery." This secret leads them to desire worship and love the church passionately. If such love and passion are not present in them, then the discipleship training is nothing more than a certificate.

You must be willing to sacrifice your life for the church (Eph. 5:25). "Loving the Church seems almost impossible. While it is possible to pretend to love the Church, sacrificial love for the Church requires going through the 'valley of tears' to the extent of tearing away one's own flesh at times."[21] This is only possible when one discovers the mystery found in Christ.

The Church Is Not the Problem; the Lack of Love for the Church Is. The Corinthian church had many issues—sexual immorality, disorderly worship, open conflicts, and divisions among the believers. Today, we face equally troubling situations. "I love the church, but it is narrow-minded, awkward, malicious, competitive, and superficial." This is a painful assessment to hear from the people both in and out of the church.[22] Nevertheless, the Lord loved this "problematic" Corinthian church. Through 1 Corinthians 13, God reveals love as the better spiritual gift, and 1 Corinthians 15 shows the true blessings of "resurrection." Love for the church should become second nature to believers.

Today, among those who criticize the church within the church, it is difficult to find someone who genuinely loves the church. If one loves the church, the love must show. They must be able to demonstrate this love by showing just how many people have heard the gospel and been led to the church because of such love. This is because "it is impossible to bring people to the church without true love for the church."[23] True love for the church is manifested in those who traverse the valley of tears for the church. Therefore, believers who criticize the church should first demonstrate evidence of their love for the church by staking their treasures for the love of the church.

Without love for Jesus Christ, one cannot love the church. Conversely, without love for the church, one cannot love Jesus. Without loving Jesus, one fails to realize that Jesus Christ is the "glorious mystery" within. In this dark and hopeless world, who will sow the seed of eternal life if there is no church? If there is no church, who will serve as the ark of the gospel? Without the church, who will proclaim the indiscriminate gospel in a society dominated by discrimination? Without the church, who will proclaim the gospel of resurrection in a society suffering from despair? Without the church, who will proclaim the absolute truth in a pluralistic society? If there were no church in this world, what hope would we offer to numerous youth who roam the streets today? If there were no church, how would we have Christian hospitals and nursing homes? In a world full of evil, if there were no church, it would become unimaginably worse. Ministers must remind believers that to love the body of Christ the church is to love Jesus. They should teach that the absence of love for the church is a more significant problem than the problems within the church. Teleios Discipleship is training to inscribe love for the church into one's entire being.

God's Glory Is the Banner of Teleios Disciple and Teleios Discipleship Training

Reflecting on Life from the End of a Teleios Discipleship

What is the life of a Teleios disciple? What kind of life should one live to showcase a life lived as a Teleios disciple? There is a person who vividly demonstrates what this life looks like by showing how the opposite of this life turned out: Uzziah. Isaiah 6:1 begins with the phrase, "In the year that King Uzziah died." Uzziah succeeded Amaziah at the age of sixteen and ruled for fifty-two years. He fortified Jerusalem and was recorded as a king who ruled justly before the Lord. Uzziah developed agriculture, strengthened the military, and made Israel a powerful nation, fulfilling the meaning of his name, "the strength of the Lord." Uzziah was a successful king to the point that the Bible portrays him as a king who received God's remarkable help (2 Chron. 26:15).

However, as the nation became powerful, Uzziah became proud, committed evil, and sinned against God, leading to God's punishment. He spent his last years in solitude and departed this world lonely. Isaiah notes the gravity of this event by stating, "In the year that King Uzziah died." Uzziah's life teaches us what the life of a Teleios disciple, a Teleios saint, and a Teleios pastor should be. "Finishing well" is the evidence of a Teleios disciple's life. The life lived in total surrender, then being able to end one's life on earth with peace, and never swaying from allegiance to God are the true appearances of a Teleios disciple.

In this regard, Teleios Discipleship entails a way of life that continues to grow, become whole, develop further, and is never static.[24] The apostle Paul expressed this attitude of life as "forgetting what lies behind and straining forward to what lies ahead, I press on toward the goal for the prize" (Phil. 3:13–14). A life that advances in spiritual maturity every day, a life that progresses toward the goal of the God-given purpose is the outlook of a Teleios disciple. A Teleios disciple and Teleios Discipleship training heighten their hunger for the Lord, clinging to Him no matter the circumstances or how advanced in years they get. Teleios Discipleship seeks to train disciples to embody such pursuits.

Then why did the life of Uzziah, who was once on God's side, face a tragic end? Why do many saints who followed the Lord for a long period sometimes arrive at an unwanted ending? It is because they are "trampling of [God's] courts," as stated in Isaiah 1:12. They are treading the courtyard by not enjoying the presence of God in the holy of holies as they go through the mundane routine of worship. These people do not always start out this way, but as time goes on, their worship becomes centered on people rather than God as time goes on.

With the normalization of online worship after the COVID-19 pandemic, the danger of courtyard-only worship has only increased. Warnings about the dangers of courtyard-only worship have surfaced here and there. Even when offering online worship, the fact that the number of people watching the live stream drops frighteningly as soon as the sermon ends indicates that there are a concerning number of people who are not in worship but watching the worship. Remote worship can be a dangerous land mine created by Satan after the pandemic. Pastors must be vigilant to teach and train the members so that the land mine does not explode in front of their congregation. Pastors should devote their lives to growing believers as Teleios worshippers so that they will no longer just tread the church courtyard. Moving them into the holy of holies is essential.

The True Image to be Imprinted on the Retina of a Teleios Disciple

The opening of Isaiah 6 speaks of what the eyes of a Teleios disciple should see. Isaiah and the seraphim saw God's glory filling the temple like dense clouds. The tragedy today is that many are not seeing God's glory in their lives.

The reason seeing the glory of God is the refreshing source of Teleios is because such glimpses restore the glorious image of ourselves as we were created at the beginning. Anticipating the glory of God to be revealed is the holy excitement, hope, and motivation that allows saints to live a complete life on earth.[25] As these saints reach the fountain of Teleios, they are led to shout, "I have seen the glory of God." While efforts may result in slightly better expressions of morality in one's life, true Teleios is only associated not only with morality but with the overwhelming glory of God. Teleios involves a fundamental transformation of destiny, character, and temperament inside and out. This fundamental transformation is possible only when one is impacted by the view of the overwhelming glory of God. This is biblical Teleios. Boasting about our ethics or morality before the glory of God is like holding a small candle in front of the sun and marveling at its brightness. In this sense, the Teleios we pursue has an eschatological element. When Christ returns, the ultimate purpose of the salvation work will be fulfilled, and our completeness will be transformed into a new dimension of Teleios completeness through the fullness of Christ.

The Cornerstone That Reveals Whether One Has Seen the Glory of God or Not

So, how can we know if we have truly seen the glory of God as Teleios disciples? Without exception, those who have seen the glory of God despair at their own wretched state and fall before God. This explains why Isaiah confessed, "Woe is me! For I am lost; for I am a man of unclean lips" (Isa. 6:5). Those who have seen the glory of God are overwhelmed by the radiance and holiness of God's glory; they are bound to fall to bow down. This was true for Isaiah, as well as for Ezekiel (Ezek. 1:28) and John (Rev. 1:17). Job, who recognized the deficiency and insignificance of human existence in the face of God's awe and glory, confessed directly before the splendor of God, "Behold, I am of small account; what shall I answer you? I lay my hand on my mouth" (Job 40:4). The conflicts, divisions, and fractures within the church today are a result of not beholding the glory of God and, therefore, failing to prostrate ourselves before Him.

The Weight of Life That Senses the Glory of God Even in Pain Is the Weight of Teleios

People of the world fail to understand that the pain or challenges one experiences in life can produce a Teleios life. They often view pain or adversity as mere imperfections in life, thinking at most that they play a role in refining one's life. For Christians, pain and difficulty become tools to make life complete. Scripture vividly illustrates this teaching: "For this light momentary affliction is preparing for us an eternal weight of glory beyond all comparison" (2 Cor. 4:17). The crown of thorns on Jesus became a crown of glory and honor (Heb. 2:7).

The importance of the "weight of glory beyond all comparison" lies in its role as a decisive touchstone and measure that distinguishes between "true Christians" and "nominal Christians." Many believers, and even pastors, often regard expressions like "It is good for me that I was afflicted, that I might learn your statutes" (Ps. 119:71) as mere empty confessions, at worst, or beneficial only to the extent that it makes life deeper, at best.

However, for those on the path of a Teleios disciple, suffering becomes the substance that achieves the glory of God. Suffering is beneficial in that it serves as the path to achieving the glory of God within us. Telios pastors must not stop short of merely comforting those who are suffering without showing them how it will eventually lead them to glory. The pinnacle of Teleios Discipleship training is to make individuals live in awareness and pursuit of the glory of God. Teleios Discipleship cumulates in raising disciples who seek after the light of the glory of God that shines down on them under any circumstances.

As Isaiah once did, those who ascend to the height of Teleios by opening their ears to the voice of God always echo two life questions in their hearts: "How can I please the Lord?" and "How can I fully bear the mission the Lord has given me?" The glory of God is the secret of saints living in this world. "Even if storms of life come one after another, those who see the glory of God never become dismayed, surprised, or disappointed by anything. The weight of the affliction we receive is not light. However, if we place the exceedingly great and eternal weight of glory on one side, the weight of life's affliction or pain on the other side becomes light. A weight of 10 kilograms is heavy, but compared to a ton, it is light. Even a weight of 1 ton becomes nothing compared to the 'exceedingly great and eternal weight of glory.'"[26]

The Banner Fluttering at the Summit of Teleios

"We become what we behold. We are changed into what we see. . . . We are transformed from glory to glory as we behold the glory of the Lord."[27] We often pray, "Lord, change me," which is indeed a precious prayer. But if we truly desire transformation, we must wholeheartedly focus on beholding God's glory. What might be written on the banner waving at the summit of Teleios once we ascend its peak? Wouldn't it be, "Behold the God of glory!"?

When asked about the meaning of discipleship training, various answers will emerge depending on each individual inclinations and experiences. However, when it comes to the question of what the goal of Teleios Discipleship training is, there is only one answer. It is to enable saints to see the glory of God in their lives. The goal is to progressively embed the jewels of God's glory in their bodies as they experience these moments of glory, filling the bosoms of the saints with the radiance of God's glory despite sufferings. It is to fill the heart of a saint with the light of God's glory. Even during adversity, it is to live like Stephen who, even in death, "looked up to heaven and saw the glory of God, and Jesus standing at the right hand of God" (Acts 7:55 NIV). The glory of God is the dream, goal, and pinnacle of Teleios Discipleship training. Engraving this in the soul of saints, always prioritizing the glory of God, and reacting to that glory spiritually is the mission of a Teleios disciple-making pastor.

PART 3

Fruits of Teleios Discipleship: Practical Application of Teleios Discipleship

"There is not a square inch in the whole domain of our human existence over which Christ, who is Sovereign over all, does not cry: 'Mine!'"

Abraham Kuyper, Inaugural speech at the Free University

CHAPTER 7

Five Personal Dimensions of Teleios

"Discipleship, which requires lifelong obedience toward the same direction, is truly a challenging task that goes against the current of modern life. Nevertheless, in the advanced contemporary world, discipleship remains an unavoidable and crucial top priority for our time."[1] What is the reason for placing discipleship at the forefront of life's priorities at all costs? It is to be transformed into a person God desires and to live as a pleasing sacrifice unto Him.

From the moment of conversion, the goal of sanctification is to reach the glory of God by "being transformed into the same image from one degree of glory to another" (2 Cor. 3:18). Speaking from the perspective of Teleios Discipleship, sanctification involves a complete transformation of a believer, opening the eyes to the shepherd's mindset and gladly carrying their cross in self-denial. This process invites a believer to embark on the transformative journey of a missional life.

Teleios Discipleship training is continuous training of holy disciplines and avenues of grace to keep the outworking of the holiness manifested within us. The process of abandoning sin and living toward God is "gospel-centered sanctification."[2] The driving force behind such transformation is grace.[3] Grace is the agent that works to transform our nature; but at the same time, we also apply the grace to our lives through the works of the gospel-centered sanctification in our intellect, will, and emotions to ensure that grace abides in each dimension.[4] Through grace, our nature is transformed, and our transformed nature longs for more grace.

How can we receive this grace? God provides grace in, by, and through Jesus.[5] The gospel of grace transforms our entire being into the image of God. "God has given us intelligence, heart, and will to humans. One of the greatest glories of the gospel is that it captures the entire person."[6]

What It Means to Holistically Resemble the Lord

When we deny ourselves and walk the path of repentance and faith, our entire personality begins to become like Jesus. When we say we become like Jesus, how so? First is the realm of mind. Our thoughts tend to lean toward evil if left unchecked (Matt. 15:19). Therefore, we need to capture our thoughts and make them obedient to Christ (2 Cor. 10:5). Second is the realm of emotions. The joy and delight experienced as he walked with the Lord around the tree of life in Eden instantly vanished as Adam took a bite of the other tree. Due to Adam's disobedience, bitter emotions like thorns and thistles (Gen. 3:18) took hold of humanity. This sinful nature thus has solidified in us. Is there any antidote to these icy and rigid emotions? The greatest evidence of our wounded emotions being healed is joy. When joy begins, sorrow and sighing will depart (Isa. 51:11). This joy is given when we personally encounter Jesus, just like the disciples. Third is the realm of will. Originally, Adam had the will to follow God. But when this will was shattered by sin, it degenerated into a will that rebels against God. Fourth is the realm of relationships. Adam's sin resulted in a severed relationship with God. The broken relationship with God also caused disruptions in relationships with other people. The most evident proof of the transformation is the restoration of the relationship with the Creator God. Being in the right relationship with the Creator God gives meaning to even the most trivial aspects of life.[7] Fifth is the realm of actions. The actions of a saint serve as evidence of being a child of God and act as a mirror for unbelievers to see God (Matt. 5:16). However, the sinful actions caused by Adam's transgression are squirming instinctively within us. To kill evil actions that somehow find their way into us, a determined and forceful struggle is required. God has given us "the sword of the Spirit" to oppose and attack Satan, "which is the word of God" (Eph. 6:17). Teleios Discipleship training involves mastering the sword of the Spirit as the decisive technique for holy actions.[8]

Jesus took upon Himself our sins on the cross and renewed the entirety of our being. When we respond to the gospel of the cross, our character naturally transforms into the likeness of Jesus (2 Cor. 3:18). This is because Jesus is the essence and substance of the gospel is Jesus (Mark 1:1). The life in repentance and faith results in transformation that aims to reflect the work the cross. The resemblance of Christ begins at the core of our personality, then expands out to resonate in and out of our lives as it shapes our entire being.

Teleios of Mind

The realm of mind is the most intense battlefield within us.[9] Although we have already achieved victory in spiritual warfare through the blood of Christ, the remaining sins of our old selves are diligently working to construct an unrighteous stronghold within our thoughts. They strive to turn us back to the state before the freedom from sin whenever there is an opportunity. "Wretched man that I am! Who will deliver me from this body of death?" (Rom. 7:24). While there may be countless literary works, it is unlikely to find a passage that vividly captures the inner fierce battle as the words Paul uttered above. Satan is lying in wait at the door, eagerly watching for an opportunity to enter and prowl within us (Gen. 4:7). How can we rescue the doorknob of our thoughts from the hands of Satan?

The Mind Is the Battlefield

While the world urges the liberation of human thoughts, the Bible instructs us to submit them to Christ. The battle waged within our mind is brutal and unforgiving. "Satan, who seeks to destroy God's plan for humanity, primarily uses concepts and images. Therefore, these become the main battlegrounds for spiritual formation."[10] Satan is sinister and evil. He is the father of all lies (John 8:44). He corrupts our thoughts to rebel against God. The challenge lies in facing temptations and trials as we live in the flesh until the day we meet the Lord, the day of ultimate sanctification (1 John 2:16). Unbelievers may not experience such intensity. They may internally struggle with a conscience but do not necessarily wage the internal war as we do. Unbelievers lack the absolute truth about right and wrong, making it impossible for them to engage in a battle for biblical absolutes. However, since we believe in Jesus and live in Him, the clash between the driving force of sanctification and the old nature is more intense than in preconversion days. Conflict arises in our hearts, preventing us from fully resembling the Lord and focusing on His perfection.

Even with a deep experience of faith, there is no room for complacency. Peter, who received praise for confessing, "You are the Christ, the Son of the living God" (Matt. 16:16), immediately earned a severe rebuke for attempting to oppose Jesus when He spoke about the cross (Matt. 16:23). Peter's sudden disagreement shows how his thoughts were significantly influenced by Satan. It truly shows that the mind is a spiritual battleground.

The Path to Teleios of Mind

Self-Denial, Not Self-Examination. If we divert our attention even slightly toward human affairs instead of God's work, our minds become devastated like a bombarded ruin. In that case, how can we place our thoughts under the dominion of the Holy Spirit for true Teleios maturity? To achieve the Teleios of mind, there is a crucial point that must be addressed: excessive self-examination that places the self on the throne of thought, robbing the inner space where Jesus should dwell. "Are we ready to discard the pathological self-examination that endlessly questions our worth? Constantly gauging our value on our own, we cannot be useful to God at all."[11]

Some assert that constant self-examination is necessary for wholesome thoughts and a wholesome heart. However, the Bible suggests that self-examination can lead to spiritually detrimental results by making the self the subject. Self-examination dominated by the human ego can lead to the addiction to self. Self-addiction is the essence of sin and the most significant hindrance to what God wants to do within us and through us.[12] Excessive self-examination creates a paradox by idolizing the self as the "idealized me" and placing it on the throne of their minds. In such a state, there is no room for Jesus. Christ's disciples triumph in the battlefield of mind through biblical self-denial.

Biblical Thinking, Not Positive Thinking. "Therefore, as we think, we act; as we act, we develop habits; as we develop habits, we shape character; as we shape character, we determine destiny."[13] This tells us that our thoughts determine our destiny. However, the reason why believers need to train and constantly examine their thoughts is not for the benefit of positive thinking. Romans 8:6 provides the reason why we must thoroughly examine and handle our thoughts: "For to set the mind on the flesh is death, but to set the mind on the Spirit is life and peace." Again, the thoughts of fallen humanity will gravitate opposite to God if left unchecked. If left alone, human thoughts flow toward atheistic thinking, are drawn to unrighteous and arrogant thoughts, and are led toward vanity and emptiness. In this regard, the pulpit should be a holy place that goes beyond actively promoting positive thinking or optimistic thinking. Disciple-making pastors must use the pulpit to train the thoughts of believers to stand on God's side.

Again, Teleios Discipleship training is about training in biblical thinking that prompts believers to stand on God's side. Emphasizing positive thinking blurs the image of God that needs to be cultivated in us. It often leads to emphasizing individual, family, or business success in the world's terms. In doing so, pulpits can easily become indistinguishable from worldly lectures on success stories or just another self-help. The fatal result of this is the crumbling of the boundaries between the church and the world.

Faith Reporting, Not Fact Reporting. Somewhere along the way, the church and believers have fallen into a cynicism of faith. Phrases like "Praying doesn't work. Worshipping doesn't change anything" have spread within the community, and cynicism has grown into a frightening defeatism, penetrating even the roots of the church. This is a sign of secularism infiltrating the church. The secular mindset rejects eternal and absolute authority. This kind of thinking prioritizes human thoughts about God over God's thoughts about humanity. How can a community steeped in such a mindset turn its course and progress into Teleios maturity in faith?

You will not find the practice of "faith reporting" amid the prevalence of "fact reporting" in a community steeped in the worldly mindset. Why is this a problem? Because, as John Owen once said, in places dominated by unbelief, human thoughts cannot be conscious of God's glory.[14] Some who claim to be experts in church ministry project a continuous decrease in the church's vibrancy and warn of looming darkness in the church's future. They add weight to their case using the European church as historical evidence. As a result, even the average members of the church community are buying into their argument. The cynicism that contaminated the garden of Eden is also corrupting the church and believers. Cynicism within the church is eating away at the hearts of pastors and believers.[15]

Reflecting on past ministries, cynicism has proven to be a significant obstacle to the advancement of God's work. Why should pastors and discipleship leaders be vigilant against cynicism? We find the answer as we behold the glorious work of God in creation. The most repeated phrase in that account is, "God saw that it was good" (Gen 1:10, 12, 18, 21, 25). There is no cynicism in God's assessment.

How can the church overcome cynicism and stand on God's side? Disciple-making pastors must engage in "faith reporting," going beyond mere "fact reporting." Today, one of the major factors weakening the church is its sole reliance on "fact reporting." To elaborate, the issue is not reporting facts—it is relying only on facts. For believers, facts are not everything; the most important thing is God, the Sovereign of facts. In Numbers 13, the twelve spies reported the facts. "There we saw the Nephilim (the sons of Anak, who come from the Nephilim), and we seemed to ourselves like grasshoppers, and so we seemed to them" (Num. 13:33). Is the problem the facts? No, it is how they saw things. *Seeing* is the problem. People have a bias toward seeing only what they want to see. "Everyone did what was right in his own eyes" (Judg. 21:25) reveals the inner bias of fallen humanity. If left unchecked, human thoughts naturally flow according to personal opinions rather than God's perspective. Before being trained as a disciple, the believers may have been doing "what was right in [their] own eyes." But for those who have undergone the training of the mind, operating solely on facts before the God is simply not permissible (Deut. 12:8).

Seeing is dominated by thinking. What one usually thinks is what becomes both noticeable and visible through one's sight. Human bias is dominated by the bias of sin. The atheistic culture, anti-Christian ideologies, and secularism chained by materialism—all whisper to people's minds that life on this earth is all there is. They evidence how human thoughts are captive to the bias of sin. Training the thoughts of a believer is training to reject cynicism and the bias of sin. It is the training of the mind to see what God sees, not with the eyes of the flesh.[16] Training in thinking that looks at what God sees lifts believers to the dimension of "faith reporting," not "fact reporting." This training elevates believers from a mindset of cynicism coupled with the bias of sin to a dimension of "faith reporting." Do you want true success in ministry? Do you want believers to live set apart from the world? Train the thoughts of believers to embody "faith reporting," not "fact reporting."

Teleios in Emotions

Our society is currently immersed in an intense emotional furnace, to the point where the phrase "normalization of anger" does not sound out of place. This is not just a phenomenon in one society but a global trend. Captivated by ideologies and partisan logic, it seems that the moment the coverings of issues are lifted, anger that was withheld inside is immediately poured out. Anger in our society seems to be seeping through the gaps in the torn emotions of church members. It is not difficult to find instances where emotions erupt over trivial matters. Wounds of anger take deeper roots, and red-hot disputes frequently rise against one another inside the church community. These people may have the appearance of good Christians, but the lack of integrity between the spiritual and emotional indexes result in the loss of balance in the pursuit of Teleios faith.

While it may be natural for nonbelievers to have broken emotions and false knowledge due to their fallen nature, those who have accepted the gospel are expected to have transformed emotions that are aligned with their faith. John Calvin said, "If one truly accepts the gospel, it must penetrate the deepest emotions of the heart, taking root and transforming the entire person."[17] Therefore, if someone claims to believe in Jesus but has no change in their life and still experience emotional unrest, it is an indication that the gospel has not penetrated their hearts. Gospel transformation and healthy emotions go hand in hand.

I fear that we have not always handled the issue of emotions sufficiently. While emphasizing spirituality, subjective emotions were undervalued and distrusted. As a result, there were instances where the emotional index and spiritual index did not align. The unresolved issue of emotions led to the misapplication of the Word, resulting in a distorted faith that patterns after the world in selective love and prejudiced forgiveness.

Looking back on more than forty years of ministry, I witnessed how the bitterness was used as Satan's tool to bring people down. The Bible states that bitter roots trouble and defile individuals (Heb. 12:15). Unhealed wounds, when ignored, eventually erupt in unexpected times and spaces.

Ultimately, the neglect of unhealed emotions can lead to significant leakage personally and pastorally. Satan, in any way possible, lays the groundwork within us for guilt, fear, anger, worry, disappointment, and sadness to flow continuously. Unhealed emotions pervade today's church. Without healing emotions, it is impossible to walk the path of a disciple of Jesus. How, then, can emotions be healed?

The Position and Significance of Emotions in Faith

Emotions were an important aspect even for Jesus. During His earthly ministry, many of the imperatives He gave, such as "do" and "do not," were related to emotions: "Do not fear," "take comfort," "forgive," "love," "rejoice," and "be glad." Jesus recognized the significance of addressing emotional issues in the disciples' journey. This implies that pastors, too, without deeply observing and examining the emotions of believers, cannot ensure the health of the community and the individual's spiritual growth.

With the development of various disciplines that delve into human inner life and emotions, it has become evident that there are factors deeper than knowledge that move people. That factor is none other than emotions. Recognizing this, Jesus, who already knows this truth, did not ask His disciples, "What do you know?" or even "What do you believe?" Instead, He asked, "What do you want Me to do for you?" "Will you follow Me?" and "Do you love Me?" These three questions are essentially on the same level, touching not on knowledge or actions but delving into the deeper realms of our thoughts, affections, and desires (emotions). If discipleship fails to address the realm of emotions, it may be successful in imparting biblical knowledge but will completely and inevitably miss the most crucial aspect of human experience.

Emotions as a Part of the Image of God

Emotions are an area of the human soul that must be deeply examined in the process of discipleship training. Joy, gratitude, hope, peace, mercy, and more are all emotions that transformed saints express after repentance.

"The fact that a saint experiences emotions at a specific moment and expresses them in those moments reveals the spiritual condition of a being as it is closely connected to one's character."[18] But if emotions were not part of discipleship training, Paul would not have mentioned forming, controlling, and using emotions, such as being thankful (1 Thess. 5:18) or rejoicing (Phil. 4:4). Therefore, "emotions can be shaped, even decided intrinsically, but it must be done through the concept of grace. Emotions that can influence the spirituality of saints are theological issues and areas that require teaching."[19]

To internalize the Bible's teachings, one must use emotions. The Synoptic Gospels depict Jesus as a person rich in emotions. Matthew describes Him as a merciful king, Mark as a compassionate one, Luke as God's Son full of empathy, and John as a loving Lord. The Gospels portray Jesus with emotions. Therefore, Christ followers should learn and be trained to possess healthy and diverse emotions—expressing them appropriately.

How does our identity from creation shape the reason we consider emotions as a part of discipleship training? Reflect on the creation account's recurring phrase, "And God saw that it was good" (Gen. 1:4, 10, 12, 18, 21, 25, 31). Notice it does not say, "Upon analysis, it was good." Instead, it was good at the sight! The garden of Eden was a place filled with perfect emotions—complete harmony, perfect beauty, and perfect order that filled human emotions. Thus, since we are created in God's image, we hold a part of God's bursting emotions within us. In Genesis 2, when God said, "It is not good for man to be alone" (Gen. 2:18 NLV), we can equally see the exposure of emotions. The statement that emotions are also part of the image of God demonstrates why believers should train their emotions.

Reasons Why Korean Pastors Should Pay More Attention to the Emotional Training of Believers

Teleios beauty of emotions has been shattered by Satan's attacks. Put differently, Satan is a destroyer of Teleios of emotions. In *The Screwtape Letters*, C. S. Lewis intriguingly states how the devil perceives and attacks a believer's emotions. Screwtape advises his nephew Wormwood, "When you see the mistakes he has made, this was because they were beyond your ability. However, it will be worthwhile to try to attack his emotions."[20] From the devil's perspective, even a deeply faithful person has enough vulnerability when it comes to emotions.

For Koreans, emotions are both a treasure trove of sentimentality and a source of wounds. Koreans have a unique word called "Hwabyeong" which does not have an exact English equivalent but refers to a Korean culture-bound illness that includes symptoms of insomnia, depression, and somatization in the lower abdomen, causing sleepless nights, and even much worse related conditions. There is also a term for a sudden burst of anger that cannot be controlled, known as *Uk* in Korean as well. For instance, in the 1920s, crimes related to arson, specifically self-inflicted arson, were frequent in Korean society. The act of setting fire to one's own house out of anger seems to be a unique phenomenon and happens with extreme intensity among Koreans.[21] On the other hand, Koreans also have the concept of "Heung," which refers to an exhilarating and rhythmic joy that cannot be logically explained. It denotes that burst of energy, vibrancy, and rapture welling up from inside. It remains a mystery how *Heung* translates to a power that allows one to accomplish seemingly impossible tasks when ignited.[22] It is not an understatement to claim that the success or failure of pastoral ministry targeting Koreans depends on healing the national emotion of *Uk* with the gospel and transforming *Heung* into a mission-conscious enthusiasm that leads to holy dancing.

Pastors committed to disciple-making who also aim to lead their people to redeem their emotions must pay attention to cultural sentimentality that may be present in a believer. Moreover, they must affirm that the understanding and discerning the emotions of believers are not mere considerate efforts but an essential aspect of pastoral ministry because it is based on the shepherd's heart. Jesus, our Shepherd, treated the flock in the same way. His heart was compassionate when He saw the crowds. In Jesus's constant emotion was the unchanging compassion for His people. Disciple-making pastors replicate such emotion in their hearts.

Total Commitment and Teleios in Emotions

More critical than training the emotions of believers is the pastor's self-training of emotions. There are numerous instances where pastors, who have lived all their lives in exemplary faith worthy of commendation and respect, suddenly fall into scandal and cannot rise again. When a pastor falls, it creates a tsunami-like impact on the emotions of the congregation. The self-management of a pastor's emotions is truly crucial, especially when dealing with instincts rooted within. I have a type of maxim for myself: "Reason cannot overcome instincts." No matter how educated and outwardly composed a person may be, no logical restraint can rein in emotions and behavior when instincts are triggered.

The reason for addressing the side of instinct in emotions is because as emotions break, weaken, suffer, or become corrupt, the power of instinct grows in its place. Healthy emotions in a pastor are crucial in ministry. A pastor's broken emotions resonate prominently from the pulpit and become contagious to the members. Emotions spread as a contagion in the hearts of the believers can easily cause complications in the lives of believers.

How can a pastor maintain healthy emotions? Pastors must avoid situations where instincts are triggered. Even more important than this is creating an environment or space that brings emotional recovery. For example, when I feel emotionally exhausted, I refresh my pastoral instinct through several methods. The first is reading. Engaging in conversations with characters in books while reading helps me gain emotional recovery. The second is art. I gain emotional healing and insight through music concerts and art exhibitions. The third is nature. When I am especially fatigued, I climb the hill and sit behind my house. This hike helps me experience a reversal of undesired emotions. Disciple-making pastors must recognize that their healthy emotions are not only fundamentals needed for themselves but also an asset for the congregation and the ministry. Being aware of this, all pastors must work to establish their own routines for emotional recovery. The emotional training of pastors is practically more than half of the emotional training of believers.

The Teleios of Believers' Emotions Comes When the Pulpit Is Filled with Joy

The four hundred years between the last proclamation in the Old Testament and the coming of Jesus were a time when revelation was interrupted, spirituality dried up, and emotional wounds abounded. When the era of the gospel began with the coming of Jesus, joy erupted like a spring fountain. The messages of the angels announcing the arrival of Jesus were the trumpets of joy. The joy that started in Luke 1 continues through to the end of Luke 24:52. It showcases the biblical way is the joy that breaks in—the joy is God's way of healing broken emotions and alleviating pain. The joy of believers, as mentioned in Luke 15:32 (NIV), is inseparable from the spirit and essence of the gospel, illustrated by seeing what was "dead and is alive again; . . . was lost and is found." The gospel signifies that through sin we died and through the cross we came to life. Through sin we lost our lives, and through the gospel we gained them. Since this is the source of joy, a pulpit filled with the gospel is the origin of the most complete healing of believers' emotions. If emotional issues are frequently evident among believers and cause problems among them, it may be worth considering whether the lack lies in not proclaiming the gospel of joy from the pulpit.

"Not only did our Lord pay the price for our righteousness but also for our joy."[23] The joy of believers needs to be deeply rooted in the fact that it is not self-generated, nor is it situational happiness. The joy of believers is the joy the Lord paid the price for. We must recall that God allowed His sheep to live an abundant life in this challenging world by His Son taking the agony of the cross.

One of the core key concepts in the apostle Paul's ministry is "rejoicing in the Lord." Joy shines like a jewel throughout Paul's letters. In fact, joy in the Lord was a holy emotion that captured his heart despite all the twists and turns of his life as a disciple of Jesus. As an apostle, his life was a series of suffering, hardship, shame, and continuous defamation. Nevertheless, the reason his wounded and torn heart could be healed and further maintained healthy emotions was the joy in the Lord. Rejoicing in the Lord means being joyful because I am a beloved one in the Lord, rejoicing because I have embraced the source of joy, Jesus. We are delighted because I can share the most Jesus with others in the circumstances that God allowed me to be in. This is why Paul rejoiced. When the pulpit of a pastor is filled with joy, believers can live not with torn emotions but with healed hearts and healthy emotions.

Teleios of Will

The world often thinks that one's volition becomes whole when making greater resolutions, stronger vows, and more significant actions. However, the Bible teaches that our free will was already corrupted by Adam's disobedience, and with this corrupted free will, we cannot achieve the Teleios of will on our own. "We were given the gift of being able to freely glorify and serve God. However, humanity, through the misuse of that freedom, thwarted the perfection that God intended."[24] How can we restore the wholeness of our corrupted will? It is through complete obedience to Jesus.

God's Noble Gift: Will

Our souls bear the image of God. Within the soul, there is the mind (intellect, thoughts), emotions, and will. To activate the mind is to engage emotions, to express intentions is intellect, and the exertion of one's strength is connected to volition. Because God made us volitional beings, our soul is inherently volitional.[25] If the mind is the engine, the will can be likened to the steering mechanism. The will is not a temperament, but temperaments are expressed through the will. The will is the operational center of human agency. In human existence the will is central. "The essence of faith is the will, and the essence of righteousness is also the will. The only good recognized by God is that which comes from the will, and true holiness is only the holiness derived from the will. . . . The will is like an automatic adjustment device that keeps the soul from deviating off course."[26]

The will plays a unique role within our inner selves. It allows us to "permit" ourselves to think something and feel something intentionally. No matter how fanciful a thought may be or primitive an emotion may seem, without the control of the will, thoughts do not wander on their own, and emotions do not rise or subside spontaneously. "What thoughts you entertain is in the direction the will has conceived, and it flows along that direction."[27]

The will bestows nobility upon humanity. "The will has a clear, intrinsic, and surpassing value."[28] Additionally, the will is a source of creativity. Human dignity cannot exist without the will. If there is no dignity for humans, there is no reason for Jesus to die or express satisfaction in the results produced by His death.

What Ever Happened to the Will?

People often blame the will. Whether it is a child getting addicted to games and neglecting studies, a family member unable to quit tobacco and alcohol, or someone struggling to lose weight, they all attribute it to a "weak will." Is the will truly weak? The will cannot function alone. The will is always accompanied by thoughts and emotions.

The fallen human will is ensnared by the gravitational pull of sin that rebels against God. At creation, humans had the ability to both commit sin and refrain from it. But after the fall, humans lost the ability to abstain from sin. Augustine expressed this as "a will arrived in chains that cannot escape the devil's binding."[29] The fallen human has completely lost all the willpower to perform any true good. If there is a will, it is solely the will to sin.

With a fallen free will, there is no capacity to seek God, nor the ability to carry out God's pleasing will and work. Paul expressed this truth by saying, "You . . . were . . . slaves to sin" (Rom. 6:17). In our attempt to be free from God, we have become even more enslaved to sin. The fallen will is, in fact, a formidable weapon used for the rebellion against God. Look at the prodigal son in Luke 15; he indulges in his own willfulness. There is a boundary to the will, and crossing it leads to dysfunctional willpower. One overlooked truth is that the elder son also displays the dysfunctional aspect of the will. "But he was angry and refused to go in" (Luke 15:28). He made a deliberate decision, driven by will, not to join the celebration feast. Both sons possessed strong wills, but they both were wills entangled with sin.

Humans have lost their complete willpower and are captivated by a distorted will. The world might commend a stubborn person as having a "strong will." Yet the Bible describes them as sinners who hold onto dysfunctional wills. Human strength alone cannot restore a Teleios will. It changes only when we receive a new heart through God's grace.

Restoring the Will Through Dependence

The path to restoring the corrupted free will, which entered through disobedience, is opened through the absolute dependence and obedience accomplished by Jesus Christ. The supreme example of willpower is Christ's act of surrender and humility on the cross (Phil. 2:6–11). This is a crucial core of the gospel. Even after enduring the cross with complete obedience, Jesus entrusted Himself to the Father. This Jesus helps us fully entrust ourselves to God through His example and righteousness secured, as well as the power to make us anew. When we completely depend on God, our corrupted will is made whole.

"Total commitment" is not a term commonly used in the world today. However, for us, disciples of Jesus, it is a matter of life and death. If Jesus entrusted His soul solely to the Father after carrying out the salvation of the world through life-costing self-denial and by becoming obedient to the Father's will on the cross, then we, the disciples of Christ, must equally and diligently follow His words, "Commit your way to the LORD" (Ps. 37:5).

Setting Priorities and Teleios of Willpower

To reach the Teleios of willpower through total commitment, one must prioritize. "Whoever loves father or mother more than me is not worthy of me, and whoever loves son or daughter more than me is not worthy of me. And whoever does not take his cross and follow me is not worthy of me" (Matt. 10:37–38). The key message the Lord conveys here is, "Do you truly want your will to be whole? Do you desire a will of obedience? Do you want total commitment?" If so, you must establish clear priorities in your life.

To make our will complete, it is crucial to establish a relationship of total commitment with the Lord, prioritizing it over parents and children. "If anyone comes to me and does not hate his own father and mother and wife and children and brothers and sisters, yes, and even his own life, he cannot be my disciple" (Luke 14:26). The term *hate* in this verse does not mean genuine hatred but rather emphasizes that total commitment to the Father takes precedence over parents and children in terms of priority. The best way to save parents, spouses, brothers, and sisters is through wholehearted reliance on the Lord.

Why did the loving Lord emphasize total commitment? Why did He set priorities through such a combative tone and instruct us to make our will whole? It is because without the path of love, total commitment, and Jesus-like obedience, our love, trust, and fellowship will be constrained and will not endure. Although the world encourages strong and stronger autonomy, we must practice strengthening total obedience and total commitment. Only through this training can our love and trust become genuine. One must learn to love God first, before parents, children, or spouses. Training in total commitment-based willpower exposes and corrects our hypocrisy. With the steering of a will entirely reliant on God, shaky households become secure, broken relationships are restored, and feeble faith comes to life.

When training for the Teleios of willpower, caution must be taken not to fall into legalism or self-righteousness (Matt. 23:23). The Pharisees meticulously adhered to rules and regulations they created, proudly boasting of their will to keep the law. However, they ended up fulfilling their own will rather than God's righteousness. Their pride in strict adherence to the law hindered the life found in Christ, causing dismal consequences. They kept the small laws but abandoned the law's foundation, which is justice, mercy, and faith.

Teleios of Relationships

We are bound not only by a powerful vertical relationship with God through faith in Jesus as our Savior but also by strong horizontal relationships among fellow believers. This constitutes a "peculiar and new genealogy" of relationships.[30] The Teleios of relationships among believers, or the relationships they form, possesses a uniqueness that cannot be replicated by popular human relationship books or psychological prescriptions.

"Faith is fundamentally relational as much as is about trusting in God."[31] Discipleship training too takes place with personal encounters, times of sharing, and relationships with one another before it is a theory of Christian life.

Humans are relational beings. This has been our destiny since creation. The history of humanity can be seen as a trial-and-error process of seeking the perfect relationship that leads everyone to happiness. However, because relationships are broken by sin, the world, unable to resolve sin, cannot find a solution.

Are you on the path to the Teleios of relationships? Are you loving those who are difficult to love all because of Jesus (Matt. 5:43–47)? The Bible commands us to reconcile with our brother before presenting an offering if we remember that someone has something against us (Matt. 5:23–24). This may seem impossible with the sinful nature of human beings. Nevertheless, why does God emphasize relationships to the extent of commanding us to love our enemies (Matt. 5:44)? It is because, for God, our relationship with Him is everything. God sent His Son into the world and allowed Him to die on the cross (John 3:16; 1 John 2:2). God has gone all-in for the sake of establishing right relationships.

The Bible frequently uses the language of family when talking about the transformation of relationships through the gospel. When sinners become children of God and creatures begin to call the Creator their Abba Father, a relational transformation occurs. The language of reconciliation in the New Testament is also relational (2 Cor. 5:16–21). "After receiving the gospel, people need to learn a lot about the prospect of reconciliation. We do not realize how much God has prepared. Reconciliation with God is not complete until we reconcile with others, conform to the order of providence, and submit to the unchanging laws of the spiritual world."[32]

The Human Longing for Relationships

Korea, influenced by Confucian philosophy for more than five hundred years during the Joseon Dynasty, learned to value five key relationships: parent-child, ruler-subject, senior-junior, spousal, and friendship relationships.[33] The Bible also places great importance on relationships. In some respects, the faith presented in the Bible is profoundly relational. Even in the creation narrative, the first occurrence of something "not good" takes place. This verdict hits like an abrupt interruption in the unfolding of creation. Understandably, this expression carries deep significance. It was "not good" when God saw that Adam was alone (Gen. 2:18). This statement vividly and forcefully shows that humans were created from the beginning to be social beings, destined to live in relationships with others.

Disciples of Christ need to think about relationships for more fundamental reasons. First, the triune God is social and communal (Matt. 3:16–17). The highest model of relational intelligence is the relationship within the triune God. The relationship formed by the triune God is an eternal economy of love, truth, and justice. From this Trinity, the grace of eternal salvation flows. Jesus, despite being equal with the Father, identified Himself as the Son who has a Father—defined relationally. When He prayed in the garden of Gethsemane, He revealed His being in the deep relationship with God by saying, "My Father."[34] Since the triune God is personal and communal, humans created in His image are also relational.

Second, the creation of man and woman in principle reveals the relational nature of humanity. Created man and woman share an equal relationship in terms of value and dignity. Especially through a man and a woman becoming one body through marriage, the union takes after union of the Godhead in the Trinity. Its goal is to create a perfect community of love and trust as one would detect in the triune God—the one that death cannot do apart.

Third, the salvation offered by Jesus is relational. A rich ruler approached Jesus, asking, "Good Teacher, what must I do to inherit eternal life?" (Luke 18:18). Jesus, recognizing the man's observance of the law from his youth, invited him to "follow me" (Luke 18:22), revealing that eternal life is obtained not through observance of the law but through a relationship with Jesus. Jesus is the ultimate authority in relationships. He interacted comfortably with Jewish elites like Nicodemus (John 3) and had no barriers in communicating with marginalized individuals like the Samaritan woman at the well (John 4). Jesus treated people with tailor-made approaches, disregarding race, gender, or status.

Fourth, the church is relational. When Paul explains the relationship between Christ and the church, he describes it as the connection between the "body" and the "head" and the relationship between a "husband and wife." This relationship is based on unity. This unity is not just legal or administrative but internal and spiritual.[35] The church is an organic community that is likened to a body and a marital relationship. This indicates that the lives, confessions, and existence of the church members should be understood within the context of this organic relationship. Believers are a spiritual family and members of the body. Furthermore, Jesus referred to his disciples as "friends" (John 15:14).

Fifth, human reality is relational. Aristotle stated, "If an individual is self-sufficient in isolation, he will not enter into any relationship with the whole. A person who cannot live in a community or does not feel the need for it is not part of the state but is either a beast or a god."[36] Aristotle seeks to explicate the idea that human beings cannot survive without belonging to a form of society. Paul goes further. He understood that not only are human beings social creatures, but he also knew what kind of society Christ must form. "For none of us lives to himself, and none of us dies to himself. For if we live, we live to the Lord, and if we die, we die to the Lord. So then, whether we live or whether we die, we are the Lord's" (Rom. 14:7–8). The ultimate goal of perfect human relationships is revealed in the relationship where life and death are entrusted to the sovereignty of our Savior Jesus Christ.

The world too sincerely emphasizes the importance of relationships. Thousands of books on relationships have been published, and countless more claiming to provide solutions for relationships will continue to be released. This phenomenon is like drinking salty water, making one only thirstier. It simply reveals that the thirst for relationships becomes more severe without passing through the path of the cross.[37] Jesus is the only way.

The Only Solution to Relationship Issues: Is Love for Our Neighbors Possible?

The commandment of Jesus, "Love your neighbor as yourself" (Matt. 22:39), is an absolute truth that all human relationships must culminate in. Yet at the same time, it seems unattainable for fallen human nature to reach. The command to love your neighbor as yourself, even beyond the level of forgiveness for an enemy who causes you harm and even takes your life, seems simply impracticable, feeling more like an abstract ideal (Luke 6:27–28).

The key to the explosive growth of the early church lies in hospitality (Matt. 7:12). Hospitality is both a manifestation of the Holy Spirit's grace and a dimension of training in relationships that all mature disciples should pursue (Rom. 12:13; Heb. 13:2). Opening one's home to strangers is the beginning of the mission.

There is a verse that makes our hearts pound whenever we talk about love for our neighbors. It is the confession of the apostle Paul, who says, "Five times I received at the hands of the Jews the forty lashes less one" (2 Cor. 11:24). Despite undergoing severe floggings, Paul says, "I could wish that I myself were accursed and cut off from Christ for the sake of my brothers, my kinsmen according to the flesh" (Rom. 9:3). After having been flogged almost to the point of death, Paul's back would have been unbearable to look at. Scars would be reminders of brutal tortures. He would have felt such deep wounds in his skin tissues that every movement of the muscle would have caused shuddering pain. Five of these beatings that took place each time the skin began to heal would be equivalent to third-degree burns. These burning sensations would have rekindled the beating and the thoughts of the Jews who had beaten him. His body might have shuddered at the thought.

However, Paul refers to those Jews who beat his body like a rag with the term "brothers of the flesh." He even says that he could lose his salvation for their sake. Even to the extent of being cut off from God's love, he did not give up on a single moment of neighborly or brotherly love. Paul could practice this seemingly impossible love because he identified himself as an enemy among sinners. Paul was only first melted by the love of the cross that called him from being the worst of the sinners to being a recipient of total grace. This was the secret of the perfect relationship that allowed Paul to love even enemies. Only Christians who truly shed tears at the grace of redemption through the blood of Jesus can pursue and enjoy the Teleios in the relationship characterized by love for even enemies.

How Can We Love Those Difficult to Love?

Jesus commands us to love our enemies and demands agape love. Agape love can only be practiced by those who have experienced God (1 John 3:16). Jesus's love is pastoral and missional. However, even if we have experienced God's infinite love, loving someone who has caused us all kinds of wounds, someone who has even ruined our lives, is not easy.

The answer lies in "advancement" in love. With a love that looks back, it is impossible to love someone unpleasant, someone who has harmed us. The issue is whether our love can move forward. A phrase that still echoes in my heart even after decades is, "How would I have known to love someone when I have never felt loved myself?" Love demonstrates that a person who has received love can properly reciprocate.

Christians may be the only ones who can love even enemies. This is because Christians have experienced the love of God. Only those who have experienced the boundless love of the cross of Christ can love even those who seem like enemies. Love that does not look back but moves forward is the love of the cross. Jesus asked for forgiveness for those who crucified Him (Luke 23:34). This is love that advances beyond hatred.

Moving forward is the beginning of agape love. When moving forward, it may be impossible to avoid the minefield of past hatred. If we are hindered by the past, every step we take will explode the mines buried in the land of the past. The lives of Peter and Judas Iscariot vividly illustrate this. Judas was a person who stepped on and exploded the mines of the past. Peter chose the advancement of love and spent the rest of his life being used by God.

As Augustine said, desire ages people, but true love rejuvenates and makes people new.[38] By embracing God's love and putting it into practice, though the outer person may age, the inner self becomes renewed day by day, providing the strength to overcome all obstacles to love and advance that love even toward enemies.

Teleios in Relationships Must Extend to All Creation

When believers obey the command to love God and love their neighbors, the Teleios of relationships they achieve extends to the restoration of relationships with all of God's created world. The Bible states that the reason the earth produces thorns and thistles is rooted in sin. Jeremiah 12:4 says that the sadness of the land, the withering of all vegetation, and the extinction of animals and birds are the results of human wickedness. The fallen natural world that is marred by sin is the neighbor that Christians must protect and care for like good Samaritans would.

Love for neighbors without the love of God ends in heartless ethics and regulations without the love of God leads to pantheism. However, the Teleios of relationships involves loving our neighbors more by loving God with all our hearts. This restoration of relationships extends to the natural world.

Through the atonement of the cross, we have already received the capacity for the Teleios of relationships, enabling us to love our neighbors as ourselves. We must recall the promise God made to Abraham, "I will bless you and make your name great, so that you will be a blessing" (Gen. 12:2). This remarkable blessing is the key to opening the gate of love to our neighbors, the pinnacle of Teleios relationships. An exemplary biblical illustration of this is found in the story of Ruth. In a fickle and dark period of the judges, Ruth, through the Teleios in relationships, saved herself, and her mother-in-law, playing a unique role in the salvation of the people of Israel.

Teleios of Action

I hear Christians say, "Being saved is enough for me." At first glance, it may seem like a commendable expression of faith, but this expression arises out of a misunderstanding surrounding the heart of God who desires to reward us. Luther's concept of justification by faith is the essence of the gospel and the core of salvation. However, since the Reformation, there has been a tendency to overemphasize faith in salvation, leading to the underestimation of the joy of deeds. We must reaffirm that faith and work go hand in hand (James 2:22).

Why should we pursue Teleios of actions? It is to "make it our aim to please him," as the apostle Paul confesses (2 Cor. 5:9). The joy of pleasing the Lord through our works is the sole motive and purpose for the actions of a Christian (2 Cor. 5:9). When our actions become the focal point of theological conversations, we often ask, "How can a loving God judge and punish human actions?" Those who raise this question often fail to see that on the other side of God's love there is God's holiness. The holy God righteously judges sin.

Do Saints Also Face Judgment?

Is there judgment for saved saints? The reason we need Teleios in action lies in the fact that our actions serve as a crucial testimony revealing the faith and faithfulness of saints at the final judgment. Christians face two judgments. The first is the great white-throne judgment (Rev. 20:11–15).[39] This judgment determines whether one enters eternal bliss or eternal punishment. It is based on whether we have accepted or rejected eternal punishment. How do we avoid this judgment? Christians have already escaped this judgement only through the blood of Christ (Rom. 8:1). However, there remains a second judgment evaluating our lives, a superior judgment based on what we have done.[40]

One reason so many Christians are confounded on how our works or actions are related to judgment is found in the confusion between the great white-throne judgment and the judgment based on deeds. Some attempt to avoid the great white-throne judgment by solely relying on their righteousness and morality instead of the righteousness and merits already achieved by Jesus Christ. Ironically, they belittle the judgment of rewards that requires our faithfulness by questioning, "Why do you seek after rewards? Do you mean to tell me there are differences in the degree of rewards? How is that fair?" People claiming to be theologically savvy have trivialized and mocked the rewards judgment, resulting in the disappearance of sermons on the rewards judgment from the pulpits. The rewards judgment must never be reduced to causal reciprocity, secular public ethics, or corruption. The rewards judgment contains profound gospel truths.

The nature and significance of the judgment based on deeds are well explained in the parable of the minas (Luke 19:11–27). In this parable, the master rewards each servant with ten or five cities based on their stewardship. Distinct from the parable of the talents, the parable of the minas makes clear differences in rewards. The Bible clearly states that there is a book that will judge "by what was written in the books, according to what they had done" (Rev. 20:12).

Why Teleios of Action Is Necessary for Saints

Why should the actions of Christ followers be Teleios in nature? There are two core theological reasons why Teleios of actions is demanded from saints. Why should the works of the disciples who follow Jesus be perfect? First, there is the principle of creation. The apostle Paul emphasizes an important point that all who are saved by grace must know: that saints were created for Teleios of action (Phil. 2:13–14). Paul explained the perfection of works in connection with salvation (Eph. 2:8–10). A Teleios disciple did not receive salvation by works but received salvation for works.[41] The reason we strive for Teleios of action is out of gratitude for the perfect salvation accomplished by Christ's sacrifice on the cross.[42] "For we are his workmanship, created in Christ Jesus for good works, which God prepared beforehand, that we should walk in them" (Eph. 2:10).

Second, there is the principle of glory. Our good deeds bring glory to God (Matt. 5:16). The New Testament authors teach and encourage believers to please the Lord through their actions. The target of our good deeds is God. It is not to gain recognition, to receive rewards, or to do good for its own sake. While doing good for ethical reasons is not inherently wrong, our motivation for good deeds goes far beyond that. Our motivation for doing good is to bring glory to God, the source and embodiment of all goodness.

The Lord rewards our Teleios action with five crowns. First, there is the imperishable crown given to the victor in the race of faith (1 Cor. 9:24–27). Second, there is the crown of life given to the martyr (Rev. 2:10).[43] Third, there is the crown of glory given to the shepherd (1 Pet. 5:2-4). Fourth, there is the crown of righteousness given to those who eagerly await the return of Jesus (2 Tim. 4:6–8). Fifth, there is the crown of boasting given to the soul winners (1 Thess. 2:19–20). These crowns are rewards that recognize Teleios in actions and deeds. The detailed biblical verses recording various crowns that reward our actions to illuminate us about the reality of the end times, to ensure that our dedication to establishing the Lord's kingdom is not in vain, and to provide us with holy motivation for the appropriate rewards recorded in the Book of Life.

Today, the faces of saints in the church bear a heavy shadow. This is true, especially among those with long years of faith. The main reason for this is that they have mistaken the role of our actions as criteria for punishment, serving only to reveal our shortcomings. Other times, they see it as a way to avoid punishment. Yet, good works and Teleios actions are not only a duty but our delight. Joy is also a litmus test to examine whether one is properly on track of the Teleios of action. Many within the church wish to have clear evidence of their salvation. Such sure evidence is the heart that is willing and eager to please the Lord through their actions.[44]

CHAPTER 8

Teleios Discipleship Training from the Perspective of Sphere Sovereignty

If we were to name a figure who significantly impacted both the theology and practice of modern Reformed thought, we cannot overlook the Dutch theologian Abraham Kuyper and his concept of "sphere sovereignty."[1] This idea advocates that God exercises sovereign rule not only in the church but in all areas such as society—namely the state, science, the arts, and all areas of life as the sovereign Creator of all. This concept provides disciples walking the path of Teleios Discipleship with two crucial insights.

First, this tells us that there is not a single realm in this world that is outside the kingly rule of Jesus Christ. Second, when God governs each domain, He uses unique methods of governance suitable for that domain. God knows and governs the distinctiveness of each realm, whether it is the church, the state, or the family. In contrast to the narrow or mistaken concept of sphere-subsidiarity that limits the church's representation of God's sovereignty to specific domains, the concept of sphere sovereignty is not only more biblically sound but also balances general and special revelation well.

In dealing with sphere sovereignty, it is crucial to be aware that misunderstanding or misinterpretation of this concept can lead to the weakening of the church. One must be cautious not to mistake the sovereignty of God over a domain as if the domain itself has some type of autonomous sovereignty. When this happens, one might wear the cloak of God's sovereignty in their desired domain and assert a self-given authority. For instance, when someone claims their version of justice and righteousness as an exercise of their unique sovereignty from such a sphere as the political arena, it will certainly deviate from the kind of justice and righteousness that God desires to see roll like a river, depriving the world of genuine justice that only God can grant.

Focusing solely on justification by faith as the work that God is concerned with, this emphasis may cause one to overlook how comprehensively discipleship allows the principles of the gospel to be embodied in various areas of life. For instance, worship, family, workplace, mission, and cultural spheres are essential areas where the spirit of discipleship should be lived out. Yet, most traditional discipleship training efforts have not sufficiently discussed how these various spheres are the very places for discipleship to take place. In the mission field, there is a risk of falling into the paradigm of "either planting or watering," possibly missing the most critical element in the Great Commission: making disciples. Regarding the cultural sphere, there has been a lack of training that challenges believers to see what cultural behaviors and practices align with the Teleios of a disciple. The fuller understanding of discipleship training involves not only the internal life of the soul but all aspects of life—living as a disciple of Christ in both the church and daily living, serving as a witness of the gospel in every moment, every space, and every sphere of the created world.

Worship Discipleship

Lord, Revive Our Worship!

Since the planting of SaRang Community Church in Southern California, there has been a rallying cry echoed every week from the pulpit of Saturday Morning Prayer Meetings. The cry is, "Lord, revive our Lord's

Day worship tomorrow!" Before concluding Saturday Vision Morning Prayer Meetings where the members of the church gather for early morning prayers, and representatives of each branch involved in the operations of the worship service, including prayer leaders, worship leaders, directors of worship music, directors of the education department, ushers, parking, and other service ministries, kneel together on the floor, crying out, "Lord, revive our Lord's Day worship tomorrow!" They fervently pray together. Without exaggeration, for over thirty-five years, this prayer contained in this desperate cry has been lifted up every Saturday morning in my ministry.

I am a worshipper, simultaneously serving as a worship leader. Worship is the DNA of my faith and ministry. I have experienced both highs and lows in life's valleys, but unwaveringly, I have considered worship the central focus of my life. Even in my college years, when I had nothing in my pocket and no glimmering path for the future, I consistently woke up at 3:00 a.m. every Sunday, heading to Seoul Yongsan Railway Hospital by 4:00 a.m. for visitation ministry. With fellow members who breathed the same cold air of the early morning, we prayed and sang hymns, circulating the hospital beds on each floor. The hospital predominantly treated patients with severe trauma from railway accidents, and many patients had experienced horrifying injuries such as limb amputations. While worshipping with these patients, I often felt a mysterious divine presence and witnessed the paradox of the gospel. Over the eight years of visiting the railway hospital for early morning worship, I became convinced of something: Regardless of life circumstances or worldly judgments, the quality of life depends on whether one worships or refuses to worship.

Over my forty-year journey of discipleship training in ministry, I have realized that if one's worship is vibrant, discipleship training cannot be dull or formal. Conversely, if there is a dynamic force and transformative power in discipleship training, worship cannot succumb to traditionalism or dead ritualism. The spiritual health of worship directly influences the vigorous drive of discipleship training, and as discipleship training becomes actively applicational, grace abounds in worship.

Until the church I planted in Southern California grew to be about two thousand people, I knew where everyone sat for the Lord's Day worship by heart. In preparation for Sunday morning, I prayed, "Lord, this is the seat where Mr. So-and-So always sits to worship. Lord, I pray that he will have an encounter with the living hope through worship tomorrow. Oh God, this is where Ms. So-and-So usually sits but was missing last week. Please lead her back to this seat tomorrow, receiving the power to live in victory throughout the week as she receives the heavenly glory and hope," as I held onto those chairs every Saturday. I was greatly encouraged to hear the person who used to sit in one of those seats went on to become a missionary in Thailand and replicated my practice in his mission field years later.

Plausible Myths About Worship

There are some common myths about worship. First, let us consider the notion that the absence of one's engagement in communal worship is acceptable as long as one's relationship with God is right. The biblical understanding of an individual is far from the notion of a self-exalted, self-elevated individualism suggested by the existentialistic mindset. Such a mindset undermines the real worth of an individual as the Bible sees a person—an individual is precious not as an isolated entity but because one holds a God-breathed soul in the being. Worship never cultivates a lone "special forces operatives' soldier" abandoned behind enemy lines.

Every element in worship holds significance—from the opening hymn to the closing song led by the choir. However, a considerable number of believers seem to view the sermon as the entirety of worship. Even after wholeheartedly offering praise, when it comes time for public prayer, someone might say, we are now beginning to offer our worship.

Worship readied with preparation nurtures the saints. While the preparation for worship is crucial, a prepared "worshipper" is even more important. Worship that God receives, that brings transformation to lives, and that changes the course of history is brought forth by a prepared worshipper. The conversation between the Samaritan woman and Jesus concludes with the importance of the preparation of the worshipper.

The gathering of all saints on Sundays to worship God is like the first ripple created by a pebble dropped into a calm lake. Even when a single pebble falls into a tranquil lake, energy—or ripples—spread out. What then would happen if the meteorite of heavenly worship falls into the depths of the human soul? The concentric circles move and swirl from the center, ultimately causing ripples across the entire lake surface. When Sunday worship comes alive with grace and truth, then daily worship, private worship, workplace worship, family worship, and worship in small and large groups all come alive in vibrancy. Not only Sundays but every day becomes a sacred day that should be kept holy. Vibrant worship turns the entire spheres of life into a holy place, not just the building where worship takes place.

The statement that the sending of the believers concludes the worship is only half true. In reality, worship extends out to life in Christian ministry. Worship is service, evangelism, and mission. At least four times a year, SaRang Church holds Communion in the Sunday main service, two baptisms, and two confirmation ceremonies. During these events, we celebrate together with the new believers, hearing their testimonies.

If you want to know how God calls, touches, and heals people through worship today, listen to the testimonies presented during the baptism ceremony at SaRang Church. You will hear: "I felt as if God was speaking to me in worship." "Tears welled up as I listened to the worship music." "I was drawn by the serenity and gentleness reflected in the faces of those worshipping." "I was overwhelmed by a solemnity not felt in any other ceremony or ritual." "I came to the church because of the tranquility and meekness reflected in the worshippers." This does not mean that worship alone negates the need for service, evangelism, and mission. Rather, it emphasizes that there is no more vibrant arena for service, evangelism, and mission than in the context of worship.

Comprehensive Understanding of Worship

Discipleship training provides a profound and biblical reflection on worship, leading to a renewed understanding concerning worship, worshippers, and the outcomes of worship. Worship should be a place where we can offer all our thoughts to glorify God. "Worship is . . . a storage room of imagination where our love and longing grow."[2] When we begin to envision what kind of worship we can offer and how we offer it, we can eagerly anticipate worship with excitement and anticipation as we utilize all our imaginative faculties. Discipleship training cleanses our sin-contaminated thoughts through the work of the Holy Spirit, allowing us to approach the place of worship with a holy imagination. This is the outcome of Teleios Discipleship training. Through discipleship training, we can learn and offer worship in a new way, becoming more robust and mature as disciples of Christ. We become true worshippers, with abundant and fruitful practices in public and private worship.

Telios discipleship offers worship that is, above all, an offering of the highest and best. When God instructed the offering of an unblemished one-year-old lamb as the sacrifice for the Passover, it signified the highest dedication. What difference would this make when God does not lack anything? The point then of this offering is not to discuss what God needs but rather to shape and emphasize the attitude we should have in worship. The success of worship is determined by the holy anticipation for it even before the worship service begins.

Sunday Worship as a Weekly Celebration of the Resurrection, Not a Repetition of Rituals. Worship is participating in the life of Jesus Christ who annihilated sin and death. It is being present at the scene of resurrection, marveling at the empty tomb and the neatly folded graveclothes. Worship is also a jubilant celebration, rejoicing in the profound truth that, though we, as sinful beings deserving of destruction, now have full access to true life. Therefore, every worship we offer is a small Easter experience, a weekly celebration of the resurrection. Alister McGrath insightfully recognized that during true worship, the boundaries between heaven and earth are dissolved, and genuine worshippers experience the mystery of stepping onto the doorstep of heaven.[3] McGrath shows why weekly worship should become a small Easter and why we should engage in worship as such.

Yet, there are many cases where worship is no longer a celebration of what Christ has done to defeat death but an event that has morphed into a religious ritual. With this transgression of worship, people participate in empty liturgy while missing the encounter with the risen Jesus. How can we determine whether our worship is a small Easter or not? The Bible provides criteria: First, when listening to the Word, our hearts should burn within us (Luke 24:32). Second, there should be an overflow of joy. The Scriptures record that the disciples were overjoyed when they encountered the resurrected Jesus (Luke 24:41).

Worship as the Cleanser of the Secular Stains and a Transcendent Coronation Ceremony. We are all too susceptible to take on stains from the secularized world, soaked in the shame of past regrets. The term *image of God* means being marked with God's imprint, yet this mark has become too faint. Is there any way back? Is there any way to restore the glory of the soul as a child of the Creator God? Worship guides us along that path.

Looking at the Samaritan woman to whom Jesus went near the well of Sychar (John 4:9–38), we learn what kind of person a worshipper should be. When the Samaritan woman became aware of her sin, what did she prioritize? It was worship. When one truly receives grace and awakens to the light, they become a worshipper who first offers themselves entirely to God. Worship should be directed toward a personal, absolute being beyond my existence. In this sense, the significant transformation in the Samaritan woman's way of addressing Jesus is remarkable. In verse 9, she calls Jesus a "Jew," but in verse 11, she addresses him as "Sir." Later, in verse 19, she refers to him as a "prophet," and finally, in verse 29, she acknowledges him as the "Messiah" (CSB). The Samaritan woman's inner journey to find the object of worship portrays her shedding the stains of secularity and participating in the transcendent coronation ceremony of glory and grace inherent in worship. No matter how wretched the person, when they worship, they undergo a holy metamorphosis, putting on the radiant garment of God's children, testifying to the majestic and glorious reign of the King.

Worship Full of the Holy Elation of the Lamb's Wedding Feast. After history, the new heaven and new earth are revealed, and we look forward to the worship that will take place. The scene begins with the kings of the earth laying down their glory before King Jesus, the Christ of all kings (Rev. 21). There is no more resistance or hesitation against the authority of Christ. All the powers of the world surrender before the cosmic reign of Jesus, reaching the climax of worship. Worship is the feast of the Lamb, a celebration enjoyed only by those who acknowledge Jesus Christ as the Lamb chosen by God.

Discipleship aims for such worship. Worship should be a scene where the elation of the bride welcoming the Groom, Jesus, overflows. Worship is the Lord's banquet.[4] We participate in worship longing for the final fulfillment that will take place at the promised heavenly wedding feast.[5] Whether traditional or contemporary, worship is the banquet of the kingdom of God where all people participate regardless of the form of worship (Luke 13:29). It is a place where the daughters of Zion sing, rejoice, and exult with joy (Zeph. 3:14). Therefore, saints attending worship should enjoy the festive nature of worship.

When saints worship, their hearts must overflow with jubilation. Those hearts, pressed down by the world throughout the week, should be bursting with the holy joy of heaven. The festive nature of worship has always been my pastoral conviction and the spirit of worship since the day I began as a pastor. As a pastor, I consistently endeavored to make sure that no one goes home without grasping at least a drop of heavenly elation. This reflects the shepherd's heart of Jesus, who could not send the crowd away hungry (Matt. 15:32).

Worship: The Spirit-filled Space Where the Banner of Ego Tears Down

Stephen is the archetype of a true worshipper. Like Jesus, he was rejected by the world. His adversaries attempted to kill him, bringing him before the council when all other attempts proved unsuccessful—the same council where Jesus was tried. Like Jesus, Stephen was rejected and despised. However, in the very place where the world rejected him, Stephen was "full of the Holy Spirit" and saw "the glory of God, and Jesus standing at the right hand of God" (Acts 7:55). The worship we offer turns where we stand into a space filled with the Holy Spirit, allowing us to witness God's glory. It also allows us to follow Jesus even when we are faced with rejection from the world. The ultimate form of worship we pursue is none other than being filled with the abundance of Jesus and reproducing the likeness of Jesus.

The most significant feature of Teleios worship is the fullness of the Spirit. To be filled with the Spirit means, in a word, to be thoroughly broken in self-ego. It is to "tear down the banner of ego from top to bottom, just as the Lord tore the curtain of the temple from top to bottom."[6] What does it mean to tear down the banner of ego for the fullness of the Spirit? It is "to expel the trash accumulated over centuries from the time of Adam out of our hearts, emptying all the rooms of our hearts to welcome the heavenly guest."[7]

This is the power of the Spirit's fullness coming down from above. Just as the curtain is torn from top to bottom, there must be a rupture in our ego. Unless the victorious and arrogant self is broken, one cannot enter Spirit-filled worship. A person with an unbroken ego is like someone who keeps the door to their life shut even at the knocking of the Spirit, but a person with a broken ego is the one who opens the door to the Spirit. A person with an unbroken self is like someone who has turned over a vessel upside down. No matter how much rain pours, not a drop can be contained in the overturned vessel. However, when the vessel is turned back to its correct position, it can receive the pouring blessings of the Spirit like water. Worship is a time to recharge power. Instead of living a life trapped in limitations, struggling, and drying up like a wrung-out towel, a mature and fulfilling life dawns when we receive the overflowing grace of heaven through the cracks in our broken egos during worship.

Living like Cain Throughout the Week and Pretending to Be Abel Only on Sundays

The Bible views worship as a communal act from beginning to end. Solitary worship is something we have wrongly created. Anyone who is convinced that they can partake in the Word alone or understand the Word by themselves while persisting in isolated faith will quickly learn that something is significantly off. To prevent this, we must always be a part of communal worship. More importantly, we should enjoy the blessing of worshipping together in a glorious community all our lives. This is discipleship through worship. The motivation for us to participate in the fellowship and sending of the triune God is "not to achieve a sense of individual moral excellence or personal experience of God, but to worship God as a part of the community."[8]

Even when the Bible mentions "where two or three are gathered in my name" (Matt. 18:20), we should not simply view those two or three people as a small number. In Israel's legal system, the testimony of two or three witnesses could lead to the death penalty. The testimony of two or three people had significant legal and law-abiding power. The worship offered by two or three people thus reveals its public nature. Worship is a public act from start to finish. Hence, prioritize communal worship over individual worship and personal devotion.

However, keep in mind that you cannot live a Cain-like life throughout the week and then come to Sunday worship pretending to be an Abel. Conversely, someone who has lived the week as a righteous person like Abel would not dismiss the communal worship on Sunday as a solitary religious act. True worship and a complete spiritual life align precisely. Discipleship is not a program that stimulates religious knowledge or emotions; it is training to live a life in the presence of God.

Family Discipleship

Family discipleship is unfamiliar to many believers. Many commonly perceive that discipleship training is something handled in the church, under the guidance of pastors and alongside fellow trainees. Typical experiences at church often reinforce this view. However, the term *family discipleship* carries significant weight, not only for the family but also for the future of the church. What determines the future of the church? Today's state of European churches, where Christianity has declined dramatically, speaks volumes. The decline of European churches is attributed to the failure of passing down faith through generations.

Teleios Discipleship is a training effort that is seriously committed to passing down the parents' faith to their children and subsequently to the grandchildren. Jesus said, "For what will it profit a man if he gains the whole world and forfeits his soul? Or what shall a man give in return for his soul?" (Matt. 16:26). This translates to the idea that gaining the whole world but failing to pass down faith to the next generation is futile. Family discipleship serves the warning that if your wealth, fame, power, or possessions cannot aid the generational transmission of faith, they are merely illusions and dust.

"We are links in a longer chain, notes in a grander melody, scenes in a larger story. But among the long line of faith generations rooted in God, there is no link more critical to the next generation than ours. . . . As always, our greatest priority is to pass on something worth passing on to the next generation, in the direction of loyal commitment of allegiance to our Lord."[9] Without the transmission of faith through generations, no one will play the cosmic melody composed by God, or narrate the cosmic story revealed by God or narrate the cosmic story revealed by God. Who will bear the holy mission of being the connecting link in God's hands for the coming generations?

In the Bible, there is a tragic example of the failure of faithful generational succession. Jonathan, the descendant of the great spiritual leader Moses, became a priest of idolaters, leading to the complete disappearance of one tribe in Israel (Judg. 18:30). The tribe of Dan played no role in Israel's history thereafter, and even in Revelation 7, where the chosen tribes are counted, the name of the tribe of Dan cannot be found. The tragedy of the tribe of Dan, which vanished from the Bible due to the failure of faithful generational succession, serves as a dire warning to the church and faithful households today.

Discipleship Training: In the Home or for the Home?

Does family discipleship imply that those involved in discipleship training should behave well in their families? It goes beyond that. It means considering the family as an important arena for training as well as transforming the family through discipleship. Family discipleship means living as disciples of Jesus, evaluating all aspects of family life according to the values of a disciple, reforming it, bearing witness to the gospel to family members through words and actions, making the home the center of daily and life worship, and turning the home into a hub for evangelism to share the gospel with neighboring families.

There are reasons why the concept of discipling the family is still unfamiliar for many. First, there has been a tendency to confine faith or spiritual life to the public domain. The concept of discipling more personal areas, such as the family, was scarce because faith was seen as pertinent only to the limited domains like the social relationships outside the home, the church, a few doctrines, or specific issues. Despite acknowledging the need to minimize the gap between the faith expressed on Sundays and daily life, we have still neglected a deep exploration of why this gap exists and how to bridge it.

Second, more particularly in the Korean context, the remnants of Confucian notions, such as prioritizing public duties over private matters have persisted. Even if there were problems in the family, taking care of church "business" was considered a priority. Consequently, family matters were either avoided altogether or, if brought up, their importance was often downplayed. There is thus a natural tendency to still believe that prioritizing church work and service over personal issues reflects a strong faith. Moreover, in the context of first-generation discipleship training, many interpreted the goal of such training as "receiving training to become a core worker in the church" or harbored the notion that "without discipleship training, one cannot become a church leader." In such situations, the gap between discipleship training and the family inevitably widens.

Family Discipleship: Restoring Distorted Relationships, Remembering the Blessings of the Past Generation, and Bestowing them onto the Next Generation. Family discipleship is about restoring distorted relationships protruding through sinfulness and remembering the blessings of previous generations to pass them on to the next. In light of this, the family is not only an essential arena for discipleship training but also a benchmark for evaluating the success or failure of discipleship training. The reasons for discipling the family can be traced back to the ancestors of faith like Abraham. God's long and faithful response to the profound problem of sin revealed from Genesis 1 to 11 unfolds significantly from Genesis 12, continuing through Revelation 22. The initial solution God provided to overcome sin was a godly family that believed in God and His promise, following His will.[10] When God first called Abraham in Genesis 12, it might have looked like the calling of an individual, but as we progress to chapters 15, 17, and 22, we see God using a "family" trained through the covenant. This is evident in Genesis 18:19a, where God states, "For I have chosen him, that he may command his children and his household after him to keep the way of the LORD by doing righteousness and justice." The blessings, land, and the purpose for a renowned name that God gives to Abraham all aim at establishing a family that "[keeps] the way of the LORD by doing righteousness and justice."

Unlike Abraham and Isaac, Joseph did not directly receive God's promise through a personal encounter or vision. Although God appeared to him in dreams to reveal what He would do, Joseph did not receive the covenant promise directly from God as his ancestors did. Nevertheless, Joseph lived his life as if he had personally received God's promise, embracing the promises God made to the forefathers throughout his lifetime (Gen. 50:24).

Family Discipleship: An Urgent Duty of Disciples That Cannot be Delayed. Family discipleship is unavoidable for disciples. The Israelites have the Shema, beginning with the words "Hear, O Israel" (Deut. 6:4–9; 11:13–21; Num. 15:37–41). Jews, today, recite these words in daily prayers in their morning and evening worship. Israel never purposed to acquire a broader and more fertile land, a more powerful army, or to increase national wealth. The existence of Israel was rooted in raising devout descendants dedicated to God through their families, reflecting God thoroughly in every aspect of personal and social behavior. Raising a generation committed to God was nonnegotiable.

The Shema unequivocally and vividly speaks of family discipleship. First, the parental generation must disciple their children so that what they teach should be impressed on their hearts. Then, they must diligently teach it to their children. Not just any children but their children of their own. Additionally, it should not be sporadic teaching; it must be done "diligently." "Diligently" implies making discipleship a weighty mission. Family discipleship should be pursued wholeheartedly as if there is no reason for the existence of the family other than training the children. It must be done immediately, especially considering growing children do not wait for parents to be ready to train them.

Exemplary Family Discipleship Shown by Jesus and the Apostles

Some people mistakenly believe that Jesus disregarded family and prioritized faith unconditionally, citing statements like "If anyone comes to me and does not hate his own father and mother and wife and children and brothers and sisters, yes, and even his own life, he cannot be my disciple" (Luke 14:26) or "Who is my mother, and who are my brothers?" (Matt. 12:48). Jesus obediently followed and was raised by His earthly parents, Joseph and Mary, showing honor to them. As the eldest son, He faithfully fulfilled familial duties.

Luke 2 records an incident from Jesus's boyhood when He went to Jerusalem at the age of twelve for the Passover. The event concludes with the statement, "And he went down with them and came to Nazareth and was submissive to them" (Luke 2:51). It would be a mistake to skip verse 51 after seeing passages like "Why were you looking for me? Did you not know that I must be in my Father's house?" (Luke 2:49). As seen in verse 51, Jesus personally demonstrated how disciples should behave.

Another scene reveals Jesus emphasizing family and teaching how faith should manifest within a family. In the passage, Jesus, while on the cross, sees his mother and the disciple He loved standing nearby. He says to his mother, "Woman, behold, your son!" and to the disciple, "Behold, your mother!" From that moment, the disciple took her into his own home (John 19:26–27). Even in this agonizing moment, Jesus considered the well-being of His mother Mary. When he says, "Behold your son; behold your mother," Jesus is essentially saying, "Mother, this is your son, John, who will take care of you in my absence." Authenticity is proven in the family and completed through discipleship of the family.

The apostles wholeheartedly inherited the exemplary model shown by Jesus. Their letters primarily outline the conduct of saints within a family context, addressing various human relationships such as marriage, parent-child, and master-slave relationships (Eph. 5–6). The apostles recognized that the starting point of discipleship is the family.

To Succeed in Family Discipleship Training

Family discipleship training involves training the family as disciples of Christ and living as a disciple starting in the family. Deliberately aligning efforts in this direction and consistently pushing forward with focus constitutes family discipleship. In this regard, family discipleship requires several skeletal foundations. Family discipleship is not a romantic or an effortless process. If started incorrectly, it can yield mediocre results. These next ideas ensure a firm foundation and can help avoid such mediocrity.

First, while the format can be natural and free, there must be essential elements in training. Family discipleship training must include imparting and inputting the core message of the Word. This means that family discipleship training should provide solid biblical truths, a foundational worldview, and values to children and family members.[11] Despite the unpopularity of the term "inputting," it is crucial to teach God's Word and fundamental truths without compromise.

Second, a strong resolution is a must. Discipleship training, whether received by adults or teenagers, goes against the mainstream culture of society. This is what John Stott describes as the character of a radical disciple who is countercultural.[12] In family discipleship training, one must be prepared for children to become thorough outsiders, holy misfits, and even outcasts in the anti-God culture. A commitment to being a holy outsider and misfit, like Daniel, is necessary. On the other hand, family discipleship can instill a holy confidence in children, allowing them to stand confidently in public. Through discipleship training at home, children develop excellent and sociable leadership skills that can be demonstrated in school and the workplace (Prov. 22:29).

Third, one must emphasize the attitude of valuing the process over the results. We engage in family discipleship training for the glory of God. The goal should be to imprint not our image but the likeness of Jesus Christ on our children. One should cherish the process itself with a thankful heart, placing more importance on the journey than the outcome. In family discipleship, children may express resistance to authority, training, and discipline. However, parents should firmly hold onto the promises and the comfort found in the Word when facing the struggle for discipleship training in the family.

The main agents of family discipleship are not the church, school, or pastors; they are parents and grandparents. Parents and grandparents must work together to disciple the next generation. It is not a mission that can be delegated or passed on after fulfilling other missions. Family discipleship must be the top priority, the central focus of family life. It is not to be taken lightly or casually. It is an urgent and paramount mission that must be carried out promptly. Although it comes with great importance and heavy responsibility, one thing is clear: whether you are a parent with many years of experience or just starting, if you commit to starting family discipleship, the Lord will grant you strength, wisdom, opportunities, helping hands, and, above all, the joy that springs from the depths of your heart.

Strategies for Family Discipleship

Some statistics observe that about 50 percent of believers who attended church during their middle and high school years abandon their faith once they enter college.[13] Shockingly, in a telephone survey, more than ten thousand people responded that they used to attend church weekly during their youth but now rarely or never attend at all. Among those who no longer consider the Bible as truth, 40 percent doubted during middle school, 44 percent during high school, and 11 percent experienced doubts in college.[14] Children are being taken away from the spiritual battle much earlier than we think.

What can we do about children who abandon their faith? How can they be kept in the faith? We must work to plead with them that life is not merely a struggle for what becomes of them and what is gained for their comfort. We must persuade them that their lives are but rather a process of achieving the purpose for which God has sent them to this earth. Adolescence is heavily influenced by peer groups, and it is essential to encourage young individuals to resist the unbelieving influences and pressures of their peers. It is vital to introduce tools for family discipleship that consider grandparents, parents, children, and grandchildren in a four-generational context.

Family Worship. People often ask me, "How did your family get involved in church planting for generations? How did you become a household of faith with a legacy?" My response is that I received the blessings of family worship from my forebearers. From a young age, both corporate worship and family worship at home were ingrained in me. I can confidently say that the basic structure of my faith and the roots of my discipleship philosophy were established in the family worship I participated in since childhood.

Through family worship, one realizes that raising children to be "blameless and innocent, children of God without blemish in the midst of a crooked and twisted generation, among whom you shine as lights in the world" (Phil. 2:15) is never achieved by human strength alone. Family worship may not be popular, and it may seem rigid and boring today. Yet, family worship can be a way to train children to swim against the currents of the world as an adventurous undertaking. It nurtures them to gain the trait that solely relies on God's inspiration, wisdom, and power for their lives. Believers who recognize God's sovereignty will consider family worship as a significant starting point for family discipleship training.

Family worship not only vitalizes God's church but also brings transformation to society as a whole. John Calvin emphasized that parents teaching children in the home is an absolute duty, viewing the absence of religious education in children as a form of negligence worthy of correction.[15] Martin Luther referred to parents as the "shepherds" who were appointed to lead their households. Those Christians with adherence to the reformed faith, considering themselves heirs of the Reformation, saw family worship as a key to renewing both the church and the nation. For Puritans, it was before meals, for Dutch Reformed church members, it was after meals—times varied but all of them engaged in simple family worship.

Family worship must become a holy routine before it becomes any formal order or obligatory requirements. It should naturally find its place in the daily life of a family. Occasionally, the entire family can gather comfortably on a bed to engage in excellent family worship through singing, prayer, and Scripture memorization. Such family worship, woven into the fabric of everyday life, can leave a lasting impression on children as sweet memories. Every moment in family life can become an opportunity for family worship.

Four Generations Together in Worship. At SaRang Church, we gather four generations to worship together every Saturday morning at the Saturday Early Morning Vision Prayer Meetings. Having all four generations worship together forms the foundation of family discipleship. Why four generations? In terms of human lifespan and social structure, it is the most realistic unit for a household to worship together. Even if grandparents, parents, children, and grandchildren do not live in the same house, the widespread adoption of weekend breaks makes it possible for them to gather for worship if there is a will.

Even in the Bible, four generations are seen as essential for the proper establishment of faith in a family (Gen. 12–50). Abraham was a pioneer who advanced in faith holding firmly to God's covenant; Isaac fortified the covenant through gentleness and humble obedience; Jacob expanded the covenant from generation to generation; and Joseph, by bringing the covenant to an international stage, laid the foundation for the nations to enter God's blessing as Abraham was promised. Four generations of faith can be a clear demonstration of faithful transmission of the blessings of God's kingdom.

The key to this ministry is the "worship of generations." As God forbids idolatry and the making of images in the first and second commandment, he emphasizes, "You shall not bow down to them or serve them, for I the Lord your God am a jealous God, visiting the iniquity of the fathers on the children to the third and the fourth generation of those who hate me" (Exod. 20:5b). Here, the "third and fourth generation" refers to an extended family that lived together in Israel. If the worship in a household does not hold its place, no member of that family can lead a Teleios life.

For this reason, I have consistently emphasized the importance of families coming together to worship on Saturday mornings at the Saturday Early Morning Vision Prayer Meetings. Recently, I have even distributed prayer staff to symbolize Moses's staff that parted the Red Sea to families with their own designated numbers to encourage participation. I continue to urge four generations in the family to come out to worship because of the burning desire of a shepherd's heart to help saints grow spiritually. It is because of the tremendous blessings found when the four generations of faith join in prayer.

Over the past forty years of ministry, I have observed and experienced the spiritual succession of children through the earnest prayers of parents attending these prayer meetings. This experience aligns with biblical truth. First Samuel 7 recounts the famous history of Ebenezer at Mizpah. In verse 10, when Samuel offered a burnt offering, the Philistines came out to fight against Israel. Yet, "the Lord thundered with a mighty sound that day against the Philistines and threw them into confusion, and they were defeated before Israel." What we cannot fail to recognize is the connection this victory has with Hannah's prayer in 1 Samuel 2:10: "The adversaries of the LORD shall be broken to pieces; against them he will thunder in heaven." The prayer and praise offered by Hannah in the past find continuity in the present with the prayer of her son Samuel, resulting in the victory of Ebenezer. When the curtain of Ebenezer is lifted, we find the living manifestation of God's mighty power becoming a written history for God's people—as a mother's prayer is answered by a son's prayer.

What happens when generations come together to pray and worship? Through the time families gather to worship and pray together at Saturday Early Morning Vision Prayer Meeting, generational succession of faith occurs, ordinary lives transform into extraordinary lives through divine intervention, and discarded stone-like lives turn into cornerstone lives. Saturday Early Morning Vision Prayer Meeting erases generational gaps between parents and children, even grandparents and grandchildren. It produces an experience of transformation, a change in countenance, and the cultivation of holy habits and environments. It allows for the families to gain spiritual balance that equips one with the power to lead the times.

Holy Flame That Erases Generational Differences: Scripture Memorization. While traveling in Lystra, Paul encountered a remarkable household—Timothy's family. Timothy, likely born of a Hellenistic father and a Jewish mother named Eunice, was raised in a unique family. His grandmother Lois, possibly a Greek, had been teaching him the Scriptures from a young age: "And how from childhood you have been acquainted with the sacred writings" (2 Tim. 3:15). Recognizing the significance of this, Paul entrusted Timothy with the responsibility of overseeing the churches in Lystra and Iconium. Timothy, Paul's faithful disciple and a spiritual worker of the gospel, had been nurtured with a knowledge of the Scriptures from his early years.

In a child's spiritual education, Scripture memorization constitutes a crucial part. However, an even more critical piece in this education is the practical application of the memorized Word. It is stated, "If one memorizes the Scriptures, carrying them on the tip of his tongue but does not obey them, he is no different from a shepherd who counts other people's sheep, yet does not possess even a single calf himself!"[16] Scripture memorization and obedience are the two wheels interdependently needed to establish Teleios disciples.

Bible Memorization Is the Ultimate Asymmetric Strategy

While Bible memorization may seem like an ancient educational method, it is, in fact, the ultimate asymmetric strategy for believers to overcome the challenges of this atheistic era. Without making excuses or leaving room for evasions, parents must teach their children according to the unequivocal and authoritative Word of God, teaching them who God is and what He does. Through the Scriptures, children can accurately learn about the identity of Jesus Christ. Knowledge of Christ is not mere cognitive information; it penetrates the hearts of children, igniting a flame in them. Once this flame is kindled, children will live their lives as people who personally know the Bible. When they learn from the Scriptures how to hear God's Word and how to live accordingly, our children will become the blessed person described in Psalm 1.

Consider Deuteronomy 6:6, where the command is to impress God's Word on the hearts. What does it mean to engrave God's Word on the heart? It means memorization. Who does the memorization? It is the parents. Why do parents memorize the Word? To teach it to their children and to share it.

It is said that even today in traditional Jewish households, there is no generation gap between grandfathers and grandsons because they share the same faith, values, language, and traditions, regardless of age. If parents can memorize and fill their heads and hearts with Bible verses together with their children, the family will not only eliminate generational differences but also ensure the transmission of faith through generations.

In Jewish tradition, the coming-of-age ceremony, known as Bar Mitzvah for boys and Bat Mitzvah for girls, takes place at the age of thirteen. However, the significance of the age thirteen lies not in physical maturity but in the spiritual preparation that precedes it. Jewish parents actively teach and encourage their children to memorize the Torah from the moment they are born until the age of twelve. The goal is for the Torah to be fully ingrained in their lives.

At SaRang Church, we take a similar approach. At the age of thirteen, we hold a spiritual adulthood ceremony for our students. At the age of eighteen, we hold a ceremony for sending the next generation as missionaries to colleges and the world. The ceremonies for the thirteen-year-olds prompt the children to consider their relationship with God personally, urging them to take responsibility for their faith. It is a moment of blessing that empowers them to be individuals who carry their faith with a sense of ownership. The ceremony at the age of eighteen is a festive occasion where young adults are encouraged to embrace their roles as mission bearers in the broader community such as their campus and the society at large.

Parents who release their children on a safari in Africa without any preparation would be severely criticized. But how would we feel if Christians were doing the same without taking notice? Christian families indeed are sending their children into the anti-Christian secular jungle without adequate spiritual preparation. It is essential to equip children spiritually so that they can uphold their faith on their own.

The Final Puzzle Piece of Faith Succession

While it is typical for children raised under spiritually excellent parents to inherit a strong faith, there are unfortunate cases where the parents' faith does not necessarily pass on to their children automatically. It goes to prove that mere demonstration of the parents' faith is not a quick and easy solution to the succession of faith. The crucial puzzle piece that children need to experience from their parents is not just the good experience of faith but the grace embedded in their lives. Demonstration of good Christian lifestyle and life filled with experiences of God's grace appear the same, but they are two distinct matters.

Faith succession, above all, lies in parents revealing their conviction of God's grace in their lives. I still vividly remember seeing my parents singing the song "Nearer My God to Thee," sitting together by the window during their toughest times of the church. Growing up, I knew they knew God's grace. This became an unseen force that helped me preserve my faith during my turbulent adolescent years.

There is a difference between Sunday attendance as a family and being captivated by the blessings of God in worship as a family. Presenting tithes and offerings that capture the faith confession of a family, as well as the moments of family worship in Word and prayer are all those flashes of blessings that the family can cherish together. What children need to see is the parents' authentic pursuit of the blessed presence of God. For all parents aspiring for the succession of faith, these blessed moments and recognition of God's grace must flow from parents to children. Grace through faith has no expiration date, but grace to be enjoyed after being saved does have one.

Teleios Discipleship training teaches the children to long for the unexpired fresh blessings. Genuine Teleios family discipleship training teaches and imprints God's grace in their hearts so that this flow of blessings will ever be fresh in their lives.

For Discipleship Training That Takes Root in the Unconscious

As we enter the twenty-first century, we are witnessing a significant decline in children and youth ministry attendance, far exceeding the rate of population decrease. However, even more disheartening is the church's helpless posture. Some churches are quick to resign themselves to the back-seat, watching these cultural trends as an inevitability. Some propose greater efforts in nurturing Christian elites as a solution, and while this may be a valid strategy, no one is crystal clear in articulating how to cultivate them.

None of these challenges can be properly addressed without letting the faith take such deep root in the unconscious—to a degree where loyalty to Christ becomes an innate nature of a Christian. Boldness to overcome the rough waves of the world is only possible when there is a firm identity rooted in unwavering faith.

Sanctifying the Consciousness Before Words and Actions. Actions speak louder than words, and there is little doubt about it, but what is more important than actions is one's consciousness. Every revolution or practical change that transformed the world began from inner conviction or ideologization. This is precisely why education in children's ministry is crucial. Educating children to develop the gospel-shaped consciousness must begin during this early period for it to take root deeply and effectively. I wonder if children from Christian households were to engage in religious debates with Jewish or even Muslim children, it is not easy to picture our children dominating the debate against them. Our lack of preparation is perceivable even without seeing that debate in action.

When we engage in discipleship training, we can overly accommodate what others think or feel: "Could this come off too coercive? Could it feel like an attempt to brainwash?" Perhaps what is ultimately hindering the consciousness transformation of discipleship training is our excessive caution and concerns for reception. Biblically speaking, the instillation of consciousness saturated with the gospel can be expressed as the "holy stump" in Isaiah 6:13. The worldly forces may be rampant in the world like the dancing blades of a skilled butcher, and sometimes those swings of the butcher will cut down some branches. However, those who have internalized the gospel in their consciousness have a holy stump within them that cannot be cut down.

Training methods and practical actions are important, but to cultivate witnesses of the gospel, the most crucial aspect is to internalize the gospel in the heart and mind. It is a process akin to conscientization and ideologization but done with the gospel. This forms the foundation that the church must grasp for the sake of evangelization of a nation. In history, changes in the destiny of nations and people have often been brought about by a few individuals with heightened consciousness and ideologization. Why not do the same with the power of the gospel? If individuals transformed by the Word became holy revolutionaries, we will come to witness history being rewritten by the power of the kingdom. Discipleship training is a holy revolution in consciousness. This must begin as early as possible.

How to Share the Gospel with an Apathetic Generation. The language and thought patterns of the millennials are entirely different from those of previous generations. Technology is a natural part of their bodies. Their parent's generation struggles with decoding trendy street vocabulary. They feel more comfortable with light, surface-level relationships rather than deep connections. Millennials are known to express their opinions boldly, yet they may have multiple faces depending on social media accounts or even physical places. Unlike the previous generations, they are referred to as the first globally synchronized generation to appear worldwide simultaneously.

Approaching these individuals who differ in language, thought, and communication style beyond generational gaps is challenging when merely using the language and thoughts of the older generation. For them, having fun is the first, second, and third priority. So, how can we inscribe the profound meaning of the gospel into the hearts of those who prioritize fun above all else? How can we shake their emotions and souls more powerfully than any form of entertainment? In a rapidly changing world, delivering the gospel without addressing these concerns is like sending a love letter to an outdated address.

Ministers must listen to the heartbeat of the millennials and the alpha generations using a stethoscope, searching for the depth of their souls.[17] This challenge, combining decades of pastoral ministry, has led me to deep reflection and contemplation. The more I ponder, the clearer the solution becomes. Only the gospel with the anointing of the Holy Spirit possesses the power to break through the strong shell of their fun.

Workplace Discipleship

Why Do We Work in the First Place?

We often like to associate work with the consequences of the Fall, as if the first humans lived idly in the garden of Eden until they were bored and decided to indulge in the fruit of the tree of the knowledge of good and evil. However, that is far from the truth. "Be fruitful and multiply and fill the earth and subdue it, and have dominion over the fish of the sea and over the birds of the heavens and over every living thing that moves on the earth" (Gen. 1:28). When the sovereign Creator of the universe commanded, prefall Adam and Eve would have immediately obeyed God's command with all their heart, strength, and will. Considering prefall Adam and Eve as merely idling in the garden of Eden is a disregard for the depiction of the "working God" and his "to-do list" in Genesis 1 and 2. God is introduced as the "one who works" in the first chapter of the Bible, and as those made in His image, we share His nature.

Achieving a Mission Through Work Produces True Humans

In response to the question, 'Why do we work in the first place?' John Stott provides these three reasons.[18] First, we work for our accomplishments. Work is essential for self-expression for humans, who, as beings made in the image of God, rule on behalf of God. Second, we work for the community's benefit. Third, we work for God's glory.

Work shapes us into true humans. When we work, when we express ourselves through work, and when we reveal God's true goodness, we give Him glory. The one who sows and waters to make things grow is none other than God. Luther expressed this truth by saying, "God milks the cows through the vocation of the milkmaid."[19] In this way, if we do not work, God's goodness and glory will not be revealed. There is a saying about work that should be etched in our minds: "The quantity of work is not important. What truly matters is how much of the work God demands you have done."[20] This statement indicates where the priority of work lies for believers. The "future resume" of a believer is determined not by the world's concerns but by how and how much they execute God's concerns.

Jesus's Philosophy of Work

It appears that Jesus worked as a carpenter for at least twenty years (Matt. 13:55; Mark 6:3). How would Jesus have approached His work of carpentry? A significant clue is found in John 5:17, where Jesus states, "My Father is working until now, and I am working." Jesus had a profound conviction that what He did was the work of God. He did not stop there; He worked alongside God. He worked with the assurance that He was not alone but working in the presence of Father God. Moreover, Jesus's carpentry work was about serving people and laying the foundation for life. The Lord engaged in His work with the consciousness of participating in God's creative work and ensuring the completion of the tasks of creation. As disciples of Jesus, we should approach our work with the same consciousness, recognizing that "the labor of a Christian is a holy participation in God's creative work."[21]

When we believe in Jesus and become children of God, our work takes on new meaning. In Genesis 3, when Adam sinned, the result was death. The earth was cursed to produce thorns and thistles, and humans had to toil for survival. Greek philosophers viewed work with such disdain that it was considered a curse. However, the moment we become God's people, our work is renewed. Just as death is not a curse for those who are in Jesus but a transformation into the glory with the entrance into the eternal home, in the same way, our work is no longer a cursed hardship but redeemed as participation in God's creative work.

Shalom That Dawns in the World of Work

Although work itself has no inherent evil, significant ruptures have occurred in the world of work due to human corruption. Even those without faith acknowledge and strive to rectify the alienation and conflicts manifesting in the realm of work. Their often-employed method is revolution. However, we emphatically declare that such approaches cannot overcome the brokenness in the world of work. Colossians 3:22–23 (ESVUK) instructs, "Slaves, obey in everything those who are your earthly masters, not by way of eye-service, as people-pleasers, but with sincerity of heart, fearing the Lord. Whatever you do, work heartily, as for the Lord and not for men." This verse instructs that we are never to dismiss work itself or superficially try to overthrow a system no matter how severe disparities or irrationalities are found.

This passage may seem to endorse slavery and place undue obligations on slaves, seemingly taking the master's perspective unilaterally. However, the intention is not to approve of slavery but to present Christianity as a life-transforming gospel that overcomes the prevailing social norms, including slavery. History shows how Christianity has inspired societies to protect and care for not only slaves but also other vulnerable groups such as the disabled, women, the elderly, and those suffering. How could welfare for the poor, basic rights, and human rights have developed? The transformative power of the gospel has naturally led these societies to actively protect and uphold the rights of those marginalized. All of these protections have been influenced and shaped by Christian principles.

In the biblical context, slaves were in a dehumanizing position, akin to brute animals, with nowhere to descend further down in social status. Yet, the directive to work diligently for masters takes on a redemptive meaning. If the work were only about pleasing earthly masters, it might seem unfair and challenging. However, when they work, their true Master is ultimately the Father God. Therefore, loyalty to the heavenly Master becomes the enduring legacy of their service at work. This reality encouraged slaves to be faithful, honest, and loyal at their work all the while being encouraged by the fact that their heavenly Father knows all that they do. In this way, this biblical instruction went beyond providing comfort to the hearts of slaves; it proclaimed that God, the true Master, would reward them, as shown in verse 24. The earthly master may offer commendation, but God provides the ultimate reward because they are no longer wretched slaves but workers "serving the Lord Christ."

The Bible may not directly denounce the colonialism, cruel dictatorship, and inhumane slave system of Rome. However, recognizing that true historical change and the elevation of the soul begin with the liberation of slaves, the Lord waited patiently to see His disciples exert a positive influence until the time when they could bring about change. As the time came, the institution of slavery was socially overcome through the redeemed people of God.

The right to be able to work, as well as labor rights, are a message from the Creator God who enabled labor in the first place. Labor rights are the fundamental human rights of individuals created in the image of God as coworkers with God. "God who cares for every facet of his creation, made us co-laborers with him, allowing us to identify and utilize knowledge to create new and amazing things. God has designed a complex plan for us to express our unique identity as humans through work, fulfilling the needs of life, and contributing to our neighbors. Labor rights are basic human rights."[22] However, the right to work has been subverted by the greed of sin. The devil fostered Mammonism to flourish, turning what was originally neutral into the root of all evil (1 Tim. 6:10). This unbiblical love of money corrupted even the human right of labor into a tool of greed that brought the tragedy that undermines rights concerning work. Since the Industrial Revolution in Britain, work has degenerated into a cruel means of destroying rights, as it became the driving force that caused Marx to rise against the capitalists. The advent of atheistic Marxism is undoubtedly a historical tragedy; yet we must let this tragedy teach Christians why we work in the first place. All that now surrounds work propels us to both capture the importance of discipleship training for the sake of workspaces and awaken the believers to live out their discipleship at work.

Workplace Discipleship Training That Turns Work into Worship

Workplace discipleship training is not a job placement initiative. It is not about connecting mentors and mentees in a professional network. Workplace discipleship training is training for a transformation of perspective through faith. If so, what kind of mindset should disciples have as they engage in workplace discipleship training?

First, it is the mindset of the priesthood (1 Pet. 2:9). The people of God, Israel, see the path of their mission open by standing in solidarity with the weak (the hungry, the suffering), and connecting with them through their existence and life (Isa. 58:10–12). At such times, light is promised, precise guidance from God is given, and they become successors who carry on the righteous tradition. Although it may seem counterintuitive to ask, "Who can I help when I am struggling too?" the people of God can find a sense of accomplishment in fulfilling the mission given by God by turning their attention to the hungry, suffering, and those in difficult circumstances.

Second, it is the mindset of an agent. In Jesus's statement, "My Father is working until now, and I am working" (John 5:17), there is an implication that the work Jesus does is the work of God. Jesus thoroughly identified Himself as the Son of God and the agent of God the Father in His relationship with God. Our work is not done alone, but God is working in, with, and through us. Furthermore, the goal of everything God does is the establishment and sending of the kingdom. Our goal in work is to emulate God by building up others, loving them, and bringing healing.

Third, it is the mindset of mutuality. The apostolic exhortation, "Bondservants, obey in everything those who are your earthly masters" (Col. 3:22), is not given unilaterally to the slaves. The Bible says, "Masters, treat your bondservants justly and fairly" (Col. 4:1). It is not an easy task for masters to treat their slaves with justice and fairness. However, there is a source of strength given to the masters to obey this command: "Knowing that you also have a Master in heaven" (Col. 4:1). At that time, slaves or bondservants were considered expendable, and there was no reason or need to treat them justly and fairly. Yet, the reason masters could do so was that they also had a Master in heaven. In other words, they, too, had a Master. When the ultimate authority, Jesus Christ, is consciously recognized by both employers and employees, the age-old issue of labor relations may find a new horizon of resolution.

Fourth, it is the mindset of Christlike practice (Matt. 28:19). Workplace discipleship training aims to raise disciples who resemble Jesus in the workplace. It aims to nurture them to follow His methods and to know how to carry out the works that Jesus did for the world. Therefore, it is necessary to cultivate individuals whose practice at work differs from the world. Moreover, workplace discipleship training must instill a firm attitude toward everything that defiles God's temple, or our bodies. When coworkers witness our spiritual transparency, humility, boldness, and integrity, it becomes a form of evangelism. It is essential to help disciples recognize work as an act of worship in the context of life and to internalize the idea that perceives worship as work and work as worship. When work becomes worship, the task that was corrupted and distorted by Adam's sin is redeemed as an activity that is done with God who also works, with the delight that God shares through work.

Missions Discipleship

Youthful Dream I Dreamt as I Embraced the Globe

Almost a century ago, in the mid-1970s, carrying the youthful aspirations in my heart, I left my hometown and headed to Seoul. As I boarded the train, my father handed me an envelope. Naturally, I assumed it contained money for either my tuition or living expenses for my new life in the big city. I sat down in my seat on the train, and shortly after the train departed from the platform. Waving goodbyes to my parents as they disappeared out the window, I grasped the envelope in my hand, looking forward to opening this surprise gift. I imagined if my father had inserted a few months' worth of living expenses in this envelope, I knew it would have been a substantial sacrifice on his part, knowing what kind of economic situation my family was in. I also knew that it would be more than what I expected, but what I found inside almost knocked me out of my seat. Inside the envelope was nothing but a sheet of paper containing verses from 1 Corinthians 6:19–20, "Or do you not know that your body is a temple of the Holy Spirit within you, whom you have from God? You are not your own, for you were bought with a price. So glorify God in your body."

Despite being a poor student who could not even easily indulge in instant noodles, there was a church where I felt comfortable. I came to enjoy worship every Sunday and time with brothers and sisters in fellowship. This church eventually functioned as a pivotal point in my life and ministry. This church was Naesoodong Church.

I found shelter in an unadorned apartment in Yongsan with a couple of brothers in Christ who were also new to Seoul. It was a seven-story cement slab building without an elevator, heated by a coal boiler. It was a genuinely humble communal residence where power and water outages were frequent and normal. We named the place "L'Abri"(French for "shelter"), inspired by the small community "L'Abri" that Francis Schaeffer started in Switzerland. Along with the brothers I met, we began living together in spiritual community.

In winter, we carried coal on our backs climbing up seven stories by foot for heating, and in summer, we cooled ourselves in front of an old fan. Although the living conditions were harsh, we carried highly disciplined lives and strived to maintain the purity of our hearts. Even before quiet time was popularized, we started reading and meditating on a few pages of the Scripture regularly on weekdays and a few more on Sundays, then worshipping the Lord corporately. There was a special element incorporated into our worship. Placing a globe in the center, we would place our hands on the globe and pray for the nations and peoples. We had no food, the future seemed uncertain, and nothing was stable in our lives. Yet, strangely, when we prayed for world missions, tears flowed. A group of men, six in total, with their hands on a globe, praying and shedding tears is the moment I still vividly recall like it was yesterday. Looking back, it was quite a scene.

The Message Proclaimed in Edinburgh by That Young Man

In June 1910, 1,215 global mission leaders gathered in Edinburgh, Scotland, for a mission conference. Of course, the leaders who led the conference were Western Christians. Among the gathered, non-Western participants were only eighteen, accounting for 1.5 percent of the total attendees. Fast forward one hundred years, the one-hundredth-anniversary event of this conference was held in April 2010 at the University of Edinburgh. This anniversary was special because it signified the shift of Christianity's center from the Western to the non-Western world over the century.

God works in mysterious ways and with great wit. A poor and clueless young man, who used to pray with his hands on a globe in a coal-heated apartment during the winter, was chosen to deliver a message on the first evening of the 2010 Edinburgh Mission Conference. He spoke at the

Thirdrd General Assembly of the World Reformed Fellowship commemorating the one-hundredth anniversary, under the title "Biblical Living Hope for the Twenty-First-Century Church." I humbly expressed my gratitude, recalling the feelings I had when I prayed with my hands on the globe at Yongsan L'Abri, remembering the missionaries who came to Korea a hundred years ago. Here are some excerpts from that message:

"A century ago, just like the faithful forerunners who gathered in Edinburgh, we have gathered here with the same hearts. Our calling is no different from what it was one hundred years ago. . . . The world may be in chaos, but the redeemed people proclaim a hope not of this world but of heaven. Christianity is marked by the Living Hope declared in despair. A country that had no hope has become a nation that sends twenty-two thousand missionaries worldwide, because of the noble sacrifices of missionaries that shed their blood and tears in the Korean peninsula."

In 1910, Korea was under Japanese colonial rule, and Christians constituted only 1–2 percent of the population. But after one hundred years, in 2010, God allowed an ordinary Korean pastor like myself to share a message on missions in Edinburgh where global church leaders gathered. It was an event that made me capture God's way of interweaving human history to culminate in the history of God's mission.

Beyond a Missionary-Sending Church to Becoming a Church with a Missional Presence

"Which came first, the church or missions?" Many people might scratch their heads. For some, the answer may be too intuitive, "Doesn't mission exist because there was a church?" However, strictly speaking, that is not the case. The church was born because of the mission on this earth. Of course, one could argue that since the church sends out missionaries, the church comes first. But if we go back to the origin, we find the missional God, the one who "is a missionary."[23] The church is born because we have God who is missional and who is a missionary.

Can we claim that God is a missionary? Isn't mission something humans do? Not exactly. The mission is the goal of God, the Creator, who desires worship from all people on earth as the Redeemer and Judge. "I am the Lord; that is my name; my glory I give to no other, nor my praise to carved idols" (Isa. 42:8). Mission invites all human beings on this earth to confess him as Lord. Yet, the Bible reveals that before any missionary or mission works, God is the one who has a profound interest in receiving the worship of the people.

God, who created the entire universe, establishes a people, a servant (or a nation), to break the chains of oppression and the shackles of slavery, bringing them back to Himself—this act is the mission. Through this perspective, we can perceive Jesus Christ as a missionary. The people of Israel, whom God formed through His character and ministry, are also missionaries. The church, which is the fulfillment of the ancient people of Israel under the finished work of the servant of God, is a missionary. The church is inherently missional from its inception (John 20:21). The church did not engage in missionary work; rather, God initiated the mission, and the church was created. God has a great interest in receiving glory for Himself and desires to proclaim this work through His Spirit-filled servant, liberating and gathering His people who will continuously declare and move forward in this work.

The church of God was established with the purchase made by the blood of Jesus (1 Cor. 6:20). Jesus fulfills all of God's desires for the humanity and the world through His work on the cross. As God fulfilled His will toward humanity and the world through the cross, Jesus Christ ascended to the right hand of God's throne, so that the church may now be sent. The church should now understand that the most fitting response, as she is led by the Holy Spirit to become the missional presence in the world.

Reexamining the Great Commission and Missions Discipleship

There is no doubt that Matthew 28:19–20 is a key passage that illuminates the mission and purpose of the church. However, there is room for disagreement regarding the dynamics and meaning of the missionary-discipleship relationship as presented in the original Greek text, which may not have been fully captured in the translation. Let us first examine the shortcomings in the translation.

"Go therefore and make disciples of all nations, baptizing them in the name of the Father and of the Son and of the Holy Spirit, teaching them to observe all that I have commanded you. And behold, I am with you always, to the end of the age" (Matt. 28:19–20). In both verses, five important verb groups are present in these two verses: "go, make, baptize, teach, observe." Naturally, our attention is often drawn to "go" because we have learned that "mission equals the act of going." Hence, the missionary slogan, participate in missions either by "going or sending" gets popularized.

However, there is one surprising fact. We might think that mission is only fulfilled when we "go," but the main verb here is "make disciples," and the rest are participles. While the translation renders "go, baptize, teach, observe" as if they are also main verbs alongside "make disciples," the original text does not support this translation. Therefore, these verses can be translated faithfully separating the imperative and principles as follows: "Make disciples—by going to all nations, by baptizing them in the name of the Father and of the Son and of the Holy Spirit, by teaching them, and by observing all that I have commanded you."

Making disciples is the primary action, and the participles "going, baptizing, teaching, observing" describe how disciples are made. Interpreting the Great Commission with a proper understanding of the relationship between main verbs, participles, and infinitives brings a significant shift in its meaning. When we fail to see "make disciples" as the main verb, the emphasis tends to be on the act of "going," and making disciples is seen as something to be done after going. However, when we recognize "make disciples" as the main verb and the rest as participles and infinitives, a profound change occurs.

First, the definition of mission undergoes a complete transformation. Establishing schools, erecting hospitals, building churches, and providing leadership education to locals are important. However, these activities are not the essence of the mission. The core of the Christian mission is discipleship. Without it, any other splendid deeds are futile. Properly interpreting the Great Commission brings a revolutionary change in mission consciousness.

Second, when "make disciples" is considered the main verb and the rest as participles, we understand that going, baptizing, teaching, and observing are methods and effective tools for making disciples. Making disciples becomes the primary task, and other activities are seen as means to accomplish this central mission. If it becomes necessary for the sake of making disciples, we can go more, baptize more, or teach more—depending on what is required for the effective realization of disciple-making. Or it could be the other way around as well: if we need to wait rather than go, or do not see public baptism to be in the best timing for the sake of making disciples, we can exercise freedom to focus on other aspects of ministry if it serves the purpose of discipleship as the primary goal.

Third, a new translation of the Great Commission highlights the scope, content, and results of the mission. Jesus said, "Go," but to whom? Jesus's instruction to go to "all nations" tells us the answer, not just countries but intricately classified ethnic groups.[24]

Last, teaching to observe the commandments of Jesus shows exactly what kind of community the mission should result in. The newly found community resulting from the missional works is established by the Word. It is a particular community that is marked by love for God with all their mind, resolve, and life, all the while sincerely caring for neighbors. They consistently pursue this love in every circumstance. The correct relationship between the mission and discipleship produces a community that wholeheartedly loves God with mind, heart, and soul and genuinely cares for the neighbors in all contexts.

The correct outcome of the mission, as depicted by this new community, is achieved through the continuous practice of a disciple's life. This involves living out a life that mirrors the qualities of a genuine disciple, perpetually inviting people into this new community. This is the essence of the missional discipleship training.

Inseparable Twin Pillars: Discipleship and the Great Commission. Discipleship training and missions cannot be separated (Matt. 28:19; John 20:21). Jesus did not command His disciples to go until their training was complete. Even after receiving the command to go, the disciples stumbled and made mistakes. Yet, neither their calling nor discipleship was canceled as a result. Hence, we must see that the completion of discipleship and the fulfillment of the missional calling are ultimately under the sovereignty of Jesus Christ, not subject to our self-assessment.

By carefully meditating on what we explored above, it becomes evident that the places where Jesus commanded to go were not just cross-cultural locations but rather within one's own culture, lifestyle, and finely divided communities and local societies. Without the development of character through discipleship training, one cannot handle the "missions" in their everyday surroundings.

When we carefully examine the calls to mission in the Synoptic Gospels, we can see that the concepts of going, sending, and disobedience are not separate. In other words, there is no intentional categorization of the groups that are going, sending, or simply sitting. In the eyes of Jesus, all disciples were commissioned as missionaries (Luke 9:2; 10:1); no one can dare volunteer oneself to the "sitting out" category. However, the question arises: "Where should one go?" Jesus commanded His followers to go to the entire created world. Here we cannot ignore Abraham Kuyper's concept of sphere sovereignty. Reaching other cultures is not the only form of mission. Bringing Christ's kingship to places where Christ is not yet reigning is an excellent form of mission and precisely aligns with the purpose of discipleship training. Disciples living out their discipleship in their bounds, striving to become like Jesus in every aspect of life, is identical to a missional living that aims to make Christ the King in every aspect of life. Both of their purposes are essentially the same.

Discipleship training and missions are not separate, though differences in appearance or framework may exist. After recognizing that the content of discipleship should be missional, SaRang Church made changes in the discipleship training curriculum. Study topics such as "God's Mission," "Church, the Spiritual Israel Called to Be a Light to the Nations," and other biblical theology of mission were incorporated into the studies in the program. The focus extended beyond biblical and theological foundation of missions. During the summer, all who are enrolled in discipleship and leadership training at SaRang Church participate in a mandatory short-term missions trip. They are sent off to various sites of missional work both domestic and overseas. The impact was significant. Those who went to assist missionaries ended up receiving more than they were able to give. Witnessing God who goes ahead is truly astonishing, which becomes a living curriculum for discipleship training.

Why Should the Gospel Go Outward?[25]

One cannot think of discipleship without the consciousness of being sent. Jesus, who was sent from the Father God to us (John 1:14), sent the Holy Spirit to us and also sends us into the world (John 20:21). Discipleship training and mission can be considered tightly intertwined. "For too long, discipleship has been limited to our personal moral issues and brushed aside as a matter of faith to be dealt with only within the church. By doing so, the Great Commission to go and make disciples has been seriously neglected."[26]

Mission originates from God's heart. God is the missionary God. "To redeem humanity and the world, God sent Jesus Christ. The Son who came from the Father gives us strength and sends the Holy Spirit to guide us. And now, the triune God sends the church into the world to participate in the new creation."[27] Missional discipleship training is not about our own efforts but about "the missional nature of the triune God, who equips the congregation to live out the gospel so that saints can participate in God's mission of restoring and redeeming this world."[28]

People who have not crossed the boundaries of race, thought, customs, gender, ideology, and national borders cannot understand the differences in others. Mission is not just a matter of going abroad; it is about transcending cultures. Only those who have gone beyond cultures can overcome barriers, and only those who have crossed boundaries can truly understand the dynamics of exclusion and inclusion in life and faith.

When the world was gripped by fear due to the spread of the Ebola virus, thrity-three-year-old Dr. Kent Brantley went to Liberia for medical missions. Liberia was in the middle of a severe Ebola virus outbreak with a mortality rate reaching 90 percent. While treating Ebola-infected individuals, he contracted the virus himself. Similarly, Nancy Writebol, a nurse affiliated with the U.S. mission organization SIM, also became infected while caring for patients. Both missionaries returned to the U.S. for treatment.

Upon their return, a critical voice emerged, questioning, "Why did you go to such a dangerous place for missions, bringing trouble to the country?" I paid attention to this question because it reflects the fundamental attitude toward mission. Such a question challenges: Should one incur significant costs to go abroad? To illustrate, a conservative commentator from the U.S., thoroughly displeased with Brantley's missionary approach, criticized him as a "fool immersed in self-indulgence and heroism of mission." She questioned why Brantley went to Africa, risking the dangers of a 90 percent fatality from Ebola? In the U.S., fifteen thousand people are killed every year, and thirty-eight thousand people die from drug overdoses. Even so, why did he go to Africa? Was it because he could no longer serve Christ in the U.S.?[29]

Albert Mohler, president of the Southern Baptist Theological Seminary, responded to such criticism, stating, "They went in obedience to Christ's command."[30] This is the essence of the mission. There may be various solutions, but fundamentally, missions involve risking one's life. This has been the way the church has walked, and it is the way Christians live in a Christlike manner.

Gospel-Driven Peaceful Reunification Without Bloodshed: A New Path for National Missions for the Koreans

God's mission is cosmic, but His people's mission is regional. Christian mission transcends all barriers of region, class, race, gender, and more, making it a cosmic concept. However, this mission is necessarily regional in that it is accomplished only through our hands and feet. We must embrace the cosmic mission and carry out missions through our hands and feet right where we stand.

If there is a way for the Koreans to achieve the best missions at their present location, it is through "Gospel-Driven Peaceful Reunification of Koreas Without Bloodshed." I believe the greatest "mission" facing the Korean nation is the reunification of North and South Korea. If the North and South are unified, the spirit of martyrdom in the underground churches of North Korea will awaken the saints in the South.

Since childhood, there has been a prayer engraved in my soul: "Protect the 155-mile truce line and the 850-mile coastline of this nation." Such prayers from our ancestors supported South Korea in overcoming the ashes of war and achieving economic growth in just over half a century, transforming a recipient of aid to a donor country after World War II.

Upon this foundation, there was an episode where my ingrained love for the nation was taken to the next level—into the missional dimension. In March 2015, I had a meeting with members of the German Christian Democratic Union, including party leader Volker Kauder. As we were discussing reunification together, the phrase "without shedding blood" came into my heart like a flash, embedding itself deeply in my heart. "Gospel-Driven Peaceful Reunification Without Bloodshed" is fundamentally rooted above all in the shepherd's heart that embraces the nation. This path is a missional journey that rescues our brothers and sisters in Christ still horrendously persecuted in North Korea and awakens the South Korea Christians entangled in mammon.

To become the cornerstone of prayer for unification, SaRang Church began committing to prayer for reunification. The Jubilee Unified Prayer Meeting, which started in 2004 with SaRang Church's college ministry and the mission organization, Revival Korea, is approaching its one thousandth session. Water boils at one hundred degrees Celsius. There is an explosive threshold in ministry as well. The labor of the Korean church in prayer for unification is approaching that tipping point. "Gospel-Driven Peaceful Reunification Without Bloodshed" is the way to restore the priestly responsibility for this era and open a new dimension of mission for Korea. Unification should be a gift from God, a grace without anyone's merit. "Gospel-Driven Peaceful Reunification Without Bloodshed" will be an answer to the saints' prayer, fueled by the love of the nation and passion for mission. It would be God's gift that opens a new dimension of mission for Korea. Every nation has an opportune regional mission to undertake.

Cultural Discipleship

The Cultural Leadership DNA in the Church

Sometimes, when reminiscing about my childhood, memories arise of my father's humble church plant in the poor neighborhood of Busan. Whenever it rained, raindrops would drip from the ceiling. My father was always abstractly and fiercely strict with me, and as the eldest son, I had to endure his stern discipline faithfully. However, if those times were just filled with cold, hunger, and a sense of inferiority, I would not want to recall them no matter how many valuable lessons were embedded.

For me, that period was not just a vague memory of harsh times but the sweet embryonic stage that sprouted and grew my faith, sense of ministry, and cultural sensibility. And this is because of the church. Even in the

1960s and 70s, the church was cutting-edge. Despite the church's leaking ceiling, it was filled with state-of-the-art cultural tools. There was a poster hang-board displaying hymns, sermon points, and other visual aids. This was an advanced communication tool that could be only found in schools, government offices, and military bases. Later, it evolved into overhead projectors and screen projectors.

Back then, one could only find one or two households affluent enough to own a piano or harmonium in the entire neighborhood; yet, small churches had harmoniums and large churches had pianos. People at church learned to sing hymns precisely to the rhythm of these instruments. They might not have recognized Christian doctrines, but everyone in the neighborhood knew that "church songs" were called "hymns." Even small churches organized choirs, and friends with talent in singing formed vocal groups, when most of the people did not know how to read music. Later, the popularization of "culture nights," where members of the church showcased their artistic gifts through the means of musical numbers, poetry reading, skit dramas, or choral music, in the public also began in the church.

Even in urban schools, people came across mimeograph papers on term exams only a few times a year. Meanwhile, churches published bulletins with mimeograph papers every Sunday. Looking back, all the communication that was used every Sunday was crafted using the standardized and most sophisticated language and sentences. Attending church immersed me in this standard of language. Moreover, various age-appropriate groups were organized, creating an environment where familiarity with healthy communication practices and the development of skills for constructive debate were inevitable. This culture laid the foundation for Korean society to enter the highly intelligent social climate.

Why Did the Church Lose Cultural Hegemony?

Why did the Korean church lose its cultural dominance over society and be pushed to the outskirts after the mid-1990s? Even in the 90s, the Korean church was culturally dominant in society. It quickly embraced early media culture and demonstrated its response to popular culture through contemporary Christian music (CCM), seeker-driven worship services, and other artistic expressions in worship. During that time, no social organizations were more conducive for small groups as in Korean churches. Every church had dedicated spaces for young people and promptly purchased learning materials for Sunday school. Modern instruments began to appear in churches as well. This was also when nontraditional media like simple PowerPoint presentations were introduced into ministry. Churches were receptive to cultural changes, and, in terms of cultural utilization, there were no institutions or organizations that could keep up with the pace of the local church.

However, compared to the 1960s and 70s, the church missed one crucial element. The church failed to extend the ministry of the gospel that reaches the souls in the culture. The Korean church began to lose its cultural dominance after the mid-1990s. It began to emphasize cultural relevance and lost its true purpose for having cultural relevance. While culture is not the sole means of gospel preaching and missions, it should have been transformed and positioned under the guidance and supervision of the gospel. However, the crucial link between the gospel and culture was broken in the church's attempt to utilize cultural tools for the sake of culture. This imbalance seems to have brought tragic results to culture itself after the mid-1990s and into the 2000s. It did not happen because cultural investment was neglected but because the church sprained her ankle—losing her balance and missing the opportunity to focus on the reason it should pay attention to cultural forms and what the results should be. It missed the mark by losing sight of the mission of God in cultural transformation and the purpose of using those cultural forms to propel God's mission.

The Necessity of Cultural Discipleship

How can we heal the underlying illnesses of the social culture in our world today? The current secular worldview is a monster with various faces: combining individualism, consumerism, extreme nationalism, moral relativism, scientific naturalism, and postmodern tribalism. The solution to this problem is not merely a matter of temperament change or creating an atmosphere of dialogue. The roots of this problem lie in values and worldviews; it involves spiritual dimensions. For this reason we must recover cultural discipleship.

Culture varies. North American culture is not the same as East Asian culture. I am not advocating for cultural relativism. However, one cannot evaluate the whole of European culture based on the standards of Asian culture. Europe and Africa differ in this regard as well. When discussing cultural transformation, the unique characteristics of the history, region, ethnicity, and society must be carefully considered. Indiscriminately passing judgment on other cultures due to ethnocentrism is a sign of cultural imperialism.

Culture is like the air. We often do not realize the severity of air pollution until fine dust and UV warnings are issued. While discipleship training over the years has focused on elevating the issue of individual forgiveness, character transformation, and development, not much attention has been given to the air quality of the atmosphere—namely the culture and various spheres of our society. Jesus demands discipleship that goes beyond the personal soul, reaching into the realms of rulers and authorities of this world (Eph. 6:12). Why have we regarded discipleship as being solely related to the individual soul and personal life?

The Cultural Mandate and the Great Commission Are Not in Opposition but Are Oriented in the Same Direction

Those with a conservative faith often consider the Great Commission of Matthew 28:19–20 as more important than the cultural mandate of Genesis 1:28. Yet, such a perspective does not contain a comprehensive view of the entire Bible. When God called Abraham in Genesis 12, He promised forgiveness of sins and salvation of souls and also a great nation, blessings, and land. These areas had been corrupted due to human fall in

Genesis 1–11, and God promised to restore them. Salvation and cultural restoration are not two distinct causes.

These two commands do not face different directions. Both arise from the shepherd's heart to bless and preserve the created world, based on the work of salvation and redemption accomplished in Jesus Christ. The Great Commission completes the cultural mandate, and the cultural mandate is realized through the Great Commission. They are two sides of the same coin, in a relationship like a locomotive and its cars. Faithfully following the Great Commission and producing disciples of Jesus is to bring forth the restored image of God that can carry out the cultural mandate at a higher level on this earth.

We are reaping the result of positioning the cultural mandate and the Great Commission as opposing forces. This led to churches suffering significant losses by slipping away from Christian presence in the culture. While evangelistic efforts were successful to a certain extent, the practical demonstration of what it means to think and live as a Christian in various areas of life was lacking. Consequently, the positive influences of early Christian missionary efforts, starting from public domains like politics, economy, and education to private domains like arts, popular culture, leisure, and sports, have gradually faded away. The beneficial impacts of early Christian missions on society are diminishing, not only due to the secularization of the society but also because we failed to understand the implementation of the cultural mandate and the Great Commission as a joint venture. Concerns have been raised, and the news of victory may not come easily. So, what do we do now?

Examine the Lens Through Which You View Culture

We are called to resemble and follow Jesus, and culture and its spheres are the very places we do so. This is another axis of discipleship training. Sin did not just strike the human heart, but it brought a curse to the earth. As seen in the Tower of Babel, sin thoroughly divided and confused people, causing hostility with one another. Discipleship training should address the task of exploring what it means to be Christ's disciples in those areas of culture and civilization, including in the spheres of society, politics, economy, and education.

How the church views the surrounding culture and the relationship it establishes, and the question of how the church responds in faithfulness to its essence and mission are not merely problems of yesterday or today. The question of how to be in the world without being of the world will find its first answer key in understanding how Jesus approached worldly culture. What attitude did Jesus show toward worldly culture? We bear the responsibility to transform the entire culture. While there is a need for an attitude that rejects some aspects of culture while accepting others, above all, we should be like the "leaven that a woman took and hid in three measures of flour" (Matt. 13:33). We are called to be leaven not for a certain portion of a culture but for the whole of culture, aiming for its total transformation.

Cultural discipleship should firmly instill in learners how Jesus Christ is introduced as a cultural transformer in the Bible. Since the Bible does not explicitly provide answers about which political system ultimately aligns with the kingdom of God or offer specific policies for current issues such as education, labor relations, diplomacy, and defense, especially North-South Korean relations, it is impossible to directly extract them. However, a theological and philosophical foundation can be established by intellectually engaging with the message of the Bible and relying on divine guidance.

God has a purpose and plan for the world. He revealed it to us, and it is being unfolded through the church. Our role in discipleship is to offer an introduction and provide implementation of God's fundamental purpose for the world. We have continuously witnessed how the world cannot offer reasonable hope for the future or fundamental solutions to issues. Therefore, cultural discipleship must present the true and alternative foundation for human culture, including its answers from reasons of spirituality, meaning for morality, and the purpose of life.

Creative Separation and Nonviolent Engagement in Cultural Discipleship

The methods employed in cultural discipleship are also crucial, especially when we are confronted with a clearly evil culture. What should we do when faced with an evil culture? While it is appropriate to use biblical means to eliminate or collapse evil culture whenever possible, what should be done in situations where that is not readily feasible?

First, as Christians, we should be separated from the world's culture. This entails living in the world but not being contaminated by it, not escaping from the world, and yet maintaining a distinct identity in Christ (John 17:14–16). An example from the Bible is Obadiah in 1 Kings 18. Despite being in the palace of Ahab, one of the most wicked kings in Israel's history, Obadiah kept his identity as a believer in God. Through holy and creative separation amid a corrupted political culture, he exerted a positive influence without being assimilated into the world. It is truly challenging for Christians to live in the world without conforming to it. This is because "the world is more invasive, destructive, and coercive than ever."[31] The world enhances its influence, destructiveness, and compulsion, hence captivating the hearts and minds of believers with worldly pleasures and stimulating pleasures. It is leading people inexorably toward the path of destruction. Escaping the destructive gravitational pull of secularism is undeniably difficult. What is required in cultural discipleship is a firm resolve to guard and embrace the disciple's loyalty and identity.

Second, we must employ nonviolent engagement when the culture of the world challenges the Christian faith. When Christian beliefs meet cultural hostility, the response should not be made with violent resistance. Daniel, in the heart of Babylonian culture that opposed God at that time, adopted a stance of nonviolent engagement. When Christian values clash with worldly values and society attacks Christianity, how should Christians respond to these attacks? In a world that is increasingly following the path of secularization and where such secular standards are imposed as the right ones, what should we do?

Jesus said that what belongs to Caesar should be given to Caesar, and what belongs to God should be given to God. We should never compromise by giving to Caesar what belongs to God. This attitude should guide us when standing against the values of the world in any situation. Jesus desired that God's children endure hatred from unbelievers but endure it until the end. Our nonviolent engagement involves standing firm against them; endurance, boldness, and uncompromised are the ways of Christ followers. We must remember that Jesus promised glorious salvation to those who endure (Matt. 10:16–18).

How Can We Overcome Secularization?

"Is the Christian church finished, and is the Christian faith going into a great museum of history?"[32] How would you answer this question? This question, reminiscent of the tragic collapse of European churches, rings a frightening alarm for the future of the church. The sense of helplessness in the Christian community is prevalent as Christians face the storm of secularization that leaves the aftermath of spiritual ruins everywhere. As a result, churches build their own fortress, and congregants believe that they can live safely on this earth if they stay in that bubble until they go to heaven.

To be certain, the hope of heaven became a precious nourishment for the saints, providing spiritual peace even amid life's hardships. For Korean Christians, it was especially true during the Japanese occupation and extreme poverty after the Korean War. The anticipation of Jesus's return and the dream of a heavenly kingdom that dries our tears are indeed central pillars of Christianity, bringing joy that is unique to Christians on this earth. Therefore, this hope should be intensified and strengthened for every believer who confesses Jesus Christ as their Savior. However, the hope of heaven should not serve as an escape from the harsh reality of secularization. Instead, it should become the foundation for a combative faith and a combative church that opposes secularization with a martyr-like spirituality.

The axes of time and space have changed completely from before. We are in an era of nonlinear time, where traditional linear time has disappeared, and societies can predict and manipulate future outcomes. Today, even before a child is born, diseases in their genetic code can be removed. As humans gain the ability to predict and alter the future through super artificial intelligence and acquire the power to manipulate life, secularization deepens with its increasing disbelief. In such times, how can the church rein in on secularization?

The solution to the secularization problem is intricately linked to an accurate and precise understanding of the contemporary era. "Secularization is a process in which an increasing number of people abandon religion, and simultaneously, sectors operating without religious values and ideologies expand in society and life."[33] The Bible depicts secularization as "Let us eat and drink, for tomorrow we die" (1 Cor. 15:32), "Who is self-indulgent" (1 Tim. 5:6), and "The more words, the more vanity" (Eccles. 6:11).

Therefore, the most crucial and only path to overcoming secularization is to unmistakably demonstrate the gospel of Christianity to people as the promise of eternal life rather than a life that ends tomorrow, a joy greater and more astonishing than worldly pleasures, and a meaningful life rather than a futile one. For this reason, the pastor preaching about life, joy, and the eternal gospel every week from the pulpit is not only vital for sustaining the believers but also is laboring to form the most important foundation for cultural discipleship, conquering the culture of the secular world running toward secularization.

Epilogue

When I became the senior pastor of SaRang Church, I had a pastoral dream and vision for the church. It was to stand together with the saints all over the world on the horizon of the "global standard." I am convinced that this dream was a vision that would freshly breathe a much-needed vitality into the global church.

The global church has constantly suffered from internal divisions, resulting in chronic leakage that drains the energy of evangelism and weakens the progress of global missions. The energy that should be directed outward has been diverted inward, depleting each other's strength. Many within the church are aware of this condition and are concerned, but a solution focused on internal matters alone will be ineffective in alleviating this ailment.

Mountain climbers ascending Everest do not boast about conquering the peaks of local mountains like Bukhansan or Seoraksan in Seoul. Navigators crossing the Pacific do not settle for sailing on rivers or lakes, and explorers journeying to Antarctica do not make rural villages their goal. The gospel, by nature, loses its life force when confined to a specific region. Similarly, churches founded on the same gospel also cannot exert their strength as a community of divine life when trapped in internalization or strict adherence to certain ideologies. As Brennan Manning said, "Churches trapped in coffins of so-called orthodoxy bring discord and division to the body of Christ."[1] The inability to break free from this trap is due to the lack of experience with the "global standard" of the gospel. Excessive denominational loyalty that hinders the advancement of the gospel becomes an obstacle that prevents the fulfillment of the missional commission to make disciples of all nations.

This task of awakening the people of God to stand together on a global level for a global collaboration for a globally focused mission has become my lifelong mission, incarnated through the serendipity of my past ministry journeys. I grew up in a church where I recited Presbyterian confessions. I obtained spiritual and theological nourishment from a conservative seminary and denominational. I then studied at a nondenominational seminary, Talbot School of Theology in the United States, and graduated from Calvin Theological Seminary and Potchefstroom Theological School. I also experienced the borderline of progressive thoughts while being a Fellow at Harvard University.

Serving for fifteen years as the International General Secretary of KOSTA (Korean Students Abroad), I witnessed the dynamic movement of the gospel in various settings and contexts. Through the "Westward Movement of the Gospel" initiatives, I began sowing seeds for the planting of a thousand churches in Europe. Traveling to twenty provinces in China and meeting fellow believers, I was able to experience breakthroughs in the thresholds of my ministry. Simultaneously, working in South America to promulgate disciple-making ministry for fifteen years, particularly in Brazil—halfway around the globe from Korea, I felt the boundless universality of the gospel. Additionally, traversing the five oceans and six continents to preach the word, I experienced the contextualized realities of the gospel in various cultures.

On the one hand, I experienced not only the revival of ministry but also had to come to places where I sought God's guidance amid situations that were too harsh to articulate personally. I suffered and asked God to even take my life in those times. Having experienced it all, there is only one reason and purpose for sharing the theological, ministerial, cultural, and pastoral side of the journey I walked so far through this writing. That is to ensure that we see the big picture of ministry and not waste energy on nonessential matters. To grasp this, one must read the fervent heart of God, who called the timid Gideon a "mighty warrior" (Judg. 6:12 HCSB). Only then can one respond like a true warrior when God calls the church that is struggling with both external and internal threats to rise again. Only when the church senses this aching heart of God for the church will it be able to respond boldly when He pronounces: "You are called for a great purpose."

The path of ministry, a journey of both glory and tribulation, is the way of the cross. One cannot walk this path of the cross without having the heart of Jesus who wishes for not a single soul to perish. The shepherd's heart is the heart of Jesus who lays down His life for the sheep. The shepherd's heart required in the twenty-first century is the heart that refuses to relinquish the adventure of faith even in the presence of adversity, the heart that vows to take steps of faith with steadfastness and courage even during great storms, and the heart that is marked by *splagchnizomai* (σπλαγχνίζομαι)—to be moved as to one's bowels, hence, to be moved with warm compassion that no single soul is overlooked. This shepherd's heart is the source of the clarity of calling that aligns the pastor with God's will even in the fog of confusion, the fountain that makes the shepherd rise again even in the direst situations.

After crossing the raging river of COVID-19, many seem to believe that recovering the glorious days and moving toward the season of revival is a distant, unimaginable reality. However, on the "9.26 National Pastors' Conference," as I knelt in prayer on the summit of Mount Woomyeon in Seoul, I received a fire from heaven. The insight allowed me to see that for a minister to stay awake throughout the ministry, moments of tribulations along with situations that require a leap of faith will have to accompany the minister. Moreover, I became convinced that someone must lead the way for these ministers. This is the twenty-first-century Awakening I came to realize through my reflection on the shepherd's heart. Upon this reflection, I committed my life to sharing this shepherd's heart, along with the passion that makes the heart of ministry beat and the pulse of Christ's body palpitate, with my beloved coworkers as the direction of my ministry.

In various pastoral contexts that allowed me to witness numerous revivals and declines in ministries, one thing has remained firm in my heart: Only what was done for the Lord is eternal. Not only is this a biblical truth, but it is an echo resounding through the fervent cry of pastors engaged in intense spiritual battles with the devil in their ministry. Theologians who have not been inside the bloody trenches of pastoral ministry may not fully understand the situation described by the apostle Paul as the "snares of the devil" (see 1 Tim. 3:7) or the "scheme of the enemy" by heart. The cry is a deep understanding in the hearts of pastors who passionately fight against the devil on the front lines of ministry. For the body of Christ to enter into life, to empower the pastors and believers to face the tidal current of anti-Christian attacks and atheism, it is now necessary to cut off the shackles tied to doctrines, denominations, and organizations and enter the horizon of the global horizon of the gospel, the "global standard," and the Christian Shalom Pax Mundi.

That is why I wrote this book. Our bodies and gaze should no longer look down to the bottom from the mountaintop. Instead, from this summit, let us shift our focus to turn toward the world with discipleship training that is open to the world. May our sights be focused on saving neighbors through discipleship training with the heart of a shepherd. May our hearts beat for the ministry of discipleship training not as an artificial flower rooted in the spirit of competition and self-righteousness but as a living flower that is revitalized and bearing much fruit through the power of life in Jesus. Let us long to offer discipleship training with sincerity to people and wholeheartedly to God, all the while giving glory to God through a missional life. That is Teleios Discipleship.

Notes

Prologue

1. Charles Spurgeon, *Lectures to My Students* (Word of Life, 2000), 393.2. Dietrich Bonhoeffer found clues to the instinctive longing for human wholeness in human shame and concealment. "Covering oneself with leaves is a sign of shame felt at being undressed and losing the wholeness of life" (cf. Gen. 3:7). He believed that within the shame of one's imperfect state and the concealment of one's deficiencies lies a fundamental longing for wholeness. Dietrich Bonhoeffer, *Ethics* (Bokissunghansa, 2022), 51–52.

3. John Stott yearned for the spiritual longing for wholeness in humans by examining the strong homing instinct that birds possess. He lamented, saying, "If God is truly the real home where our spirits can rest, and without Him, we are wanderers and lost, then how wonderful it would be if we, humans, also had a strong homing instinct spiritually?" John Stott, *The Birds, Our Teachers* (IVP, 2001), 21.

4. Saint Augustine, *The Confessions of St. Augustine*, translated by J. G. Pilkington (The Heritage Press, 1963), 26.

5. Andrew Murray, *Perfection* (People of God Press, 2022), 95.

6. Murray, *Perfection,* 132.

Preface

1. The powerful gravity of the secular world prevents us from escaping the forces of fleshly desires, worldly perspectives, and the pride of this life. A. W. Tozer describes this as our "morbid impulse towards

spiritual suicide." A. W. Tozer, *The Pursuit of God* (Gyujang, 2017), 61. A moderate faith cannot pull us out of the morbid impulse toward spiritual suicide caused by the gravity of the secular world.

2. The term *spiritual family* holds various dimensions, including "spiritual family." Detailed explanations can be found in part 2, "Ecclesiology for Teleios Discipleship: The Growth of Teleios Disciples and Church Community."

Chapter 1

1. Robert Coleman aptly pointed out the significance of discipleship training practiced in life. In his book *Maximizing Pastoral Ministry*, he expresses the end of theology without practice as simply a rebellion. He states, "I think future church theologians will conclude that one reason for the loss of influence by the church in the twentieth century is that those directing the church's course, the clergy and theologians, pulled laity into scholarly theories, distancing them from practical theology and practical spirituality in daily life." Robert Coleman, *Maximizing Pastoral Ministry* (Korean LPM Research Institute, 2003), 18. When discussing discipleship training, it is crucial to avoid falling into this trap. Entering the holy orbit of the ministry of the Word requires the right direction and strategy for discipleship training.

2. Contrary to the perception that being a "Teleios disciple of Jesus" denotes a select few that reach a distinctive state achieved in the distant future, the first-century Christians did not hold such a view. In the first century, anyone who believed in Jesus became a disciple. The term *disciple* was merely transformed into the term *complete one*, or the Teleios ones in the New Testament. If the term *disciple* was familiar to Jews, the term *complete one* was the term used for disciples in the Greco-Roman world. Therefore, from the moment of believing in Jesus, it is appropriate to pursue and emphasize the name of the "complete one" or "those mature in Christ." Michael Wilkinson, *Following the Master* (DMI Press, 2015), 54–58.

3. A. W. Tozer, *Passion for God* (Kuyjang, 2016), 32.

4. John Owen, *Reformed Pneumatology* (Yesurun, 2017), 427.

5. Wilkinson, *Following the Master*, 58.

6. Alister McGrath, *Alister McGrath's Christian Apologetics* (DMI Press, 2014), 210.

7. National Religious Composition Trend in 2022/2023: Domestic religious believers 36.6 percent, nonreligious 63.4 percent, Protestants 15 percent, Buddhists 16.3 percent, Catholics 5.1 percent. "Religious Status and Perception of Koreans," Ministry Data Research Institute, September 5, 2023, https://url.kr/s9m6p2.

8. Refer to "Global Standards" in chapter 6 for "What is the Gospel Global Standard?"

9. James Packer, *Knowing the Knowledge of the Spirit* (Hongseongsa, 2002), 327.

10. Packer, *Knowing the Knowledge of the Spirit*, 328.

11. Regarding believers who experience a false fire while neglecting the true fire, A. W. Tozer insightfully stated: "They are people who stand by a fire other than the fire of the Holy Spirit, trying to warm themselves by learning how to stoke a fire next to it." A. W. Tozer, *Worship or Show?* (Kyujang, 2016), 138.

12. According to IDC's Worldwide Global Datasphere Forecast 2021–2025, the amount of data generated in the next three years will surpass the data generated in the past thirty years.

13. Google's former CEO Eric Schmidt has warned about the rapid development of artificial intelligence, suggesting that AI may pose a real threat to humanity.

14. According to Datareportal's Digital 2021 report, there are approximately 4.48 billion active social media users worldwide.

15. A study published in the *American Journal of Health Promotion* (2017) indicates that individuals who use social media for more than two hours a day are twice as likely to feel social isolation compared to those who use it for less than thirty minutes.

16. Steve Raybey and Lois Modi Raybey, *Handbook of Discipleship Ministry in the 21st Century* (Blessed People, 2003), 371.

17. Leonard Sweet, *Success Keywords A to Z for the Future Church* (Words Written on Earth, 2007), 21.

18. Carl Truman delves into the scholarly explanation of modern identity in his recent book. Refer to Carl R. Truman, *The Rise and Triumph of the Modern Self* (Crossway, 2020).

19. Ray Kurzweil, *The Moment Technology Transcends Humanity: The Singularity Is Coming* (Kim Young Sa), 2007.

20. Augustine, *Confessions* (Penguin Books, 1963), 213.

21. Timothy S. Lane and Paul David Trip, *How People Change* (New Growth Press, 2008), 24.

22. John Piper, *Desiring God, Rev. Ed.* (Multnomah Books, 2011).

23. John Calvin, *Sermons on Genesis* (Banner of Truth, 2009), 93.

24. Jae-Chun Cho, *Hebrews* (Hongseongsa, 2016), 71–72.

25. Horst Balz and Gerhard Schneider, *Exegetical Dictionary of the New Testament, Vol. 3*, (Eerdmans, 1993), 345. Refer to Exodus 29:9–35; Leviticus 8:21–33; 16:32; 21:10; and Numbers 3:3.

26. Jae-Chun Cho, *Hebrews*, 71–73.

27. Timothy S. Lane and Paul David Trip, *How People Change* (New Growth Press, Third Edition, 2008), 15.

28. Dallas Willard, *The Spirit of the Disciplines* (HarperOne, 1999), 45.

29. Tim Chester, *You Can Change* (IVP, 2013), 38.

30. Josh MacDowell and Bob Hostetler, *Two Faces of Tolerance in Toleranz* (Steps Stone, 2009), 31–32.

31. French abbreviation for "répondez s'il vous plait," meaning "please reply."

32. John Owen, *Mortification of Sin* (Chapel Library, 2018), 6.

33. John Stott, *The Living Christ* (Blessed People, 2020), 165.

34. C. S. Lewis, *The Weight of Glory* (Hongseongsa, 2008), 12.

35. Tim Keller, *Center Church* (Duranno, 2016), 72.

Chapter 2

1. Jungeun Kim, *Jesus Column 1* (Suncheon Books, 2013), 25.

2. Alister McGrath, *Luther's Theology of the Cross* (Concordia Publishing, 2015), 295.

3. McGrath, *Luther's Theology of the Cross*, 295.

4. A. W. Tozer, *The Pursuit of God* (Word of Life Press, 2003), 108.5. Charles Spurgeon, *Evening by Evening* (Crossway, 2007), 147.

6. R. C. Sproul, *Biblical Worship* (Jiphilseowon, 2015), 33.

7. John Piper, *The Pleasures of God* (Multnomah, 2012), 255.

8. Horst Robert Balz and Gerhard M. Schneider, *Exegetical Dictionary of New Testament, Vol. 3* (Eerdmans Publishing, 1993), 265.

9. Alister McGrath, *Seeing God's Face* (Blessed People, 2006), 82.

10. John Bevere, *John Bevere's Grace* (Duranno, 2010), 309.

11. Charles Swindoll, *The Greatest Life of Jesus* (Timothy, 2009), 106.

12. "Jesus is the first person to fully live out Psalm 23:1. Just as Jesus is our shepherd, His Father was His shepherd." Dallas Willard, *The Divine Conspiracy* (Kyujang, 2018), 75.

13. Henri Nouwen, in *Eternal Seasons*, reflects on the perpetual nature of God's love. Henri Nouwen, *Eternal Seasons* (Stump House, 2005), 84.

14. Charles Swindoll, *When Life Isn't Fair* (Mission World Library, 2007), 87.

15. Michael Card, *Writing on the Sand* (IVP, 2003), 15–16.

16. Alister McGrath, *How to Communicate Jesus in a Postmodern Era* (Duranno, 2020), 64.

17. Charles Swindoll, *When Life Isn't Fair*, 88.

18. R. A. Torrey, *Power in the Blood* (Youth with a Mission, 2010), 44.

19. John Stott, *The Cross of Christ* (IVP, 2015), 528.

20. Martin Lloyd-Jones suggests that Paul's use of the phrase "I am under obligation" implies a sense of compulsion, reminiscent of a legal obligation that entails punishment for noncompliance. This corresponds to the meaning of 1 Corinthians 9:16, which states, "Woe to me if I do not preach the gospel!" Paul is expressing, "I am under pressure. I am a debtor. . . . I have the gospel, and I feel a compulsion to share it." Martin Lloyd-Jones, *Share the Water* (Kyujang, 2012), 138.

21. Marva Dawn, *Walking with God Without Getting Tired* (Blessed Person, 2010), 69.

22. Christopher J. H. Wright, *The God I Don't Understand* (Zondervan, 2008), 132.

23. R. T. Kendall, *Jealousy* (Innocent Nard, 2016), 222.

24. Publisher's Column, *Disciple* magazine, December 2022, DMI.

25. Martyn Lloyd-Jones, *The Core of the Gospel* (Pastoral Materials, 2019), 102.

26. Martyn Lloyd-Jones, *Revival* (Blessed Person, 2006), 541.

Chapter 3

1. Leslie Newbigin, *Sin and Salvation* (Blessed Person, 2013), 161.

2. R. C. Sproul, *Unexpected Jesus* (Joy Church, 2008), 111.

3. John Calvin, *Calvin's Institutes of Christian Religion: French First Edition 1541* (Christian Renaissance, 2015), 388.

4. Alister McGrath, *Return to the Cross* (Word of Life, 2014), 2.

5. "Relativism explains why humans are more inclined to adjust the truth to their desires than align their desires with the truth." Os Guinness, *Truth Be Told* (Nuga, 2002), 174.

6. Guinness, *Truth Be Told*, 182.

7. Guinness, *Truth Be Told*, 181.

8. Martin Lloyd-Jones, *Revival* (Blessed Person, 2006), 16.

9. McGrath, *Return to the Cross*, 189.

10. Lloyd-Jones, *Revival*, 27.

11. John Stott, *The Cross of Christ* (IVP, 2015), 602.

12. Stott, *The Cross of Christ*, 543.

13. Lloyd-Jones, *Revival*, 247.

14. Timothy S. Lane and Paul David Tripp, 177–92.

15. Alister McGrath, *Return to the Cross* (Word of Life, 2014), 212.

16. Erwin Luther, *Beholding the Cross* (Timothy, 2007), 159.

17. Luther, *Beholding the Cross*, 161.

18. Alister McGrath, *Luther's Theology of the Cross* (Concordia, 2015), 285.

19. Stott, *The Cross of Christ*, 529.

20. Dietrich Bonhoeffer, *The Cost of Discipleship* (Macmillan, 1980), 89.

21. *Disciple Magazine*, July-August 2019 (DMI), 87.

22. Henri Nouwen views death as the "great return to the place where one can become the most perfect child of God and ultimately the moment that completes perfection." Henri Nouwen, *This Is My Beloved* (IVP, 2002), 118.

23. Charles Spurgeon, *Spurgeon's Sermon Compilation: Psalms (3)* (CH Books, 2013), 765.

24. Andrew Murray, *Andrew Murray's Hebrews Devotional: Holy of Holies* (Bethel House, 2015), 304.

25. Os Guinness, *Fool's Talk* (Blessed Person, 2016), 183.

26. A. W. Tozer, *GOD* (Kyujang, 2007), 291.

27. A. W. Tozer. *Do Not Kneel to the World* (Kyujang, 2010), 85–86.

28. Chris Prejean and Marjorie J. Thompson, *Life Asks, Nouwen Answers* (ElPage, 2021), 235.

29. John Owen, The Nature and Causes of Apostasy (Revival and Reformation, 2018), 17.

30. Charles Spurgeon, *Spurgeon's Sermon Compilation 30: Colossians, 1 and 2 Thessalonians* (CH Books, 2011), 281.

31. Charles Spurgeon, *Spurgeon's Sermon Compilation 30: Colossians, 1 and 2 Thessalonians*, 159.

32. Stott, *The Cross of Christ,* 539.

33. Bonhoeffer, *The Cost of Discipleship*, 97.

34. David Platt, *Counter-Culture* (Duranno, 2016), 313.

35. David Platt, *Follow Me* (Duranno, 2019), 23.

36. Cleon L. Rogers Jr. and Cleon L. Rogers III, *The New Linguistic and Exegetical Key to the Greek New Testament* (Zondervan, 1998), 85.

37. Stott, *The Cross of Christ*, 95.

38. Stott, *The Cross of Christ*, 535.

39. Stott, *The Cross of Christ*, 535.

40. Stott, *The Cross of Christ*, 535.

41. A. W. Tozer, *Discipleship* (Kyujang, 2019), 15.

42. Stott, *The Cross of Christ*, 541.

43. Acts 1:8, the term *witness* implies a martyrdom.

44. C. S. Lewis, *An Experiment in Criticism* (Hongseongsa, 2021), 17.

45. Refer to David Platt, *Radical* (Multnomah, 210), 59–60.

46. C. S. Lewis, *Mere Christianity* (Hongseongsa, 2021), 208.

47. A. W. Tozer, *God Pursuing Man* (Blessed Person, 2016), 52.

48. Martin Lloyd-Jones, *The Cross of God's Salvation* (Duranno, 2021), 46, 48.

49. R. C. Sproul, *Acts: A Strong Defense* (Solomon, 2018), 321.

50. John Piper and Justin Taylor, *A God-Centered Worldview* (Revival and Reformation Press, 2013), 37.

Chapter 4

1. Alister McGrath, *What Is Theology?* (Blessed Person, 2022), 139.

2. Roger W. Gehring, *House Church and Mission* (Hendrickson Publishers, 2004), 295.

3. Wayne A. Grudem, *Systematic Theology* (Zondervan, 1994), 867.

4. Yong-kyu Park, *History of World Revival Movement (Korean Christian History Research Institute*, 2022), 578.

5. A. W. Tozer, *Nail It to the Cross* (Kyujang, 2015), 77.

6. Depending on the study, some claim a 40 percent growth every decade. Alan Kreider, *Worshipping Communities of the Early Church* (Heaven's Seed, 2021), 31. Others argue for a 50 percent growth. See Rick Warren, *Christianity Today*, June 2023, https://lrl.kr/INKw.

7. "Studies in Christian Living" series (all 10 volumes) and the "Design for Discipleship" series (all 6 volumes) by The Navigators.

8. PBS: Personal inductive Bible Study, also known as personal Bible study. Inductive Bible study involves observing, interpreting, and applying Scripture.

9. Oak Han-Heum, Awakening the Laity (DMI Press, 2019), 67–68, 71.

10. "What is the church? . . . It is naturally and organically connected body and members of that body, connected between the Lord and the members through that same Lord." James Packer, *Firm Christians* (Kyujang, 2002), 147.

11. Nils Witmer Becker, *Fireseeds from Korea to the World* (Campus Crusade for Christ International, 2007), 145.

12. James Packer, *Weakness Is the Way* (Timothy, 2014), 74.

13. Michael Horton, *The Christian Faith* (Zondervan, 2011), 721; see also Michael Horton, *People and Place* (Westminster John Knox, 2008).

14. David J. Bosch, *Transforming Mission* (Orbis Books, 1991), 390.

15. Michael Horton refers to the church as "missional people." Michael Horton, *The Christian Faith*, 717.

16. Oak Han-heum, 87.

17. Michael Horton, *The Christian Faith*, 828.

18. John Clark and Marcus P. Johnson, *The Incarnation of God* (Crossway, 2015), 189.

19. Wayne Grudem, *Systematic Theology* (Zondervan, 1994), 1050.

20. Grudem, *Systematic Theology*, 1055–57.

21. Gorden Fee, *God's Empowering Presence: The Holy Spirit in the Letters of Paul* (Hendrickson Publishers, 1994), 707.

22. The Cape Town Commitment (Lausanne Library, 2010), 26.

23. Grudem, *Systematic Theology*, 1050.

24. Darrell L. Guder, *Missional Church: A Vision for the Sending of the Church in North America* (Eerdmans, 1998), 184–85.

25. This phrase was first mentioned in *The Future That Has Already Happened*, published in *Harvard Business Review* in 1997.

26. Edward Gibbon, *The Decline and Fall of the Roman Empire* (Kkachi Geulbang, 2021), 243.

27. Os Guinness, *The Gravedigger File* (Jeongyeon Sa, 2011), 223.

28. Martin Lloyd-Jones, *Signs of the Times* (CLC, 2007), 443.

29. John Calvin, *Calvin's Institutes of Christian Religion: French First Edition 1541* (Christian Renaissance, 2015), 40.

30. Our History Net, accessed May 7, 2025, https://url.kr/wgis4r.

31. Myung-soo Park, "March 1st Movement, Christianity, and South Korea," *Theology and Church*, no. 11 (Summer 2019), 195.

32. Oak Han-heum (2019), 103–4.

33. Philip Schaff, *Church History, Vol. 1: Apostolic Christianity* (CH Books, 2004), 358.

34. George E. Ladd, "The Gospel of the Kingdom," in *Perspectives on the World Christian Movement* (William Carey Library, 3rd ed., 1999), 77.

35. Kim Hoi-kwon, *Reading Acts 2 with Kingdom Theology* (Blessed Person, 2023), 202.

36. Dallas Willard, *Divine Conspiracy* (Blessed Person, 2007), 92.

37. Currently, SaRang Church gathers 816 men's Upper Room Small Group leaders and 1,918 women's leaders weekly.

38. Publisher's Column, "Towards the Globalization of Discipleship Training," *Disciples* magazine, January 2005 (DMI), 72.

Chapter 5

1. Allan Heaton Anderson, *An Introduction to Pentecostalism* (Cambridge University Press, 2004), 23.

2. Anderson, *An Introduction to Pentecostalism*, 23.

3. Anderson, *An Introduction to Pentecostalism*, 38.

4. James Packer, *Knowing God's Spirit* (Hongseongsa, 2002), 329.

5. Anderson, *An Introduction to Pentecostalism*, 216.

6. James Packer, *Knowing God's Spirit* (Hongseongsa, 2002), 329.

7. R. A. Torrey, *Baptism with the Holy Spirit* (Nathan, 2002), 115.

8. Packer, *Knowing God's Spirit*, 44.

9. Park Yong-gyu, *History of Korean Christianity* vol. 2 (Word of Life Press, 2004), 72.

10. John Stott, *Pastoral Theology According to Spurgeon* (Revival and Reformation Press, 2005), 183.

11. Douglas Moo, *A Theology of Paul and His Letters* (Zondervan, 2021), 291.

12. Andrew Murray, *Abide in Christ* (Kyujang, 2012), 56.

13. John C. Ryle, *Holiness* (CLC, 2012), 554.

14. John Stott, *Basic Truths of Evangelism* (IVP, 2005), 150.

15. Alistair McGrath, *Finding Faith with Alistair McGrath* (Duranno, 2019), 290–91.

16. Charles Spurgeon, *The Message of Charles Haddon Spurgeon on the Holy Spirit* (CLC, 2021), 109.

17. Charles Spurgeon, *Saints and the Savior* (CH Books, 2011), 181.

18. Jonathan Edwards, *The Life and Diary of David Brainerd (November 26, 1745 Diary)* (Blessed Person, 2011), 594.

19. Oh Dae-won, *Meditating Christian* (Youth with a Mission, 2005), 209.

20. James Packer, *Knowing God's Spirit*, 128.

21. Mark Buchanan, *Opening Eyes to the Things Unseen* (Kyujang, 2023), 170.

Chapter 6

1. Martin Lloyd-Jones, *Christians in Crisis* (Horizon Publishers, 2008), 393.

2. Charles Spurgeon, *Prayer and Spiritual Warfare* (Christian Digest, 2002), 154.

3. John Stott, Contemporary *Issues and the Christian's Responsibility* (IVP, 2005), 233.

4. Michael Frost uses the term "Missional Imagination through Incarnational Ministry" in *The Coming of the New Church*. Michael Frost and Alan Hirsch, *The Coming of the New Church* (IVP, 2009), 12.

5. Oswald Chambers quoted in Calvin Miller, *Into the Depths of God's Grace* (Little Happiness, 2002), 49–50.

6. Park Yong-gyu, *History of Korean Christianity, Vol. 2* (Word of Life Press, 2004), 731.

7. Eugene Peterson, *Praying with the Psalms* (Hongseongsa, 2010).

8. John MacArthur et al., *Jesus Christ, King of Heaven* (Timothy, 2020), 247.

9. John Piper, *Pray!* (IVP, 2017), 62.

10. Tom Wright, *Surprised by Hope* (IVP, 2009), 128.

11. Charles Swindoll, *Insights on Life (4 Seasons)* (VoiceSa, 1992), 583.

12. Martin Lloyd-Jones, *Spiritual Depression* (Blessed Person, 2014), 78–79.

13. In *Streams of Living Water*, Richard Foster discusses six spiritual disciplines: meditation, holiness, charisma (Spirit-filled life), social justice, preaching the gospel (Word), and the sacraments (Eucharist). Richard Foster's *Streams of Living Water* (Duranno, 1999). On top of this list, I have further considered the spirituality of community and spirituality in training through my pastoral field.

14. Leslie Newbigin, *What Is the Church?* (IVP, 2010), 185–86.

15. Ralph D. Winter and Bruce A. Koch, trans. Han Cheol-ho, *Finishing the Task: The Unreached People Challenge, In Perspectives on the World Christian Movement* (William Carey Library, 1999), 349.

16. Stott, *Contemporary Issues and the Christian's Responsibility*, 25.

17. Allen P. Ross, *A Commentary on The Psalms, Vol. 1* (Kregel Academics, 2011), 42.

18. Larry Crabb, *Safest Place on Earth* (Yodan Publishers, 2005), 246.

19. Wayne Cordeiro, *My Life's Mentor Met in the Bible* (Duranno, 2009), 28.

20. Jonathan Edwards, *Jonathan Edwards's Resolutions* (Word of Life Press, 2015), 113–26.

21. Henry Nouwen, *Food for My Soul* (Duranno, 2001), October 24.

22. Dallas Willard, *The Divine Conspiracy* (IVP, 2016), 147.

23. Nouwen, *Food for My Soul*, October 24.

24. Michael Wilkins, *Following the Master* (DMI Press, 2015), 346.

25. James Packer, *Knowing God's Spirit* (Hongseongsa, 2002), 145.

26. Martin Lloyd-Jones, *Behold the Glory* (Jipyeongseowon, 2014), 40–42.

27. John Piper, *The Bible and the Glory of God* (Duranno, 2017), 353.

Chapter 7

1. Os Guinness, *Impossible People* (Togijangi, 2017), 115.

2. John Owen, *Mortification of Sin* (Chapel Liberty, 2018), 435.

3. Owen, *Mortification of Sin*, 443.

4. John Owen, *Indwelling Sin in Believers* (Revival and Reformation Press, 2010), 128.

5. Owen, *Mortification of Sin*, 443.

6. Martin Lloyd-Jones, *The Greatest Message* (Hope Press, 2011), 177.

7. Leonard Sweet, *The Most Precious Three Words* (IVP, 2009), 120.

8. John Piper, *The Joy of Living by Faith* (Good Seed, 2009), 169.

9. John Owen, *Overcoming Sin and Temptation* (Word of Life Press, 2008), 62.

10. Dallas Willard et al., *The Kingdom Life* (DMI Press, 2012), 56.

11. Oswald Chambers, *He Shall Glorify Me* (Togijangi, 0210), 143.

12. Larry Crabb, *Let Church Be Church* (Duranno, 2011), 158.

13. Ronald Anton, *God's Seven Ways to Ease Suffering* (Xulon Press, 2007), 219.

14. John Owen, *The Evidence of Saving Faith* (Word of Life Press, 2018), 41.

15. A. W. Tozer, *Renounce Me* (Kyujang, 2008), 247.

16. A. W. Tozer, *Burning Faith* (Kyujang, 2017), 68.

17. John Calvin, *The Christian Life* (Calvin Academy, 2007), 34.

18. Robert C. Roberts, *Spiritual Emotions: A Psychology of Christian Virtues* (Eerdmans, 2007), 9.

19. Roberts, *Spiritual Emotions*, 9.

20. C. S. Lewis, *The Screwtape Letters* (Hongseongsa, 2002), 177.

21. Lee Gyu-tae, *The Emotional Structure of Koreans 1* (Shinwon Cultural History, 1994), preface.

22. Lee Gyu-tae, *The Emotional Structure of Koreans 2* (Shinwon Cultural History, 1994), 226.

23. John Wesley, How to Pray: The Best of John Wesley on Prayer (NCD, 2010), 72.

24. Walter Kaiser, *Jesus, the Healer* (Missionary Flame, 2009), 24.

25. Neil T. Anderson, *Discipleship Counselling* (Regal, 2003), 64.

26. A. W. Tozer, *The Pursuit of God* (Kyujang, 2007), 75.

27. Dallas Willard, *Renovation of the Heart: Putting on the Character of Christ* (NavPress, 2002), 142.

28. Willard, *Renovation of the Heart*, 145.

29. Augustine, *Confessions*, trans. Han-yong Sung, 199.

30. R. C. Sproul, *Do You Really Believe That?* (Good Seed, 2000), 58.

31. Alister McGrath, *Mere Theology* (Society for Promoting Christian, 2010), 3.

32. J. Gary Millar, *Changed into His Likeness* (IVP, 2021), 226.

33. L. Robert Kohls, *Learning to Think Korea* (Intercultural Press, 2002), 101.

34. Robert Letham, *The Holy Trinity* (P&R Publishing, 2004), 35–40.

35. Donald G. Bloesch, *The Church* (IVP, 2002), 43.

36. Aristotle, *Politics* (Forrest, 2022), 21–22.

37. Peter Scazzero, *Emotionally Healthy Discipleship* (Duranno, 2021), 219.

38. Willard et al., *Kingdom Life*, 276.

39. Wayne Grudem, *Systematic Theology* (IVP, 1994), 1143.

40. James Packer, *A Quest for Godliness* (Kyujang, 2002), 71.

41. Michael Horton, *The Christian Faith* (Zondervan ,2011), 564.

42. Clinton E. Arnold, *Ephesians in Zondervan Illustrated Bible Backgrounds Commentary, Vol. 3* (Zondervan, 2002), 315.

43. Mark Wilson, *Revelation in Zondervan Illustrated Bible Backgrounds Commentary, Vol. 4* (Zondervan, 2002), 264.

44. Charles Spurgeon, *Spurgeon's Sermons: 1 & 2 Corinthians, Galatians* (CH Books, 2011), 359–77.

Chapter 8

1. Refer to Abraham Kuyper's *Sphere Sovereignty* (Daham, 2021).

2. James K. A. Smith, *You Are What You Love* (Viatore, 2022), 11.

3. Alister McGrath, *Hope of Heaven* (Christian Herald, 2005), 278.

4. Marva Dawn, *Worship: A Precious Jewel of Heav*en (WPA, 2017), 490.

5. Marva Dawn, *A Royal Waste of Time* (Iresewon, 2004), 452.

6. A. W. Tozer, *Holy Spirit* (Kyujang, 2006), 85.

7. Tozer, *Holy Spirit*, 52.

8. James Torrance, *Worship, Community, and Triune God* (IVP, 2022), 188.

9. Os Guinness, *Impossible People* (Togijangi, 2017), 270–71.

10. Christopher J. H. Wright, *The Old Testament in Seven Sentences* (IVP, 2019), 35.

11. Matt Chandler and Adam Griffin, *Family Discipleship* (Crossway, 2020), 32.

12. John Stott, *The Radical Disciple* (IVP, 2010), 21.

13. Fuller Youth Institute, accessed May 9, 2025, https://url.kr/iyomj1.

14. For all the mentioned social surveys and statistics, refer to Chap Bettis, *The Disciple-Making Parent* (Diamond Hill Publishing, 2016), 9–10.

15. Luther's Small Catechism of 1529.

16. A. W. Tozer, *God's Wisdom Cannot Be Gained by Knowledge* (Kyujang, 2018), 64–66.

17. Trends in the US Content Industry, "Understanding Generation Alpha," August 23, 2023 (Korea Creative Content Agency).

18. John Stott, *The Disciple of Christ* (IVP, 2019), 59–62.

19. Stott, *The Disciple of Christ*, 63.

20. Wayne Cordeiro, *Recharge Your Leadership* (Word of Life, 2009), 89.

21. Timothy Keller, *Every Good Endeavor: Connecting Your Work to God's Work* (Penguin Books, 2014).

22. Ronald Sider, *Scandal of the Evangelical Politics* (Hongseongsa, 2010), 169.

23. John Stott, *The Living God Is a Missionary God in Perspectives on the World Movement* (William Carey Library, 1999), 3–9.

24. Ralph D. Winter and Bruce A. Koch, "Finishing the Task: The Unreached People Challenge," in *Perspectives on the World Christian Movement* (William Carey Library, 1999), 511–12.

25. Publisher's Column, *Disciple*, October 2014.

26. Alan Hirsch, *Debra Hirsch, Untamed* (Baker Books, 2010), 29; Jay Richard Akkerman, Mark A. Maddix, ed., *Missional Discipleship* (Beacon Hill Press, 2013), 16.

27. Akkerman, *Missional Discipleship*, 17.

28. Akkerman, *Missional Discipleship*, 18.

29. Albert Mohler, "Are Christian Missionaries Narcissistic Idiots?—A Response to Ann Coulter," accessed May 9, 2025, https://albertmohler.com/2014/08/07/are-christian-missionaries-narcissistic-idiots-a-response-to-ann-coulter/.

30. Albert Mohler, "Are Christian Missionaries Narcissistic Idiots?—A Response to Ann Coulter," accessed May 9, 2025, https://url.kr/bczuhf.

31. Jacques Ellul, *The Christian in the World* (Daejanggan, 2008), 18.

32. Os Guinness, *Renaissance* (Blessed Person, 2016), 15.

33. David Fraser and Tony Campolo, *Sociology Through the Eyes of Faith* (IVP, 2009), 38.

Epilogue

1. Brennan Manning, *His Name Is Jesus* (Toggijangyi, 2005), 53.

About the Author

Dr. John Jung-Hyun Oh has devoted his entire pastoral life to the ministry of discipleship, grounded in his philosophy of "raising each individual as a fully mature disciple of Christ." Over the years, he has served in a wide spectrum of ministry contexts, from pioneering church plants to small, medium, large, and even megachurches.

He currently serves as the senior pastor of SaRang Church, where he is committed to the internationalization of discipleship, gospel-centered peaceful reunification of South and North Korea without bloodshed, the nurturing of global leaders for the next generation, and holistic engagement with society.

He has declared the "2033–50 Vision"—a fervent vision to see 50 percent of the Korean population evangelized by the year 2033, which marks the 2,000th anniversary of Jesus's resurrection and ascension and the birth of the church. In this era of the Fourth Industrial Revolution, he is working with the members of SaRang Church to become a platform of blessing and a Divine Commons, laying a "New Foundation for a New Future."

He currently serves as president of SaRang Global Academy (SaGA), director of Disciple Making Ministries International, chairman of the board of Soongsil University, chairman of the board of Korea OM Mission, and co-organizing chair of the 2025 WEA (World Evangelical Alliance) Seoul General Assembly. He also served as the organizing chair of The 50th Anniversary of Billy Graham Crusade Seoul Crusade. In these roles, he is wholly committed to seeing discipleship take root in homes, workplaces, and all spheres of society.

A fourth-generation Christian, Dr. Oh is married to Dr. Oh Nan-Young, and together they have two sons: Rev. Joseph Oh and Dr. Timothy Oh. Through his first daughter-in-law, Monica, he is also blessed with two granddaughters, Eden and Ayla.

Dr. Oh earned his BA in English Language and Literature from Soongsil University. He received his MDiv degree from Talbot School of Theology in the United States, and a ThM from Calvin Theological Seminary in Michigan. He pursued further doctoral studies (PhD) at North-West University in Potchefstroom, South Africa, and was a resident fellow at Harvard University. He has also been awarded honorary doctorate degrees from Baekseok University, Warner University (USA), Mackenzie University (Brazil), and Denver Seminary (USA).

His written works include *Living in Christ*, *David, the Man of God (Volumes 1 and 2)*, *Rebuilding Together*, *Vision Maker of Passion*, *The Sleepless Minister*, *Walking with God*, *Insight and Foresight*, *Declaration of Obedience*, and *Hope Flows Between People*, among many others. He has also published sixteen small group Bible study workbooks, including *Abraham, the Blessed Man*, *Zechariah*, *The Gospel of John*, and *The Book of Acts (Volumes 1 and 2)*.